STUDY GUIDE

Economics

Fifth Edition

Roger A. Arnold

California State University, San Marcos

SOUTH-WESTERN
™
THOMSON LEARNING

Australia · Canada · Mexico · Singapore · Spain · United Kingdom · United States

Study Guide to accompany Economics, 5e
By Roger A. Arnold
Vice President/Publisher: Jack W. Calhoun
Acquisitions Editor: Keri L. Witman
Sr. Developmental Editor: Jan Lamar
Marketing Manager: Lisa L. Lysne
Production Editor: Starratt E. Alexander
Manufacturing Coordinator: Charlene Taylor
Editorial Assistant: Maria T. Accardi
Cover Design: Tinbox Studio, Inc., Cincinnati
Cover Illustration: © Robert LoGrippo/Jeff Lavaty and Associates
Printer: Globus Printing, Inc.

For more information contact South-Western College Publishing, 5191 Natorp Blvd., Mason, Ohio, 45040
or find us on the Internet at http://www.swcollege.com

For permission to use material from this text or product, contact us by
• **telephone: 1-800-730-2214**
• **fax: 1-800-730-2215**
• **web: http://www.thomsonrights.com**

ISBN: 0-324-01900-9

This book is printed on acid-free paper.

Contents

Chapter 1
What Economics Is About

What This Chapter Is About

This chapter is an introduction to economics. Economics is defined and a few of the important concepts in economics are discussed – such as scarcity, opportunity cost, and more. Also, this chapter introduces you to the economic way of thinking.

Key Concepts in the Chapter
   a. scarcity
   b. opportunity cost
   c. decisions made at the margin
   d. theory
   e. positive and normative economics

- **Scarcity** is the condition under which people's wants (for goods) are greater than the resources available to satisfy those wants.
- **Opportunity cost** is the most highly valued opportunity or alternative forfeited when a choice is made.
- When we make **decisions at the margin**, we compare the marginal benefits and marginal costs of things.
- A **theory** is an abstract representation of reality.
- **Positive economics** deals with "what is," and **normative economics** deals with what someone thinks "should be."

Review Questions

1. Is scarcity the condition under which people have infinite wants? — yes

2. What is the difference between a *good* and a *bad*? - Good - Anything from which individuals receive utility or satisfaction
Bad - Anything from which individuals receive disutility or dissatisfaction.

3. Give an example of when something is a good one day, and a bad some other day?
A New Video Game: Some other day it may be obsolete; a newer game has come out.

4.   What is the opportunity cost of your reading this study guide?

5.   If the opportunity cost of smoking cigarettes rises, fewer people will smoke. Why?

6.   What is a synonym (in economics) for the word *additional*?

7.   If Harriet is thinking of studying for one more hour, she considers the marginal benefits and marginal costs of studying for one more hour—not the total benefits and total costs. Why does she consider marginal benefits and costs and not total benefits and costs?

8.   In the course the author discussed the unintended effects of wearing seatbelts. Come up with an example of an unintended effect of something.

9.   What is the relationship between scarcity and choice? Between scarcity and opportunity cost?

10.   What is the relationship between thinking in terms of "what would have been" and opportunity cost?

11.   What is a theory?

12.   Do people who have never formally built a theory still theorize?

13.   What are the seven steps of building and testing a theory?

14.   Why is it better to judge a theory by how well it predicts than by whether it sounds right or not?

15.   Give an example of an assumption.

16.   Give an example of when association is causation. Then give an example of when association is not causation.

Theory on a Television Show
Read the following account of theorizing on a television show.

Jerry Seinfeld Builds a Theory, George Tests It Out

You may think that building and testing theories is something only economists do. But ordinary people in all walks of life do it every day. Take, for example, George, Jerry Seinfeld's friend, on the hit television show "Seinfeld."

One day George walks into the restaurant where Jerry and Elaine (Jerry and George's best friend) are eating and complains that nothing ever goes right for him. He is a loser, he says. Everything his instincts tell him to do turns out wrong.

A lightbulb goes off over Jerry's head. He tells George that if everything his instincts tell him to do turns out wrong, then he should always do the opposite of what his instincts indicate. If his instincts tell him to turn right, he should turn left; if his instincts tell him to order a chicken sandwich, he should order a ham sandwich instead.

At this point, Jerry is theorizing. To see this explicitly, let's look at the following points of building and testing a theory.

- Point 1 is to *decide on what it is you want to explain or predict*. Jerry wants to explain why everything goes wrong for George.
- Point 2 is to *identify the variables that you believe are important to what you want to explain or predict*. The chief variable (or factor) for Jerry is George's instincts.
- Point 3 is to *state the assumptions of the theory*. Jerry implicitly assumes that George is concerned enough about the dismal state of his life to do whatever is necessary to make things better.
- Point 4 is to *state the hypothesis*. Jerry's hypothesis is that if everything George's instincts tell him to do turns out wrong, then he should do the opposite of his instincts and everything will turn out right.
- Point 5 is to *test the theory by comparing its predictions against real-world events*. In the television show, George puts the theory to the test. He goes against every instinct he has. For instance, he walks up to a woman at the counter in the restaurant. His instincts tell him that to arouse the woman's interest, he should pretend to be something he's not. Instead, he fights his instincts and tells the woman exactly what he is: a balding, middle-aged man, without a job, who lives at home with his parents. The woman immediately takes a liking to him. So far, the evidence supports the theory.

The storyline continues. George and his date are at a movie when two rowdy young men sitting behind them begin loudly heckling the characters in the movie. George's instincts tell him to slither down into his seat or move but never, under any circumstances, to confront the young men and tell them what he thinks of their rude behavior. George, still testing Jerry's theory, does the opposite of what his instincts tell him to do. He gets up from his seat, tells off the two men, and adds that it they aren't quiet he will take them outside and settle the matter. The two rowdy men shrink back in their seats like shivering puppies. The patrons in the movie theater applaud, and George's date is impressed.

- Point 6 states that *if the evidence supports the theory, then no further action is necessary, although it is a good idea to continue to examine the theory closely.* George continues to test the theory as the show continues, each time the evidence supports it: every time he goes against his instincts, something good happens to him.

The story of Jerry and George is fiction. But this fictional account is representative of what ordinary people do every day. Anyone, in any walk of life, who follows the steps for building a theory is theorizing. The theorizing can be about something as esoteric as the nature of the universe or as ordinary as George's life.

1.   Jerry built a theory, George tested it, and the evidence supported the theory. But what might the evidence have been if it had not supported the theory? In other words, what might have happened on the "Seinfeld" show if Jerry's theory had been wrong instead of right?

2.   What are some of the things that you think economists theorize about?

Problems

1.   Draw a flow chart that shows the relationship between scarcity, choice, and opportunity cost.

2. Jim is considering going to college. He knows there are benefits and costs to attending college. In the table below you will see various factors identified in the first column. Determine whether the factor relates to the cost of going to college or to the benefit of going to college. Next, identify whether the specified change in the factor raises or lowers the cost or benefit of going to college. If it raises the benefit of going to college, place an upward arrow (↑) in the benefits column; if it lowers the benefit of going to college, place a downward arrow (↓) in the benefits column. Do the same for the costs column. Finally, identify whether the change in the factor makes it more likely (Yes or No) Jim will go to college.

Factor	Benefits of attending college	Costs of attending college	More likely to go to college? Yes or No
Jim thought he would earn $20 an hour if he didn't go to college, but learns that he will earn $35 an hour instead.			
His friends are going to college and he likes being around his friends.			
The salary gap between college graduates and high school graduates has widened.			
Jim learns something about himself: he doesn't like to study.			
The college he is thinking about attending just opened a satellite campus near Jim's home.			
The economy has taken a downturn and it looks like there are very few jobs for high school graduates right now.			

3. When people explain or predict something, they usually implicitly make the *ceteris paribus* assumption. For example, Jenny says, "I plan to exercise more in order to lose weight." What Jenny is holding constant, or is assuming does not change, are things such as: (a) how much she eats every day, (b) how much she sleeps every day, (c) how much stress she is under, and so on. In other words, she is saying that if she exercises more, and does everything else the same as she has been doing, she will lose weight. She is not saying that if she exercises more, and eats more in the process, that she will lose weight.

    In the first column in the table, a statement is made by a person. Next to it write something that the person must be assuming is not changing in order for the statement to be true.

Statement	The person is assuming that this does not change:
People that don't brush their teeth will get cavities.	
As people get older, they tend to put on weight because their metabolism slows down.	
If he studies more, he will get higher grades.	

4. Identify each of the following questions as related to either a microeconomic or macroeconomic topic.
   a. Why did that firm charge a higher price?
   b. When will the economy slow down?
   c. When will the unemployment rate fall?
   d. Are interest rates rising?
   e. How does that firm decide how many cars it will produce this year?
   f. What is the price of a really fast computer?
   g. Why did that restaurant go out of business?

5. There is an opportunity cost to everything you do. In the first column you will see an activity identified. In the second column, identify what you think the opportunity cost (for you) would be if you undertook that particular activity.

Activity	Opportunity Cost
Study one more hour each night	
Take a trip to someplace you have always wanted to visit	
Sit in the back of the room in one of your classes	
Talk up more in class	
Get a regular medical checkup	
Surf the Web more	

What Is Wrong?
In each of the statements below, something is wrong. Identify what is wrong in the space provided.

1. People have finite wants and infinite resources.

2. People prefer more bads to fewer bads.

3. Scarcity is an effect of competition.

4. The lower the opportunity cost of playing tennis, the less likely a person will play tennis.

5. Abstract means to add more variables to the process of theorizing.

6. Microeconomics is the branch of economics that deals with human behavior and choices as they relate to highly aggregate markets or the entire economy.

7. Positive economics is to normative economics as opinion is to truth.

8. Because there are rationing devices, there will always be scarcity.

9. The four factors of production, or resources, are land, labor, capital, and profit.

10. Karen doesn't like to study so no one likes to study. This is an example of the association is not causation issue.

Multiple Choice
Circle the correct answer.

1. Economics is the science of
    a. human relationships in an economic setting.
    b. business and prices.
    c. scarcity.
    d. goods and services.

2. Scarcity exists
    a. in only poor countries of the world.
    b. in all countries of the world
    c. only when society does not employ all its resources in an efficient way.
    d. only when society produces too many frivolous or silly goods.

3. Which of the following statements is true?
    a. Both a millionaire and a poor person must deal with scarcity.
    b. People would have to make choices even if scarcity did not exist.
    c. Scarcity is a relatively new problem in the world's history; it has not always existed.
    d. It is like that one day scarcity will no longer exist.

4. Which of the following statements is true?
    a. Coca-Cola is a good for everyone, even someone who has an allergy to Coca-Cola.
    b. If you pay someone to take X off your hands, then it is likely that X is a bad.
    c. It is possible, but not likely, that someone can obtain both utility and disutility from a bad.
    d. If there is more of good A than people want at zero price, then good A is an economic good.

5. Kristin Taylor had a safety inspection performed on her car last week and it passed with flying colors. How is this likely to affect her future driving behavior, compared to a situation in which cars did not get safety inspections at all?
    a. She will probably drive faster, and the probability of having an accident is reduced.
    b. She will probably drive slower, and the probability of having an accident is reduced.
    c. She will probably drive faster, and the probability of having an accident is increased.
    d. She will probably drive slower, and the probability of having an accident is increased.

6. Frank is 19 years old and is an actor in a soap opera, "One Life to Ruin." He earns $100,000 a year. Cassandra is also 19 years old and works in a local clothing store. She earns $6 and hour. Which of the two persons is more likely to attend college and for what reason?
    a. Cassandra, because she is smarter.
    b. Frank, because he has higher opportunity costs of attending college than Cassandra.
    c. Cassandra, because she has lower opportunity costs of attending college than Frank.
    d. Frank, because he earns a higher income than Cassandra.

7. A theory
    a. is a simplified abstract representation of the real world.
    b. incorporates critical factors or variables.
    c. is an accurate and complete description of reality.
    d. a and b

8. Which of the following is the best example of a hypothesis?
    a. If a person eats too many fatty foods, then his cholesterol level will rise.
    b. If it is 12 noon in New York City, it is 9 a.m. in Los Angeles.
    c. The daytime temperature is often over 100 degrees in Phoenix in July.
    d. If someone yells "fire" in a crowded theater and everyone runs to the exit, you will be worse off than had everyone walked but you.

9. Evidence can
    a. prove a theory, but never disprove it.
    b. reject (disprove) a theory, but never prove it.
    c. both prove and reject (disprove) a theory (although not at the same time).
    d. change the assumptions of the theory to fit the facts.

10. If an economist tests his or her theory and finds that it predicts accurately, he or she would likely say that the
    a. evidence fails to reject the theory.
    b. theory has been proved correct.
    c. the theory is true.
    d. the theory is better than alternative theories.

11. When an economist says that association is not causation, he or she means that
    a. event X and Y can be related in time (for instance, if one occurs a few minutes before the other) without X causing Y or Y causing X.
    b. if X occurs close in time to Y, it must be that either X is the cause of Y or Y is the cause of X.
    c. what is good for one person is good for all persons.
    d. what is good for one person is usually bad for all persons.

12. *Ceteris paribus* means:
    a. the correct relationship specified
    b. there are too many variables considered in the theory
    c. all other things held constant or nothing else changes
    d. assuming that people are rational human beings

13. Which of the following is an example of a *positive* statement?
    a. If you drop a quarter off the top of the Sears building in Chicago, it will fall to the ground.
    b. The minimum wage should be raised to eight dollars an hour.
    c. There is too much crime in the United States; something should be done about it.
    d. People should learn to get along with each other.

14. Which of the following topics is a microeconomics topic?
    a. the study of what influences the nation's unemployment rate
    b. the study of how changes in the nation's money supply affect the nation's output
    c. the study of prices in the automobile market
    d. the study of what affects the inflation rate

15. "Productive resources" include which of the following?
    a. land, labor, money, management
    b. land, labor, money, entrepreneurship
    c. land, labor, capital, entrepreneurship
    d. land, labor, natural resources, entrepreneurship

True-False
Write a "T" or "F" after each statement.

16. A good is anything from which individuals receive utility. ____

17. If there is no explicit charge for a good, it is not a scarce good. ____

18. Scarcity implies that choices will be made. ____

19. The higher a person's opportunity cost of time, the more likely a person will stand in a long line to buy a ticket to a concert or some other event, *ceteris paribus*. ____

20. According to Milton Friedman, theories are better judged by their assumptions than by their predictions. ____

21. As economists use the term, a "good" is a tangible item that you can see and touch (rather than an intangible service). ____

Fill in the Blank
Write the correct word in the blank.

22. If one person talks louder than others at a cocktail party, he or she will be better heard. If everyone talks louder at a cocktail party, though, not everyone will be better heard. This is an illustration of the _____ of _____.

23. Imo believes that an event that occurs first must be the cause of an event that occurs later. Imo believes that _____ _____ _____.

24. If calorie intake causes weight gain and there are numerous things that cause weight loss, then the more cookies you eat, the more weight you will gain, _____ _____.

25. _____ is the branch of economics that deals with highly aggregated markets or the entire economy.

26. If the evidence is consistent with a theory, economists do not say the theory has been proved correct. Instead, they say that the evidence _____ _____ _____ the theory.

27. One more unit of something is the _____ unit.

28. A good that is used to produce other goods, yet is not a natural resource, is called a _____ good.

29. The person who organizes production in a firm and is responsible for recognizing new business opportunities is an _____.

Chapter 2
Trade, Tradeoffs, and Economic Systems

What This Chapter Is About
People do it everyday—enter into trades or exchanges. They might trade $10 for a T-shirt, or $70 for a dinner for two. This chapter is about trade or exchange. It is also about tradeoffs and economic systems.

Key Concepts in the Chapter
    a.   exchange
    b.   terms of exchange
    c.   consumers' surplus
    d.   producers' (or sellers') exchange
    e.   transaction costs
    f.   comparative advantage
    g.   production possibilities frontier
    h.   efficiency
    i.   inefficiency
    j.   economic system

- **Exchange** is the process of trading one thing for another.
- The **terms of exchange** refer to how much of one thing is traded for how much of something else. For example, the terms of exchange may be $2,000 for one computer.
- **Consumers' surplus** is the difference between the maximum buying price and the price paid (by the consumer). For example, suppose John is willing to pay a maximum price of $40,000 for the car, but instead he pays only $25,000. The consumers' surplus is the difference, or $15,000.
- **Producers' (or sellers') surplus** is the difference between the price received (by the seller) and the minimum selling price. For example, if the minimum price firm X will sell good X for is $40, and the price it sells good X for is $50, then the producers' surplus is the difference, or $10.
- **Transaction costs** are the costs associated with the time and effort needed to search out, negotiate, and consummate an exchange.
- **Comparative advantage** refers to the situation in which someone can produce a good at lower opportunity cost than someone else. For example, if Jones can produce good Z at lower cost than Smith, Jones has a comparative advantage in the production of good Z.
- A **production possibilities frontier (PPF)** represents the possible combination of two goods that an economy can produce in a certain period of time, under the conditions of a given state of technology, no unemployed resources, and efficient production.
- **Efficiency** implies the impossibility of gains in one area without losses in another.
- **Inefficiency** implies the possibility of gains in one area without losses in another.
- An **economic system** refers to the way in which society decides what goods to produce, how to produce them, and for whom the goods will be produced.

Review Questions

1.   José is thinking of buying a house. Is he in the *ex ante* or *ex post* position with respect to exchange?

2. Kenny paid $7 to see a movie at the Cinemaplex at the mall. He would have paid as high as $10 to see the movie. What does his consumers' surplus (CS) equal?

3. How can you use consumers' surplus to know whether a change has made you better off, worse off, or neither?

4. Consumers prefer terms of exchange in their favor. What does this mean?

5. Are the transaction costs of buying a hamburger at a fast food restaurant higher or lower than the transaction costs of selling a house? Explain your answer.

6. Give an example of an exchange with a third-party negative effect.

7. Janet can produce either (a) 10 units of X and 20 units of Y, or (b) 20 units of X and 5 units of Y. What is the cost (to Janet) of producing one unit of X? One unit of Y?

8. Why does specialization and trade benefit people?

9. Why do people trade? What is the necessary condition for trade to take place?

10. Give an example that illustrates the law of increasing costs.

11. What does a straight-line production possibilities frontier (PPF) indicate about costs?

12. What does a bowed-outward (concave downward) PPF indicate about costs?

13. A country can be at either point A or B on its PPF. What does this fact have to do with the economic concept of *tradeoff*?

14. Identify two things that can shift a PPF outward (to the right).

    a.

    b.

15. Give an example of an advance in technology.

16. What are the three economic questions that every society must answer?

    a.

    b.

    c.

17. What is a vision?

Problems

1. If price paid is $40 and consumers' surplus is $100, then what is the maximum buying price?

2. If price received is $20 and producers' surplus is $5, then what is the minimum selling price?

3. Vernon bought a hat for $40. Identify more favorable terms of exchange for Vernon.

4. Karen's maximum buying price is $400 for good X. Randy's minimum selling price is $350 for good X. Currently, Karen and Randy have to each pay $60 in transaction costs to buy and sell good X. If an entrepreneur charges both the buyer and the seller $5, what is the minimum reduction in transaction costs that that entrepreneur must bring about (for each person) before the trade will be actualized at a price of $370?

5. Can you draw a PPF for grades? Use the data (that follows) to draw a production possibilities frontier for grades.

Hours spent studying Sociology	Grade in Sociology	Hours spent studying Economics	Grade in Economics
6	90	0	60
5	85	1	65
4	80	2	70
3	75	3	75
2	70	4	80
1	65	5	85
0	60	6	90

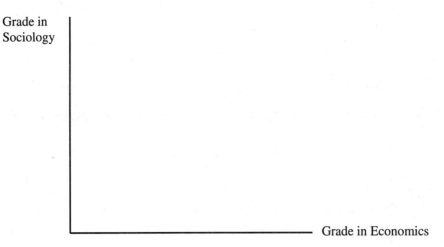

6. Using the data in the previous question, what is the opportunity cost of earning a 65 instead of a 60 in Economics?

7. Identify the points on the PPF that are efficient.

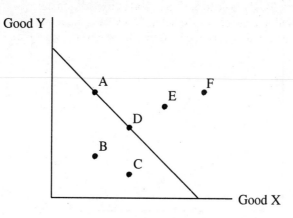

8. Which points on the PPF (in the previous question) are inefficient?

9. Which points on the PPF (in question 7) are unattainable?

10. Suppose that point C, with 100 units of good X and 200 units of good Y, is an efficient point. Could point D, with 75 units of good X and 250 units of good Y, also be an efficient point? Explain your answer.

11. Within a PPF framework, diagrammatically represent the effect of a war that destroys people and property.

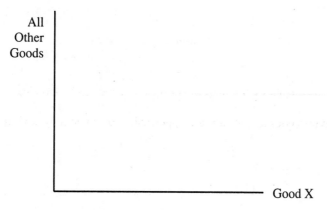

12. Within a PPF framework, diagrammatically represent the effect of an advance in technology.

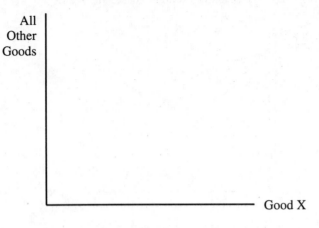

What Is Wrong?
In each of the statements below, something is wrong. Identify what is wrong in the space provided.

1.   If costs are increasing, the PPF is a straight (downward-sloping) line.

2.   Mary said that she received $40 consumers' surplus when she paid $50 for the good and only $30 consumers' surplus when she paid $45 for the good.

3.   If Jones can produce either (a) 100 units of X and 100 units of Y or (b) 200 units of X and zero units of Y, then he has a comparative advantage in the production of Y.

4.   The following PPF represents a two-for-one opportunity cost of apples.

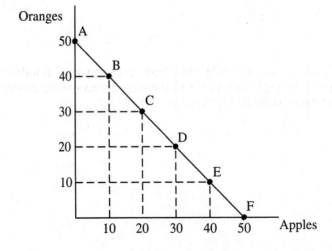

5. There are probably more unemployed resources at point A than at point D.

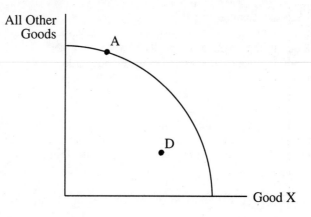

6. Efficiency implies the possibility of gains in one area without losses in another area.

7. If Georgina reads one more book, she will have to give up doing something else. This shows that Georgina is inefficient.

8. For a given quantity of output, a rise in price reduces producers' surplus and increases consumers' surplus.

9. If Bobby can produce either (a) 100 units of good X and 50 units of good Y, or (b) 25 units of good X and 80 units of good Y, then the cost of 1 unit of good X is 1.5 units of good Y.

10. John says, "I bought this sweater yesterday and I think I got a bad deal." It follows that in the *ex ante* position John thought he would be better off with the sweater than with the money he paid for it, but in the *ex post* position he prefers the money to the sweater.

Multiple Choice
Circle the correct answer.

1. Which of the following statements is true?
    a. The production possibilities frontier is always bowed outward.
    b. The production possibilities frontier is usually bowed outward.
    c. The production possibilities frontier is never bowed outward.
    d. The production possibilities frontier is usually a straight line.

2. Which of the following statements is false?
    a. A straight-line production possibilities frontier represents increasing costs.
    b. A bowed outward production possibilities frontier represents constant costs.
    c. An efficient point is located on the production possibilities frontier.
    d. a and b

3. If there is always a constant tradeoff between goods A and B, the production possibilities frontier between A and B is
    a. circular.
    b. a downward-sloping curve bowed toward the origin.
    c. a downward-sloping straight line.
    d. a downward-sloping straight line that is broken at one point.

4. Consider two points on the production possibilities frontier: point X, at which there are 100 cars and 78 trucks, and point Y, at which there are 90 cars and 70 trucks. If the economy is currently at point X, the opportunity cost of moving to point Y is
    a. 12 cars.
    b. 1 truck.
    c. 10 cars.
    d. 79 trucks.
    e. none of the above

5. If it is possible to increase production of one good without getting less of another, then currently the economy is
    a. operating efficiently.
    b. sluggish.
    c. operating inefficiently.
    d. operating at technological inferiority.

6. The production possibilities frontier represents the possible combinations of two goods that an economy can produce
    a. in a certain time.
    b. in a certain time, under the condition of a given state of resources.
    c. given that there are not unemployed resources.
    d. under the condition of efficient production.
    e. None of the answers is complete enough.

7. When the economy exhibits inefficiency, it is not producing the
    a. maximum output with the available resources and technology.
    b. minimum output with minimum resources and technology.
    c. the goods and services consumers wish to buy.
    d. b and c

8. The three economic questions that must be answered by every society are
    a. How will the goods be produced? What goods will be produced? What services will be produced?
    b. For whom will the goods be produced? What goods will be produced? How will the goods be produced?
    c. What goods will be produced? How will the goods be produced? For what purpose will the goods be produced?
    d. What goods will be produced? Who will produce the goods? Why are the goods produced?

9. When Beverly trades $60 for good X, economists assume that she is trading something
    a. of less value to her for something of more value to her.
    b. of more value to her for something of less value to her.
    c. that gives her less utility for something that gives her more utility.
    d. a and c
    e. none of the above

10. The _____ refer(s) to how much of one thing is traded for how much of something else.
    a. exchange process
    b. terms of exchange
    c. duality prices
    d. consumers' surplus
    e. producers' surplus

11. As the terms of exchange move in a buyer's favor, _____ rises and _____ falls.
    a. consumers' surplus; producers' surplus
    b. producers' surplus; consumers' surplus
    c. *ex ante* surplus; *ex post* surplus
    d. *ex post* surplus; *ex ante* surplus
    e. a and c

12. Transaction costs are
    a. the costs associated with the time and effort needed to search out, negotiate, and consummate an exchange.
    b. the costs a consumer pays in the *ex ante* position.
    c. the costs a seller pays in the *ex post* position.
    d. identical to the terms of exchange.
    e. always higher for buyers than sellers.

13. If Mark and Bob are not currently trading $10 for a book, it may be because
    a. transaction costs are too high.
    b. transaction costs are too low.
    c. at least one of the two individuals does not think he would be made better off by the trade.
    d. both individuals think they will be made worse off by the trade.
    e. a, c, and d

14. If Sean can bake bread at a lower cost than Jason, and Jason can produce paintings at a lower cost then Sean, it follows that
    a. Sean has a comparative advantage in paintings and Jason has a comparative advantage in baking bread.
    b. Both Sean and Jason have a comparative advantage in baking bread.
    c. Both Sean and Jason have a comparative advantage in producing paintings.
    c. Sean has a comparative advantage in baking bread and Jason has a comparative advantage in producing paintings.
    d. There is not enough information to answer the question.

15. Vernon can produce the following combinations of X and Y: 100X and 20Y, 50X and 30Y, or 0X or 40Y. The opportunity cost of one unit of Y for Vernon is
    a. five units of Y.
    b. two units of Y.
    c. three units of Y.
    d. one-half unit of Y.
    e. none of the above

True-False
Write a "T" or "F" after each statement.

16. Because scarcity exists, individuals and societies must make choices. _____

17. If the production of good X comes in terms of increasing costs of good Y, then the production possibilities frontier between the two goods is a downward-sloping straight line. _____

18. Economic growth shifts the production possibilities frontier inward. _____

19. It is possible for a legal institutional arrangement to be inefficient, and for an illegal institutional arrangement to be efficient. _____

20. Without scarcity, there would be no production possibilities frontier. _____

Fill in the Blank
Write the correct word in the blank.

21. The three questions (economists say) that all societies must answer are:

    a) _____

    b) _____

    c) _____

22. _____ implies it is possible to obtain gains in one area without losses in another.

23. _____ implies it is impossible to obtain gains in one area without losses in another.

24. At point A on a production possibilities frontier there are 50 apples and 60 oranges. At point B there are 49 apples and 68 oranges. If the economy is currently at point B, the opportunity cost of moving to point A is _____oranges.

Chapter 3
Supply, Demand, Price: The Theory

What This Chapter Is About

This chapter is about markets. A market has two sides—a demand side and a supply side. The chapter first discusses demand, then supply, then it puts both sides of the market together and discusses the price and quantity of goods.

Key Concepts in the Chapter

a. demand
b. law of demand
c. supply
d. law of supply
e. equilibrium price
f. shortage
g. surplus
h. consumers' surplus
i. producers' surplus

- **Demand** is the willingness and ability to buy different quantities of a good at different prices over some period of time. Keep in mind that if a person doesn't have both the willingness and ability to buy a good, then there is no demand.
- The **law of demand** states that price and quantity demanded are inversely related, *ceteris paribus*. This means that as price rises, quantity demanded falls, and as price falls, quantity demanded rises, *ceteris paribus*.
- **Supply** is the willingness and ability to produce and offer to sell different quantities of a good at different prices over some period of time.
- The **law of supply** states that price and quantity supplied are directly related, *ceteris paribus*. This means that as price rises, quantity supplied rises, and as price falls, quantity supplied falls, *ceteris paribus*.
- **Equilibrium price** is the price at which the quantity demanded of a good equals the quantity supplied. For example, if, at $40, the quantity supplied of good X is 100 units, and quantity demanded of good X is also 100 units, then $40 is the equilibrium price.
- **Equilibrium quantity** is the quantity that corresponds to equilibrium price. At equilibrium, quantity demanded = quantity supplied = equilibrium quantity.
- A **shortage** exists in a market if quantity demanded is greater than quantity supplied. If buyers want to buy 100 units of good X, and sellers only want to sell 30 units, then there is a shortage.
- A **surplus** exists in a market if quantity supplied is greater than quantity demanded. If buyers want to buy 100 units of good X, and sellers want to sell 300 units, then there is a surplus.
- **Consumers' surplus** is the difference between the maximum buying price and price paid. For example, if Smith is willing to pay a maximum of $40 for good X, and he only has to pay $10, then the difference, or $30, is consumers' surplus.
- **Producers' surplus** is the difference between the price paid and the minimum selling price. For example, if Jones is willing to sell good X for $10, but is paid $50, then the difference, or $40, is producers' surplus.

Review Questions

1. What does the law of demand state?

2. What does it mean to say that price and quantity demanded are inversely related?

3. What is quantity demanded?

4. How does quantity demanded differ from demand?

5. Demand is a function of five factors. Stated differently, if there is a change in any of these five factors, demand will either increase or decrease. What are these five factors?

    a.

    b.

    c.

    d.

    e.

6. If demand for a good increases, will the demand curve (that represents the good) shift to the right or to the left?

7. If demand for a good decreases, will the demand curve (that represents the good) shift to the right or to the left?

8. What is quantity supplied?

9. If a supply curve is vertical, what does this mean?

10. If a supply curve is upward-sloping, what does this mean?

11. Supply is a function of six factors. Stated differently, if there is a change in any of these six factors, supply will either increase or decrease. What are these six factors?

    a.

    b.

    c.

    d.

    e.

    f.

12. If the supply of a good increases, will the supply curve (that represents the good) shift to the right or to the left?

13. If the supply of a good decreases, will the supply curve (that represents the good) shift to the right or to the left?

14. Consider the standard supply and demand diagram. The demand curve is downward-sloping and the supply curve is upward-sloping.

    What is on the horizontal axis?

    What is on the vertical axis?

15. What is the difference between the relative price of a good and the absolute price of a good?

16. Demand rises and supply is constant. What happens to equilibrium price and quantity?

17. Supply rises and demand is constant. What happens to equilibrium price and quantity?

18. Demand rises by more than supply rises. What happens to equilibrium price and quantity?

19. Supply falls by more than demand rises. What happens to equilibrium price and quantity?

20. If price rises, what happens to consumers' surplus?

Problems

1. There are many factors that can directly affect supply and demand and indirectly affect price and quantity. In the first column we identify a change in a given factor. How does the change in the factor affect supply or demand? How does it affect price and quantity? Draw an upward arrow ($\uparrow$) in the demand column if demand rises and a downward arrow ($\downarrow$) if demand falls. The same holds for supply, equilibrium price, and equilibrium quantity.

Factor	Demand	Supply	Equilibrium Price	Equilibrium Quantity
Price of a substitute rises				
Price of a complement falls				
Income rises (normal good)				
Income falls (inferior good)				
Price of relevant resource rises				
Technology advances				
Quota				
Number of buyers rises				
Number of sellers rises				
Buyers expect higher price				
Sellers expect higher price				
Tax on production				
Preferences become more favorable with respect to the good				

2. Draw a rise in demand that is greater than a rise in supply.

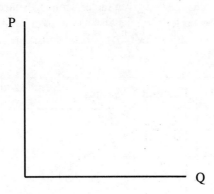

3. Draw a fall in supply that is greater than an increase in demand.

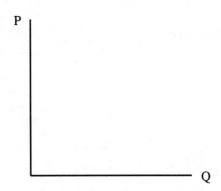

4. What area(s) does consumers' surplus equal at 75 units?

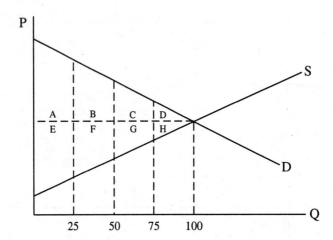

5. What area(s) does producers' surplus equal at equilibrium quantity?

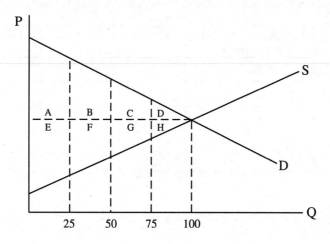

6. What is the shortage equal to at a price ceiling of $6?

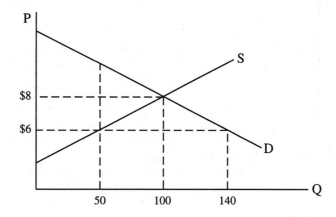

7. What is the surplus equal to at a price floor of $10?

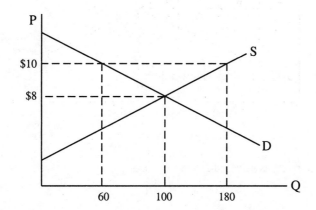

8. There are two buyers in a market, John and Mary. Below you see the quantity demanded for each at various prices. What is the quantity demanded (on the market demand curve) at each price specified? Write in the various quantities demanded in the spaces provided in the table.

Price	Quantity demanded by John	Quantity demanded by Mary	Quantity demanded (market demand)
$10	100	130	
$12	80	120	
$14	50	100	

9. If the price ceiling for good X is $4, and the maximum buying price for good X is $10, what is the highest price for a good that is "tied" to good X (as in a tie-in sale)?

10. Give an example that illustrates the law of diminishing marginal utility.

What Is Wrong?
In each of the statements below, something is wrong. Identify what is wrong in the space provided.

1. If the price of a good rises, the demand for the good will fall.

2. Consumers' surplus is equal to the minimum selling price minus the price paid.

3. As income rises, demand for a normal good rises; as income falls, demand for an inferior good falls.

4. The supply curve for Picasso paintings is upward-sloping.

5. As price rises, supply rises; as price falls, supply falls.

6. Quantity demanded is greater than supply when there is a shortage.

7. If supply rises, and demand is constant, equilibrium price rises and equilibrium quantity rises.

8. The law of diminishing marginal utility states that as a consumer consumes additional units of a good, each successive unit gives him or her more utility than the previous unit.

9. According to the law of demand, as the price of a good rises, the quantity demanded of the good rises, *ceteris paribus*.

Multiple Choice
Circle the correct answer.

1. The law of demand states that
   a. price and demand are inversely related, *ceteris paribus*.
   b. price and demand are directly related, *ceteris paribus*.
   c. price and quantity demanded are directly related, *ceteris paribus*.
   d. price and quantity demanded are inversely related, *ceteris paribus*.

2. Which of the following persons would be least likely to prefer first-come-first-served (FCFS) as a rationing device?
   a. A person who has just returned from visiting a busy city.
   b. A person who has just returned from visiting a small town.
   c. A person with low opportunity cost of time.
   d. A person with high opportunity cost of time.

3. At a price ceiling (below equilibrium price),
   a. there is a surplus.
   b. quantity supplied is greater than quantity demanded.
   c. quantity demanded equals quantity supplied.
   d. supply equals demand.
   e. quantity demanded is greater than quantity supplied.

4. Which of the following statements is true?
   a. A demand schedule is the same thing as a demand curve.
   b. A downward-sloping demand curve is the graphical representation of the law of demand.
   c. Quantity demanded is a relationship between price and demand.
   d. Quantity demanded is the same as demand.

5. Because of a price ceiling on light bulbs, the quantity demanded of light bulbs exceeds the quantity
    supplied. The owner of the light bulbs decided to sell them on a first-come-first-served basis. This is an
    example of a
    a. surplus.
    b. tie-in sale.
    c. nonprice rationing device.
    d. black market.
    e. none of the above.

6. If W_1 is the equilibrium wage rate and W_2 is a wage rate <u>above</u> equilibrium, then at W_2 there are
    a. more people who want to work and more people working than at W_1.
    b. fewer people who want to work and more people working than at W_1.
    c. fewer people who want to work and fewer people working than at W_1.
    d. more people who want to work and fewer people working than at W_1.

7. The minimum wage is an example of a
    a. price floor.
    b. price ceiling.
    c. equilibrium wage.
    d. sub-equilibrium wage.

8. If an increase in income leads to an increase in the demand for sausage, then sausage is
    a. an essential good.
    b. a normal good.
    c. a luxury good.
    d. a discretionary good.

9. Which of the following can shift the demand curve rightward?
    a. an increase in income
    b. an increase in the price of a substitute good
    c. an increase in the price of a complementary good
    d. all of the above
    e. a and b

10. Which of the following cannot increase the demand for good X?
    a. an increase in income
    b. a decrease in the price of good X
    c. an increase in the price of a substitute good
    d. more buyers
    e. a change in preferences in favor of good X

11. The law of supply states that price and quantity supplied are
    a. directly related.
    b. inversely related.
    c. inversely related, *ceteris paribus*.
    d. directly related, *ceteris paribus*.

12. A change in the quantity supplied of a good is directly brought about by a
    a. change in the good's own price.
    b. decrease in income.
    c. technological advance.
    d. fall in the price of resources needed to produce the good.
    e. none of the above.

13. Five dollars is the equilibrium price for good Z. At a price of $2, there is
    a. a shortage.
    b. surplus.
    c. excess supply.
    d. aggregate demand.

14. If supply rises by a greater amount than demand rises,
    a. equilibrium price rises and equilibrium quantity falls.
    b. equilibrium price falls and equilibrium quantity falls.
    c. equilibrium price rises and equilibrium quantity rises.
    d. equilibrium price falls and equilibrium quantity rises.

15. If supply rises and demand is constant,
    a. equilibrium price rises and equilibrium quantity falls.
    b. equilibrium price falls and equilibrium quantity falls.
    c. equilibrium price rises and equilibrium quantity rises.
    d. equilibrium price falls and equilibrium quantity rises.

True-False
Write a "T" or "F" after each statement.

16. One of the effects of a price ceiling is that quantity supplied is greater than quantity demanded. ____

17. According to Alfred Marshall, demand is more important to the determination of market price than supply. ____

18. At the equilibrium price for good X, good X is scarce. ____

19. "Supply" is a specific amount of a good, such as 50 units of good Y. ____

20. There is a tendency for price to rise when the quantity demanded of a good is greater than the quantity supplied. ____

Fill in the Blank
Write the correct word in the blank.

21. As price rises, quantity demanded _____ and quantity supplied _____.

22. A _____ is any arrangement by which people exchange goods and services.

23. If Matt's demand for motorcycles rises as his income falls, then motorcycles are a(n)

    _____ good for Matt.

24. If demand rises more than supply falls, then equilibrium quantity _____.

25. At equilibrium, the quantity demanded of a good _____ the quantity supplied of the

    good.

26. Suppose you live in New York City and are required to rent the furniture in an apartment before you

    can rent the apartment. This is called a _____ - _____ sale.

Chapter 4
Applications of Supply and Demand:
Using Supply and Demand to Explain and Predict Market and Nonmarket Behavior

What This Chapter Is About
In the last chapter you learned the basic theory of supply and demand. You learned what a demand curve is, what factors will shift it right and left, what a supply curve is, what factors will shift it right and left, and so on. The theory of supply and demand is worth little unless you can apply it. That is what we do in this chapter. We present a series of applications of supply and demand.

Key Concepts in the Chapter
- a. price of friendship
- b. price of a good grade
- c. two ways to raise price
- d. law of demand
- e. law of supply
- f. consumers' surplus
- g. producers' surplus
- h. deadweight loss
- i. price as a rationing device
- j. markets and submarkets
- k. nonprice rationing devices
- l. relative price
- m. absolute price

- The **price of friendship** refers to what someone has to "pay" in time foregone to make or sustain a friendship. Economists often use one's wage rate as a proxy for the price of friendship. For example, if Jones earns $40 an hour and Smith earns $400 an hour, the price of friendship is higher for Smith than Jones.
- The **price of a good grade** refers to what someone has to "pay" in hours spent studying in order to get a good grade. For example, consider two classes, X and Y. If one has to spend 3 hours a day studying to get a good grade in course X and only 30 minutes a day studying to get a good grade in course Y, then the price of a good grade is higher in course X.
- With some things there are **two ways to raise price**. For example, there are two ways to raise the price of speeding. The first way is to raise the probability of being apprehended for speeding. The second way is to raise the ticket price of speeding.
- The **law of demand** states that price and quantity demanded are inversely related, *ceteris paribus*.
- The **law of supply** states that price and quantity supplied are directly related, *ceteris paribus*.
- **Consumers' surplus** is maximum buying price minus price paid.
- **Producers' surplus** is price received minus minimum selling price.
- **Deadweight loss** is sometimes synonymous with net loss. Suppose that the benefits of producing the 100th through 120th unit of a good are greater than the costs of producing the 100th through the 120th unit of the good. This means there is definitely a net benefit to producing the 100th through 120th unit of the good. Now suppose the 100th through the 120th unit of the good are not produced. In other words, the net benefit is not realized; it is "left on the table." An economist would say that not realizing the net benefit is a net loss, and sometimes that net loss is referred to as a *deadweight loss*.
- In an earlier chapter we learned that because of scarcity, there is a need for some rationing device. Often, **price serves as a rationing device**. In other words, price determines who gets what of the available resources and goods.

- Is it possible to take a **market** and divide it into **submarkets**? Economists think so. For example, it might be possible to take the market for airline seats and divide it into two submarkets: (1) the market for aisle airline seats, (2) the market for middle-of-the-row airline seats.
- Just as price can serve as a rationing device, so can other things. These other things we call **nonprice rationing devices**. First-come-first-served (FCFS) is a nonprice rationing device.
- The **relative price** of a good is the price of a good in terms of another good.
- The **absolute price** of a good is the money price of a good.

Review Questions

1. Is the price of friendship higher for a 6-year-old or for a 20-year-old? Explain your answer.

2. In the text it says, "If the median wage rate is higher in city A than in city B, the people in A will have fewer friends than people in B will have." Explain the statement.

3. Give an example that illustrates that quantity demanded can be higher with a demand curve that is closer to the origin than with a demand curve further away from the origin.

4. In the text it states that the price of speeding is equal to the price of a speeding ticket times the probability of getting caught for speeding. With this in mind, what might the price of crime be equal to?

5. In the discussion of the used car market (in the text) we saw that the demand for new cars was higher with a used car market than without a used car market. Do you think this same phenomenon (higher demand if the good can be resold than if it cannot be resold) holds for any other goods? If so, which goods?

6. Do you think your supply curve of niceness is upward sloping, with the price of niceness being niceness itself? What evidence do you have to support your answer?

7. Jack says, "Companies can just pass off to the consumer any taxes they face." Is Jack correct or incorrect? Explain your answer.

8. Government places a tax on production for seller X. Is there a deadweight loss as a result of the tax? Explain your answer.

9. There is freeway congestion on Interstate 5 at 8 a.m. on Monday morning. What are three solutions to the problem of freeway congestion at this time?

10. How can the pricing scheme that a college chooses to allocate student parking spots have anything to do with whether or not a student is late to class?

Problems
1. Use the law of demand to explain why Yvonne loses her temper with her mother but not with her father.

2. Older people tend to drive more slowly than younger people. For example, a 68-year-old retired person may drive more slowly than a working 32-year-old person. Some people say this is because as people age, their reflexes slow down, their eyesight becomes less clear, and so on. All this may be true. Still, might there be an explanation that has to do with the price of driving? If so, what is this explanation?

3. "I bought things on my vacation that were way too expensive. I don't know why I did it." Is there an economic explanation why? (Hint: Think of relative price and absolute price.)

4. Suppose the equilibrium tuition at college X is $2,000 a semester, but students only pay $800 a
    semester. The $1,200 difference is paid by the state taxpayers. Do you think professors will teach
    differently knowing their students paid a below-equilibrium tuition instead of the equilibrium tuition?
    Why or why not?

5. The owners of Broadway shows charge equilibrium prices for seats to Broadway plays but hotel-
    casinos in Las Vegas do not always charge equilibrium prices for seats to a show in their main room.
    Why?

6. Richard Posner states, "The law of demand doesn't operate just on goods with explicit prices. Unpopular teachers sometimes try to increase enrollment by raising the average grade of the students in their courses, thereby reducing the price of the course to the student." Do you think the same holds, with necessary changes, for unpopular people? Do unpopular people try to change the price of being around them? Or are they unpopular because the price they charge to be around them is too high?

7. What is the difference between the price of speeding and the price of a speeding ticket?

8. Greedy people will never conserve resources. Discuss.

9. Look at the slope of the demand curve in Exhibit 3 (in Chapter 4) in your textbook. Do you think a larger percentage of the tax will be paid by the buyer if the demand curve is steeper? Draw it and see.

10. A tax on production is placed on seller X. Who gains from the tax? Who loses from the tax? How do the gainers gain? How do the losers lose?

What May Have Been Overlooked?
In each of the statements below, something may have been overlooked or ignored. Identify what may have been overlooked or ignored.

1. The higher the demand for something, the greater the quantity demanded.

2. I think how I behave is independent of the setting that I am in. I act the same way no matter what the setting.

3. If there were no flea markets or garage sales (where people can buy old furniture), new furniture companies would sell more (new) furniture.

4. The rock band has the best interest of its fans in mind. It knows it can charge $80 a ticket, but it charges only $20 a ticket so that its fans won't have to pay so much.

5. If my university doesn't charge for student parking, then I am definitely better off than I would be if it did charge for student parking.

6. The tuition at Harvard is very high, so Harvard must be charging the equilibrium tuition to students. Still, Harvard uses such things as GPA, SAT and ACT scores for admission purposes. It must be wrong that these nonprice rationing devices (GPA, etc.) are only used by colleges and universities that charge below-equilibrium tuition.

7. If a good doesn't have a money price, it has no price at all.

Multiple Choice

Circle the correct answer.

1. Who is the price of friendship the highest for?
   a. Jack, who earns $20 an hour and does nothing in his free time.
   b. Jill, who earns $20 an hour and reads in her free time.
   c. Sam, who is 45 years old.
   d. Tammy who is 23 years old.
   e. There is not enough information to answer the question.

2. If the law of demand applies to friendship, then it follows that
   a. on average, people in a high-income countries will have more friends than people in a low-income countries, *ceteris paribus*.
   b. a person is likely to have more friends when she is 12 years old than when she is 23 years old.
   c. as one's wage rate rises, one will "consume" less friendship.
   d. a and b
   e. b and c

3. Which of the following statements is false?
   a. Something that has a zero money price may have a nonmoney price.
   b. The price of friendship rises as one's wage rate falls.
   c. As the price of friendship rises, the quantity demanded of friendship falls.
   d. b and c
   e. none of the above

4. Which of the following statements is false?
   a. Low demand and low price can generate the same quantity demanded as high demand and high price.
   b. Low demand and low price can generate a greater quantity demanded than high demand and high price.
   c. The most popular professor on campus will always have more students who want to take his or her class than students who want to take the classes of less popular professors, *ceteris paribus*.
   d. The most popular professor on campus will always have more students who want to take his or her class than students who want to take the classes of less popular professors.
   e. b and d

5. As the price of speeding falls, more people will choose to speed. This is most nearly consistent with the law of
   a. demand.
   b. supply.
   c. diminishing marginal utility.
   d. increasing opportunity costs.
   e. none of the above

6. If fewer people speed the higher the price of speeding, then fewer people will speed when the probability of getting caught speeding is _____ and the price of a speeding ticket is _____ than will speed when the probability of getting caught speeding is _____ and the price of a speeding ticket is

   _____.
   a. 20 percent; $1000; 10 percent; $500
   b. 5 percent; $150; 10 percent; $300
   c. 10 percent; $200; 20 percent; $100
   d. b and c
   e. a, b, and c

7. If the "currency" you are paid in to be nice is niceness, and your supply curve of niceness is downward-sloping, it follows that you are
    a. nicer to nice people.
    b. less nice to nice people than you are to not-so-nice people.
    c. equally nice to everyone, no matter how nice they are or are not to you.
    d. b and c
    e. none of the above

8. A tax is placed on the seller of a good. The tax has the effect of
    a. shifting the demand curve (for the good) to the right.
    b. indirectly changing the quantity demanded of the good (assuming a downward-sloping demand curve and an upward-sloping supply curve).
    c. shifting the supply curve to the left.
    d. shifting the supply curve to the right.
    e. b and c

9. A $1 tax is placed on the supplier of a good. The vertical distance between the supply curve before the tax and the supply curve after the tax is equal to
    a. two times $1 if the demand curve is downward-sloping.
    b. one-half of $1 if the demand curve is downward-sloping.
    c. $1.50.
    d. one-half of $1 if the demand curve is vertical.
    e. none of the above

10. The demand curve (in a market) is downward-sloping and the supply curve is upward-sloping. If a tax is placed on the supplier of the good,
    a. producers' surplus will remain constant.
    b. consumers' surplus will rise.
    c. producers' surplus will rise.
    d. consumers' surplus will decline.
    e. b and d

11. There is no toll charge to drive on freeway A. If there is freeway congestion at 9 a.m., there will be greater freeway congestion at 11 a.m. if
    a. the demand to drive on the freeway is the same at both times.
    b. the demand to drive on the freeway at 11 a.m. is less than the demand to drive on the freeway at 9 a.m.
    c. the demand to drive on the freeway at 9 a.m. is greater than the demand to drive on the freeway at 11 a.m.
    d. fewer people carpool at 11 a.m. than at 9 a.m.
    e. none of the above

12. If goods are not rationed according to price, it follows that
    a. they won't get rationed at all.
    b. something will ration the goods.
    c. first-come-first-served will necessarily be the rationing device.
    d. there will be surpluses in the market.
    e. none of the above

13. Market X can be divided into two submarkets, A and B. The supply in each submarket is the same, but the demand in A is greater than the demand in B. If submarket B is in equilibrium, it follows that
    a. A is in equilibrium.
    b. there is a shortage in A.
    c. there is a surplus in A.
    d. there is a shortage in B only if there is a surplus in A.
    e. none of the above

14. According to an economist, people will buy relatively more of good X when
    a. the absolute price of good X falls.
    b. the absolute price of good X falls, *ceteris paribus*.
    c. the relative price of good X falls.
    d. b and c
    e. a and c

15. The demand to attend a certain college is represented by a downward-sloping demand curve. The supply of spots at the college is represented by a vertical supply curve. At the tuition that students are charged, there is a shortage of spots at the college. If the demand to attend the college falls, but the tuition stays constant, it follows that the
    a. GPA required to attend the college will probably rise.
    b. GPA required to attend the college will probably fall.
    c. SAT score required to attend the college will probably not change.
    d. a and c
    e. There is not enough information to answer the question.

True–False
Write a "T" or "F" after each statement.

16. A tax placed on a seller can lower consumers' surplus. _____

17. The deadweight loss of a tax refers to the net loss of the tax. _____

18. A higher demand means a higher quantity demanded, *ceteris paribus*. _____

19. In the face of scarcity, there must be some rationing device. _____

Fill in the Blank
Write the correct word in the blank.

20. The placement of a tax on seller X does not guarantee that seller X will _____ the full tax.

21. A tax placed on seller X will end up raising _____, lowering _____, and causing a deadweight loss.

22. If the equilibrium tuition to attend college is higher than the tuition the student pays, there will be a _____ of spots at the university and some _____ rationing device will have to be used to allocate spots at the university.

23. A $1 (per unit) tax is placed on the good a seller produces and sells (such that for every unit of the good the seller produces it must pay $1). This government action will vertically raise the supply curve (of the good) by _____.

24. A $1 (per unit) tax is placed on the good a seller produces and sells. This government action will end up raising the price the buyer _____ and lowering the price the seller gets to _____.

Chapter 5
Macroeconomic Measurements, Part I: Prices and Unemployment

What This Chapter Is About
There are many variables that economists measure—the price level, unemployment, gross domestic product (GDP), real gross domestic product (Real GDP), the economic growth rate, and so on. In this chapter we begin to discuss *how* economists measure certain variables. We focus on the price level and unemployment in this chapter; in the next chapter, we focus on GDP and Real GDP.

Key Concepts in the Chapter
- a. price level
- b. base year
- c. nominal income
- d. real income
- e. inflation
- f. unemployment rate
- g. frictional unemployment
- h. structural unemployment
- i. natural unemployment
- j. job search process

- The **price level** is the weighted average of the prices of all goods and services. Sometimes it is easier to think of the price level as an average price. For example, suppose the price of good A is $10, the price of good B is $20, and the price of good C is $30. The average price (of these three goods) is $20. In a large economy, there are many goods and services and each sells for a certain price. The average of all the prices of all the goods and services is the price level.
- The **base year** is one year in which all other years are measured up against. It is a benchmark year.
- **Nominal income** is current-dollar income. For example, suppose Suzanne earns an annual income of $60,000. This is her nominal income.
- **Real income** is one's nominal income adjusted for price changes.
- **Inflation** is defined as an increase in the price level. In a later chapter, you will learn about two kinds of inflation—one-shot inflation and continued inflation. In this chapter, we simply define inflation and show how the inflation rate is measured.
- The **unemployment rate** refers to the percentage of the civilian labor force that is unemployed.
- **Frictional unemployment** is a type of unemployment. A person who is frictionally unemployed is an unemployed person who has transferable skills. For example, suppose Joe was just fired from his job as an auto factory worker. If there is another auto factory that is hiring factory workers, then Joe has skills that can be easily transferred to another job.
- **Structural unemployment** is a type of unemployment. A person who is structurally unemployed is an unemployed person who does not have transferable skills. He or she will have to acquire some additional training to get a job. Again, suppose Joe was just fired from his job as an auto factory worker. If the only companies that are hiring currently are computer companies, then Joe may not have the skills necessary to do this kind of work. He is structurally unemployed, and will have to acquire new work skills before he gets a job with a computer company.
- **Natural unemployment** is the sum of frictional unemployment and structural unemployment. The natural unemployment rate is the sum of the frictional and structural unemployment rates. For example, suppose the frictional unemployment rate is 2 percent and the structural unemployment rate is 3 percent. It follows that the natural unemployment rate is 5 percent. When the economy is operating at the natural unemployment rate, full employment is said to exist.

- The **job search process** refers to the process of searching for a job. This process is undertaken by an unemployed person. In the job search process presented in this chapter, an unemployed person searching for a job considers both the costs and benefits of searching for a job. He or she stops searching when the benefits of the search equal the costs. Stated differently, he or she stops searching when the reservation wage equals the wage offer. A person's reservation wage is the lowest wage at which he or she will accept a job. A person's wage offer is exactly what it sounds like—it is the wage a person is offered to take a job.

Review Questions

1. What is the relationship between the price level and a price index?

2. Is the consumer price index (CPI) a reflection of the prices of all goods and services produced and purchased in an economy? Explain your answer.

3. If the CPI in a given year is 132, what does this mean?

4. Smith and Jones have the same nominal income, but they live in different countries. Does it follow that they have the same real income? Explain your answer.

5. Steve earned $40,000 income in 1987 and Jeff earned $40,000 in 1999. Was $40,000 in 1999 the same as $40,000 in 1987? Explain your answer.

6. Explain how the CPI is calculated.

7. What is the difference between the civilian noninstitutional population and the civilian labor force?

8. Not everyone who is not working is unemployed. What conditions must a person satisfy before he or she is considered unemployed?

9. If the unemployment rate is 5 percent, it does not follow that the employment rate is 95 percent. Explain why.

10. What are the four classifications of unemployed persons?

11. What is the difference between an reentrant and a new entrant.

12. Why aren't discouraged workers considered unemployed?

13. Give an example of someone who is structurally unemployed.

14. In Exhibit 8 (in the relevant chapter of the text), the wage offer curve starts off low, rises, and then levels off. Does every person's wage offer curve look like this?

15. Why does the reservation wage curve slope downard (from left to right)?

16. Explain how a change in the optimal search time can affect the unemployment rate in the economy.

Problems

1. In the table (that follows) we have identified current-year prices, base-year prices, and the marketbasket.

Market Basket	Current-year prices (per item)	Base-year prices (per item)
10X	$1.22	$1.10
15Y	$1.66	$1.16
33Z	$3.45	$2.55

What is the CPI for the current year?

2. The CPI was 72.6 in 1979 and 160.5 in 1997. What was the percentage change in prices during the time period 1979-1997?

3. Nominal income is $50,000 and the CPI is 143. What does real income equal?

4. Rebecca's income increased by 20 percent over the last year and prices increased by 2 percent. Did Rebecca's real income rise? Explain your answer.

5. Stacy earned $10,000 in 1967. If the CPI was 33.4 in 1967 and 164.3 in 1999, what was $10,000 equivalent to in 1999?

6. Use the data that follows to compute the chain-weighted price index in Year 2.

Goods	Quantities in Year1	Quantities in Year 2	Prices in Year 1	Prices in Year 2
Peaches	30	25	$0.60	$0.80
Tangerines	40	50	$0.50	$0.55

7. Fill in the numbers missing from the table that follows.

Category	Number of persons
Civilian noninstitutional population	200
Employed	100
Civilian labor force	120
Unemployment rate	
Persons unemployed	
Persons not in the labor force	

8. If the number of persons not in the labor force is 100, persons in the civilian labor force is 200, persons employed is 180, and persons unemployed is 20, then what is the labor force participation rate?

9. How does the labor force participation rate differ from the employment rate?

10. If you know the number of unemployed persons, job losers, and reentrants, is it possible to compute the number of job leavers? Explain your answer.

11. If the natural unemployment rate is 4.5 percent and the structural unemployment rate is 2.1 percent, is it possible to compute the cyclical unemployment rate? Explain your answer.

12. Diagrammatically represent the optimum search time.

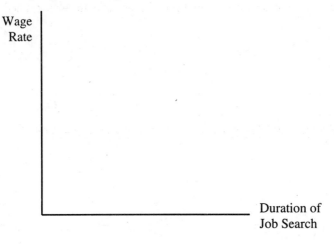

13. Diagrammatically show what happens to the optimum search time as the reservation wage falls.

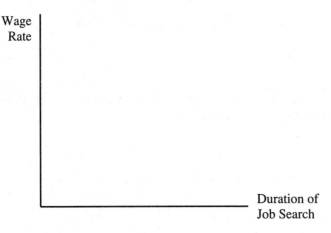

14. How will an increase in unemployment compensation affect the unemployment rate?

What is the Question?
Identify the question for each of the answers that follow.

1.   The consumer price index.

2.   Take the nominal income and divide it by the CPI. Then take the quotient and multiply it by 100.

3.   The number of persons employed plus the number of persons unemployed.

4.   The natural unemployment rate minus the frictional unemployment rate.

5.   This person is not considered unemployed (by the government), even though many people think this person should be considered unemployed.

6.   The cyclical unemployment rate.

7.   The lowest wage at which a person will accept a job.

8. Price stability, low unemployment, and high and sustained economic growth.

9. The first step is to subtract the CPI in the earlier year from the CPI in the later year. The second step is to divide by the CPI in the earlier year. The third step is to multiply by 100.

10. This happens if the CPI rises by more than your nominal income.

11. This person did at least one hour of work as a paid employee during the survey week.

12. This person quit his job.

13. This person got fired but doesn't (currently) have transferable skills.

14. The wage offer is equal to the reservation wage.

Multiple Choice
Circle the correct answer.

1. If the CPI was 72.6 in 1979 and 144.5 in 1993, by what percentage did prices rise during the period 1979-1999?
    a.   100.3 percent
    b.   160.7 percent
    c.   99.0 percent
    d.   15.09 percent
    e.   none of the above

2. Good X sold for $40 in 1945. The CPI in 1945 was 18.0 and the CPI in 1999 was 164.3. What was the price of good X in 1999 dollars?
    a. $233.88
    b. $243.76
    c. $365.11
    d. $211.89
    e.   none of the above

3. A _____ is a person who was employed in the civilian labor force and quit his or her job.
    a.   new entrant
    b.   reentrant
    c.   job leaver
    d.   job fixer
    e.   none of the above

4. The answer is: "a person employed in the civilian labor force who quits his or her job." The question is:
    a.   Who is a job loser?
    b.   Who is an entrant?
    c.   Who is a reentrant?
    d.   Who is a job leaver?
    e.   Who is a discouraged worker?

5. A _____ is a person who has never held a full-time job for two weeks or longer and is now in the civilian labor force looking for a job.
    a.   new entrant
    b.   reentrant
    c.   job fixer
    d.   job leaver
    e.   job loser

6. Which of the following statements is false?
    a.   A discouraged worker is not counted as an unemployed worker.
    b.   The frictional unemployment rate is less than the natural unemployment rate.
    c.   The natural unemployment rate is greater than the structural unemployment rate.
    d.   a and b
    e.   none of the above

7. Of all the categories of unemployment, most unemployed persons fall into the category of being a
    a.   reentrant
    b.   new entrant
    c.   job leaver
    d.   job loser
    e.   none of the above

8. If there are 35 job losers, 13 job leavers, 14 reentrants, and 10 new entrants, then there are _____ frictionally unemployed persons.
    a. 72
    b. 35
    c. 48
    d. 62
    e. There is not enough information to answer the question.

9. The number of employed persons plus the number of unemployed persons equals the number of persons
    a. in the total population.
    b. in the civilian noninstitutional population.
    c. in the civilian labor force.
    d. not in the labor force.
    e. none of the above

10. If we subtract the number of people not in the labor force from the civilian noninstitutional population, we get the number of people in the
    a. ranks of the unemployed.
    b. civilian labor force.
    c. ranks of the employed.
    d. ranks of discouraged workers.
    e. none of the above

11. The three major macroeconomic goals mentioned in the chapter include
    a. price stability, low unemployment, and happiness.
    b. price stability, high and sustained economic growth, and high unemployment.
    c. low interest rates, low unemployment, and high and sustained economic growth.
    d. low interest rates, high inflation, and happiness.
    e. none of the above

12. If your nominal income rises faster than prices, it follows that
    a. there is no inflation.
    b. there is deflation.
    c. your real income falls.
    d. your real income rises.
    e. b and c

13. The chain-weighted price index
    a. does not have a substitution bias.
    b. has a small substitution bias, just like the CPI.
    c. is similar to the CPI.
    d. has no substitution bias.
    e. is similar to the frictional CPI.

14. The civilian noninstitutional population is equal to _____ plus _____.
    a. persons not in the labor force; employed persons
    b. employed persons; unemployed persons
    c. reentrants; entrants
    d. persons not in the labor force; persons in the civilian labor force
    e. the total population; reentrants

15. The labor force participation rate is equal to the
    a. civilian labor force divided by the civilian noninstitutional population.
    b. number of employed persons divided by the civilian labor force.
    c. unemployment rate minus the employment rate.
    d. number of entrants plus number of reentrants.
    e. none of the above

True-False

16. The frictional unemployment rate minus the cyclical unemployment rate equals the natural unemployment rate. ____

17. If the economy is operating at the natural unemployment rate, there is full employment. ____

18. The price level is the weighted average of the prices of goods and services in the economy. ____

19. If the unemployment rate is 8 percent and the natural unemployment rate is 5 percent, then the cyclical unemployment rate is 3 percent. ____

20. The CPI is calculated by the Bureau of Labor Statistics. ____

Fill in the Blank

21. The _____ _____ is equal to the cyclical unemployment rate plus the natural unemployment rate.

22. The CPI is a _____ _____.

23. Nominal income adjusted for price changes is _____ _____.

24. As the optimal search time rises, the unemployment rate _____.

25. The _____ _____ is a benchmark year.

Chapter 6
Macroeconomic Measurements, Part II: GDP and Real GDP

What This Chapter Is About
In the last chapter we discussed a few macroeconomic measurements, such as the price level and unemployment. In this chapter we continue with the discussion of macroeconomic measurements. Here we discuss gross domestic product (GDP) and real gross domestic product (Real GDP).

Key Concepts in the Chapter
    a. GDP
    b. Real GDP

- **GDP (gross domestic product)** is the total market value of all final goods and services produced annually within a country's borders.
- **Real GDP** is GDP adjusted for price changes.

Review Questions

1. What is the difference between GDP and GNP?

2. GDP is defined as the total market value of all final goods and services produced annually within a country's borders. Give an example to illustrate what "total market value" means.

3. Give an example of a final good and of an intermediate good.

4. Sales of used goods are not considered when computing GDP. Explain why.

5.   Why aren't financial transactions counted in GDP?

6.   What are the three components of consumption?

7.   What is fixed investment? How does it differ from inventory investment?

8.   Why aren't government transfer payments counted in GDP?

9.   What does national income equal?

10. What is net domestic product?

11. How does personal income differ from national income?

12. How does disposable income differ from personal income?

13. If GDP rises, does it follow that Real GDP rises, too? Explain your answer.

14. How is economic growth measured?

Problems

1. Good X is made with intermediate goods A and B. The market value of A is $10, the market value of B is $13, and the market value of X is $23. Which of the three dollar amounts goes into the computation of GDP? Explain your answer.

2. The following activities (shown in the table) take place in a tiny economy.

Item	Market value of item
Nancy cleans her house.	$40.00
Bob buys illegal drugs at the corner of 5th St.	$400.00
Smithies receives a social security check written out for $654.32	$654.32
Karen buys 100 shares of stock Z	$1,255.00
Mario buys a used car from Nanette	$4,099.00
Bob mows his lawn.	$50.00
Carl produces and sells shoes.	$100.00

What does GDP equal?

3. Is it possible to compute GDP using the expenditure approach if you do not know the value of the purchases of new residential housing but do know the value of fixed investment? Explain your answer.

4. Using the expenditure approach to measuring GDP, what does GDP equal?

5. What will cause GDP to fall?

6.   Using the table that follows, compute GDP.

Item	$ Value (in millions)
Durable goods	$400
Inventory investment	30
Purchases of new residential housing	100
Nondurable goods	300
Services	100
Purchases of new capital goods	50
Fixed investment	150
Inventory investment	25
Federal government purchases	80
Government transfer payments	20
Net interest on the public debt	30
State government purchases	90
Local government purchases	70
Exports	100
Imports	190
Income taxes	80
Consumption	800
Net exports	-90
Investment	175

What does GDP equal?

7.   Using the table below, compute national income.

Item	$ Value (in millions)
Income taxes	$ 30
Net interest	20
Corporate profits	40
Consumption	300
Rental income	100
Proprietors' income	200
Compensation of employees	700
Investment	200
Excise taxes	10

What does national income equal?

8. Using the table that follows, compute personal income.

Item	$ Value (in millions)
National income	$1,200
Undistributed corporate profits	300
Social insurance taxes	160
Corporate profits taxes	40
Inventory investment	90
Government purchases	240
Transfer payments	200

What does personal income equal?

9. Using the table that follows, compute both GDP and Real GDP.

Quantities of various goods produced	Price of good in the current year	Price of good in the base year
100 X	$1	$1
200 Y	$2	$1
300 Z	$7	$3

What does GDP equal?

What does Real GDP equal?

10. Fill in the last column in the table that follows.

GDP	Population	Per capita GDP
$1,200 billion	100 million	
$500 billion	67 million	
$3,000 billion	50 million	

11. Use the terms (a) GDP, (b) income earned from the rest of the world, and (c) income earned by the rest of the world to define GNP.

12. Use the terms (a) GNP, (b) income earned from the rest of the world, and (c) income earned by the rest of the world to define GDP.

13. If you know the dollar amount of the capital consumption allowance and net domestic product, is it possible to compute GDP? Explain your answer.

14. If the first peak of a business cycle is in March, and the second peak of the business cycle is in July, is it possible to identify (in months) the length of the recovery? Explain your answer.

15. If the contraction of a business cycle is 12 months, the recovery is 13 months, and the expansion is 12 months, then how long after the first peak of business cycle does the second peak come?

What Is Wrong?
In each of the statements below, something is wrong. Identify what is wrong in the space provided.

1. The expansion phase of a business cycle is generally longer than the recovery stage.

2.   A stock variable makes little sense without some time period specified.

3.   Fixed investment includes business purchases of new capital goods, inventory investment, and purchases of new residential housing.

4.   GDP = C + I + G + EX + IM

5.   Net domestic product is equal to GDP minus capital consumption allowance. Another name for capital consumption allowance is capital good.

6.   A business cycle is measured from trough to peak.

7.   The largest expenditure component of GDP is government purchases.

What is the Question?
Identify the question for each of the answers that follow.

1. GDP divided by population.

2. Five phases: peak, contraction, trough, recovery, and expansion.

3. First, subtract Real GDP in the earlier year from Real GDP in the current year. Second, divide by Real GDP. Third, multiply by 100.

4. National income minus undistributed corporate profits minus social insurance taxes minus corporate profits taxes plus transfer payments.

5. Personal income minus personal taxes.

S

Multiple Choice
Circle the correct answer.

1. Gross Domestic Product (GDP) is
    a. the total market value of all final goods and services produced annually within a country's borders
    b. the total market value of all final and intermediate goods and services produced annually within a country's borders
    c. NDP minus capital consumption allowance
    d. personal income plus taxes plus disposable income
    e. none of the above

2. Which of the following illustrates double counting?
    a.   counting the value of intermediate goods only
    b.   counting the value of intermediate goods and final goods
    c.   counting the value of final goods only
    d.   counting the value of used car sales when measuring GDP
    e.   c and d

3. Which of the following is an intermediate good?
    a.   mustard on a ham sandwich sold at a restaurant
    b.   tires on a new car
    c.   a computer sold online
    d.   a book sold at a bookstore
    e.   a and b

4. The income approach to measuring GDP takes the sums of
    a.   consumption, net exports, and government purchases.
    b.   personal income, proprietors' income, investment, and net exports.
    c.   consumption, government purchases, investment, and net exports.
    d.   national income, exports, and imports.
    e.   none of the above

5. Government purchases consist of the total dollar amount(s) spent by the
    a.   federal government only.
    b.   state government only.
    c.   federal and state governments.
    d.   local government only.
    e.   federal, state, and local governments.

6. Leisure is
    a.   a good that is counted in GDP.
    b.   a bad that is counted in GDP.
    c.   a good that is not counted in GDP.
    d.   equal to personal income minus taxes minus savings.
    e.   c and d

7. Which of the following is often the smallest figure?
    a.   GDP
    b.   government purchases
    c.   net exports
    d.   investment
    e.   consumption

8. Which of the following is a stock variable?
    a.   the number of pencils on Harry's desk
    b.   the money supply
    c.   GDP
    d.   b and c
    e.   a and b

9. If there is a decrease in inventories, it follows that
    a.   fixed investment falls.
    b.   new residential housing purchases fall.
    c.   capital investment falls.
    d.   inventory investment rises.
    e.   none of the above

10. Which of the following is a flow variable?
    a. the money supply
    b. GDP
    c. personal income
    d. national income
    e. b, c, and d

11. Which of the following is not counted in GDP?
    a. an illegal drug transaction
    b. the production of telephones
    c. the production of shoes
    d. own-home housework
    e. a and d

12. An example of a government transfer payment is
    a. a social security check.
    b. taxes paid on income earned.
    c. excise taxes.
    d. personal income.
    e. none of the above

13. Consumption includes
    a. durable goods and services.
    b. nondurable goods.
    c. inventory investment minus government purchases.
    d. net exports minus government purchases.
    e. a and b

14. Real GDP is equal to
    a. GDP minus NDP.
    b. the sum of current-year quantities multiplied by base-year prices.
    c. the sum of current-year quantities multiplied by current-year prices.
    d. (base-year prices multiplied by current-year prices) minus current-year quantities.
    e. none of the above

15. National income equals
    a. the sum of resource or factor payments.
    b. compensation of employees plus proprietors' income plus rental income plus net interest.
    c. personal income plus personal taxes.
    d. disposable income at current-year prices.
    e. a and b

True False
Write a "T" or "F" after each statement.

16. In year 1, the chain-weighted price index was 127 and GDP was $7,000 billion. It follows that Real GDP in year 1 was approximately $6,281 billion. _____

17. Real GDP is never measured in base-year prices. _____

18. The base year is the year in which prices are the lowest. _____

19. Economic growth has occurred when Real GDP has risen over the year. _____

20. The typical business cycle is measured from expansion to trough. _____

Fill in the Blank
Write the correct word in the blank.

21. A recession is defined as _____ or more consecutive quarters of falling Real GDP.

22. A business cycle has _____ phases.

23. The bottom of the contraction is called a _____.

24. GDP is a _____ variable.

25. _____ is the sum of fixed investment and inventory investment.

Chapter 7
Aggregate Demand – Aggregate Supply

What This Chapter Is About
This is one of the most important chapters in the text. It introduces the AD-AS model, or framework, which we will use for the duration of our study of macroeconomics. Just as economists say there are two sides to a market (a demand side and a supply side), so are there two sides to an economy. We discuss each side in this chapter, then put the two sides together to discuss the economy. Our time period for studying the economy in this chapter is the short run.

Key Concepts in the Chapter
- a. aggregate demand
- b. real wage
- c. short-run aggregate supply
- d. short-run equilibrium
- e. natural real GDP
- f. long-run aggregate supply curve

- **Aggregate demand** is the quantity demanded of all goods and services at different price levels. Don't think of aggregate demand as a particular dollar amount. It is a series of quantities demanded (of Real GDP) at various price levels.
- **Real wage** is the nominal wage (or money wage) adjusted for price changes. In this chapter the real wage is equal to the nominal wage divided by the price level.
- **Short-run aggregate supply** is the quantity supplied of all goods and services at different price levels. Don't think of short-run aggregate supply as a particular dollar amount of goods and services. It is a series of quantities supplied (of Real GDP) at various price levels.
- **Short-run equilibrium** is the condition that exists in the economy when the quantity demanded of Real GDP equals the (short-run) quantity supplied of Real GDP. This condition is met where the aggregate demand curve intersects the short-run aggregate supply curve.
- **Natural Real GDP** is the Real GDP that is produced at the level of natural unemployment rate. It is the Real GDP that is produced when the economy is in long-run equilibrium.
- The **long-run aggregate supply (LRAS) curve** is a vertical line at the level of Natural Real GDP. It represents the output the economy produces when wages and prices have adjusted to their (final) equilibrium levels and neither producers nor workers have any relevant misperceptions.

Review Questions

1. Why do aggregate demand curves slope downward?

2. What is the difference between a change in the quantity demanded of Real GDP and a change in aggregate demand?

3. What are the components of total expenditures (or total spending)?

4. Will a lower price level change aggregate demand? Explain your answer.

5. Consumption will change if certain factors change. What are the factors that can change consumption?

6. What are the factors that can change investment?

7. What are the factors that can change net exports?

8. Outline the details of the sticky-wages explanation for the upward-sloping SRAS curve.

9. Outline the details of the sticky-prices explanation for the upward-sloping SRAS curve.

10. Outline the details of the producer-misperceptions explanation for the upward-sloping SRAS curve.

11. Outline the details of the worker-misperceptions explanation for the upward-sloping SRAS curve.

12. What factors can change SRAS?

13. What is the relationship between Real GDP and the unemployment rate?

Problems

1. Fill in the blank spaces in the table.

If...	AD curve shifts to the (right or left?)
consumption rises	
investment rises	
exports rise	
imports rise	
government purchases rise	
consumption falls	
net exports rise	

2. Fill in the blank spaces in the table.

If...	SRAS curve shifts to the (right or left?)
wage rates rise	
prices of nonlabor inputs fall	
productivity increases	
adverse supply shock	
beneficial supply shock	
wage rates fall	

3. Fill in the blank spaces in the table.

Factor	How does the factor change affect C, I, G, EX, and/or IM?
wealth rises	
individuals expect higher (future) prices	
individuals expect higher (future) income	
interest rate rises	
income taxes fall	
businesses expect higher (future) sales	
business taxes rise	
foreign real national income falls	
dollar appreciates	
dollar depreciates	

4.   Fill in the blank spaces in the table.

Factor	Does the AD curve shift? (right, left, no change)	Does the SRAS curve shift? (right, left, no change)	Is there a change in the price level? (up, down, no change)	Is there a change in Real GDP? (up, down, no change)	Is there a change in the unemployment rate? (up, down, no change)
interest rate falls					
wage rates rise					
productivity rises					
adverse supply shock					
wealth falls					
businesses expect lower (future) sales					
dollar appreciates					
prices of nonlabor inputs rise					
beneficial supply shock					
wealth rises					
dollar depreciates					
wage rates fall					

5.   Diagrammatically represent short-run equilibrium.

Price
Level
|
|
|
|
|
|
|
|
|_____ Real GDP

6. Diagrammatically represent long-run equilibrium.

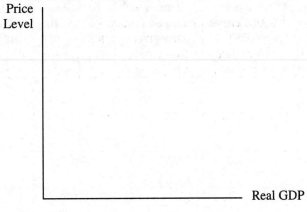

7. Diagrammatically represent an increase in aggregate demand that is greater than an increase in short-run aggregate supply.

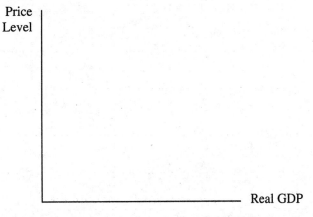

8. Diagrammatically represent a decrease in aggregate demand that is greater than a decrease in short-run aggregate supply.

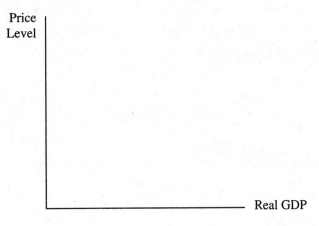

9. Fill in the blank spaces in the table.

Suppose...	Does the price level rise, fall, or remain constant?	Does Real GDP rise, fall, or remain constant?	Does the unemployment rate rise, fall, or remain constant?
AD rises			
AD rises by more than SRAS falls			
SRAS falls			
SRAS rises by the same amount as AD rises			
SRAS rises			
AD falls			

10. If the exchange rate between dollars and pounds is £1 = $1.50, a British good that is priced at £150 costs how many dollars?

11. If the exchange rate between dollars and pounds is £1 = $1.50, a U.S. good that is priced at $300 costs how many pounds?

What Is Wrong?
In each of the statements that follow, something is wrong. Identify what is wrong in the space provided.

1. Real GDP increased and the price level fell. This was because the AD curve shifted to the right.

2.   Real GDP and the price level increased. This was because the SRAS curve shifted to the right.

3.   If SRAS increases, the SRAS curve shifts upward and to the left.

4.   The price level increased and Real GDP decreased. This is because the AD curve shifted to the left.

5.   A change in interest rates will affect both consumption and government purchases.

6.   If the dollar appreciates, this means it takes more dollars to buy a unit of foreign currency.

7.   An increase in wealth will raise consumption, aggregate demand, and the price level. It will lower Real GDP.

8.   A decline in interest rates will raise consumption and investment, lower aggregate demand, shift the AD curve left, and raise the price level.

9.   The LRAS curve is vertical at the current level of Real GDP.

10. Long-run equilibrium is at the intersection of the AD curve and the upward-sloping LRAS curve, while short-run equilibrium is at the intersection of the AD curve and the vertical SRAS curve.

Multiple Choice
Circle the correct answer.

1. If the nominal wage is $100 and the price level (as measured by a price index) is 5.0, it follows that the real wage is
    a. $100.
    b. $20.
    c. $2.50.
    d. $10.
    e. none of the above

2. If wages are sticky, a decline in the price level will
    a. raise the real wage and lower the quantity demanded of labor.
    b. lower the real wage and lower the quantity supplied of labor.
    c. raise the real wage and lower the quantity supplied of labor.
    d. a and b
    e. none of the above

3. Which of the following is consistent with the sticky-wage explanation of the upward-sloping SRAS curve?
    a. The price level rises, the real wage falls, and the quantity demanded of labor declines.
    b. The price level rises, the real wage rises, and the quantity demanded of labor rises.
    c. The price level falls, the real wage rises, and the quantity demanded of labor falls.
    d. The nominal wage rises, the real wage rises, and the quantity demanded and supplied of labor rise.
    e. a and b

4. Menu costs are relevant to the
    a. sticky-wage explanation of the upward-sloping SRAS curve.
    b. sticky-wage explanation of the vertical SRAS curve.
    c. sticky-wage explanation of the vertical LRAS curve.
    d. sticky-price explanation of the upward-sloping SRAS curve.
    e. worker misperception explanation of the upward-sloping SRAS curve.

5. Which of the following is consistent with the worker misperceptions explanation of the upward-sloping SRAS curve?
    a. Workers always overestimate their real wages.
    b. Producers misperceive relative price changes.
    c. Workers initially underestimate changes in their real wages.
    d. Workers correctly perceive real wage changes in the short run but not in the long run.
    e. none of the above

6. According to the producer-misperception explanation of the upward-sloping SRAS curve, producers
    will produce
    a. less output as the relative price of their good rises.
    b. more output as the absolute price of their good rises, *ceteris paribus*.
    c. the same amount of output as the relative price of their good rises.
    d. the same amount of output as the relative price of their good falls.
    e. a and b

7. The economy suffers an adverse supply shock. As a result, in the short run Real GDP will
    _____ and the price level will _____.
    a. rise; rise
    b. fall; fall
    c. fall; remain constant
    d. fall; rise
    e. rise; fall

8. There is a fall in productivity in the economy. As a result, in the short run Real GDP _____
    and the price level _____.
    a. rises; falls
    b. falls; rises
    c. falls; falls
    d. rises; rises
    e. remains constant; remains constant

9. Here is some information: (1) the wage rises, (2) the interest rate rises, (3) any change in AD is greater
    than any change in SRAS. Based on this information, in the short run Real GDP will _____
    and the price level will _____.
    a. rise; rise
    b. fall; rise
    c. fall; fall
    d. rise; fall
    e. remain constant; rise

10. _____ identifies the level of Real GDP the economy produces when wages and prices have
     adjusted to their (final) equilibrium levels and there are no misperceptions on the part of either
     producers or workers.
     a. Short-run equilibrium
     b. Disequilibrium
     c. Long-run equilibrium
     d. Equilibrium
     e. none of the above

11. Real GDP rises and the price level falls. This can be brought about by
     a. an increase in AD.
     b. a decrease in AD.
     c. an increase in SRAS.
     d. a decrease in SRAS.
     e. none of the above

12. Real GDP falls and the price level rises. This can be brought about by
     a. an increase in AD.
     b. a decrease in AD.
     c. an increase in SRAS.
     d. a decrease in SRAS.
     e. none of the above

13. Real GDP and the price level fall. This can be brought about by
    a. an increase in AD.
    b. a decrease in AD.
    c. an increase in SRAS.
    d. a decrease in SRAS.
    e. none of the above

14. Real GDP and the price level rise. This can be brought about by
    a. an increase in AD.
    b. a decrease in AD.
    c. an increase in SRAS.
    d. a decrease in SRAS.
    e. none of the above

15. The components of total expenditures include
    a. consumption, investment, and government purchases.
    b. exports and imports.
    c. national income, personal income, and income taxes.
    d. wealth, interest rate, and wage rates.
    e. a and b

True-False
Write a "T" or "F" after each statement.

16. The real-balance effect deals with the change in the purchasing power of dollar-denominated assets that results from a change in the price level. _____

17. An increase in interest rates will raise investment. _____

18. If the dollar depreciates, net exports will rise. _____

19. If the dollar appreciates, exports will fall. _____

20. A rise in wage rates will shift the SRAS curve to the right. _____

Fill in the Blank
Write the correct word in the blank.

21. If the price level rises, the real wage _____.

22. If the nominal wage rises, and the price level is constant, the real wage _____.

23. _____ describes the output produced per unit of input employed over some period of time.

24. If wealth rises, consumption rises, and the _____ curve shifts to the right.

25. As the prices of nonlabor inputs fall, the SRAS curves shifts to the _____.

Chapter 8
The Self-Regulating Economy

What This Chapter Is About

Economists don't all agree as to how the economy works. In this chapter, we present the view of some economists as to how the economy works. For some economists, the economy is self-regulating. This means if the economy is in either a recessionary gap, or in an inflationary gap, it can "heal" itself and move into long-run equilibrium and produce Natural Real GDP.

Key Concepts in the Chapter
    a.   Say's law
    b.   recessionary gap
    c.   inflationary gap
    d.   wage and price flexibility

- **Say's law** holds that supply creates its own demand. Production creates demand sufficient to purchase all goods and services produced.
- A **recessionary gap** exists in the economy if the economy is producing a Real GDP level that is less than the Natural Real GDP level. Alternatively, a recessionary gap exists if the unemployment rate in the economy is greater than the natural unemployment rate. For example, if the unemployment rate in the economy is 5 percent, and the natural unemployment rate is 4 percent, then the economy is in a recessionary gap.
- An **inflationary gap** exists in the economy if the economy is producing a Real GDP level that is greater than the Natural Real GDP level. Alternatively, an inflationary gap exists if the unemployment rate in the economy is less than the natural unemployment rate. For example, if the unemployment rate in the economy is 3 percent, and the natural unemployment rate is 4 percent, then the economy is in an inflationary gap.
- **Wage and price flexibility** refers to wages and prices adjusting to shortages and surpluses in markets. For example, if there is wage flexibility in the labor market, then if there is a surplus in the labor market, the wage rate will fall; if there is a shortage in the labor market, the wage rate will rise. If wages were inflexible, then it might be the case that a surplus exists in the labor market, but the wage rate does not fall. In this case, the wage rate is inflexible in the downward direction.

Review Questions

1. In a money economy, a person may earn $1,000 a month, but spend only $900 of it on goods and services. In other words, $100 is saved each month. Does Say's law still hold, according to a classical economist? Explain your answer.

2. In the classical view of the credit market, the amount of investment increases as a result of saving increasing. Explain how an increase in saving can lead to more investment.

3.   What is the classical position on wages and prices? Are there economists today who take the classical position on wages and prices?

4.   What does it mean to say "the economy is self-regulating"?

5.   What condition defines a recessionary gap?

6.   What condition defines an inflationary gap?

7.   If the economy is in a recessionary gap, is the unemployment rate (that exists in the economy) greater than or less than the natural unemployment rate?

8.   If the economy is in an inflationary gap, is the unemployment rate (that exists in the economy) greater than or less than the natural unemployment rate?

9. If the economy is in a recessionary gap, is the labor market in shortage, surplus, or equilibrium?

10. If the economy is in an inflationary gap, is the labor market in shortage, surplus, or equilibrium?

11. Explain the process by which a self-regulating economy removes itself from a recessionary gap.

12. Explain the process by which a self-regulating economy removes itself from an inflationary gap.

Problems

1. Fill in the blank spaces in the table.

State of the economy	The labor market is in (shortage, surplus, equilibrium)	The wage rate will (rise, fall, remain unchanged)	The SRAS curve will shift (right, left)
Recessionary gap			
Inflationary gap			
Long-run equilibrium			

2. If the price level is rising, which is more likely: (a) the economy is removing itself from a recessionary gap, or (b) the economy is removing itself from an inflationary gap? Explain your answer.

3. If Real GDP is falling, which is more likely: (a) the economy is removing itself from a recessionary gap, or (b) the economy is removing itself from an inflationary gap? Explain your answer.

4. If Real GDP is rising, which is more likely: a) the economy is removing itself from a recessionary gap, or (b) the economy is removing itself from an inflationary gap? Explain your answer.

5. If the price level is falling, which is more likely: a) the economy is removing itself from a recessionary gap, or (b) the economy is removing itself from an inflationary gap? Explain your answer.

6. Suppose the economy is in long-run equilibrium in Year 1. Then aggregate demand rises. In Year 2 the economy is in long-run equilibrium again. If the economy is self-regulating, is the price level in Year 2 higher than, lower than, or equal to the price level in Year 1? Explain your answer.

7. Suppose the economy is in long-run equilibrium in Year 1. Then aggregate demand falls. In Year 2 the economy is in long-run equilibrium again. If the economy is self-regulating, is the price level in Year 2 higher than, lower than, or equal to the price level in Year 1? Explain your answer.

8. Suppose the economy is in long-run equilibrium in Year 1. Then short-run aggregate supply falls. In Year 2 the economy is in long-run equilibrium again. If the economy is self-regulating, is the price level in Year 2 higher than, lower than, or equal to the price level in Year 1? Explain your answer.

What Is the Question?
Identify the question for each of the answers that follows.

1. These economists believe that Say's law holds in a money economy.

2. (Current) Real GDP is less than Natural Real GDP.

3. The economy is operating at Natural Real GDP.

4. (Current) Real GDP is greater than Natural Real GDP.

5. The economy is operating beyond its institutional production possibilities frontier (PPF).

6. The economy is operating below its institutional production possibilities frontier (PPF).

7. In the long run, the price level is higher, but Real GDP is unchanged.

8. In the long run, the price level is lower, but Real GDP is unchanged.

What Is Wrong?
In each of the statements that follow, something is wrong. Identify what is wrong in the space provided.

1. The economy is initially in long-run equilibrium. Then, aggregate demand rises. In the short run, the price level and Real GDP rise. If the economy is not self regulating, in the long run the price level has risen and Real GDP has been unchanged (from its initial long-run position).

2. The economy is initially in long-run equilibrium. Then, short-run aggregate supply falls. In the short run, the price level and Real GDP rise. If the economy is self regulating, in the long run the price level has fallen back to its original level and Real GDP has been unchanged (from its initial long-run position).

3. The economy is in a recessionary gap if it is operating at the natural unemployment rate.

4. The economy is in an inflationary gap if the unemployment rate is greater than the natural unemployment rate.

5. The diagram (that follows) shows an economy in a recessionary gap.

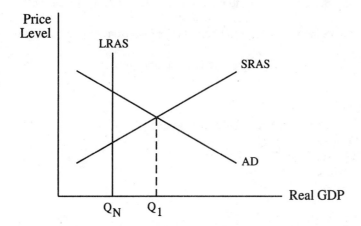

6. If wage rates fall, the SRAS curve shifts to the left.

Multiple Choice
Circle the correct answer.

1. An economy is producing its Natural Real GDP when the rate of unemployment is the
    a. cyclical unemployment rate.
    b. structural unemployment rate.
    c. natural unemployment rate.
    d. frictional unemployment rate.
    e. equal to the natural unemployment rate minus the cyclical unemployment rate.

2. If the SRAS curve intersects the AD curve to the right of Natural Real GDP, the economy is in
    a. a recessionary gap.
    b. an inflationary gap.
    c. a cyclical inflationary gap.
    d. a recession.
    e. an economic expansion.

3. Smith believes the economy is self regulating. Which of the following describes what he believes will happen if the economy is in a recessionary gap?
    a. Wage rates will fall, the SRAS curve will shift to the left, the price level will rise, and Real GDP will fall.
    b. Wage rates will fall, the SRAS curve will shift to the right, the price level will fall, and Real GDP will rise.
    c. Wage rates will rise, the SRAS curve will shift to the left, the price level will rise, and Real GDP will fall.
    d. Wage rates will rise, the SRAS curve will shift to the left, the price level will fall, and Real GDP will rise.
    e. none of the above

4. Jones believes the economy is self regulating. Which of the following describes what she believes will happen if the economy is in an inflationary gap?
    a. Wage rates will fall, the SRAS curve will shift to the left, the price level will rise, and Real GDP will fall.
    b. Wage rates will fall, the SRAS curve will shift to the right, the price level will fall, and Real GDP will rise.
    c. Wage rates will rise, the SRAS curve will shift to the left, the price level will rise, and Real GDP will fall.
    d. Wage rates will rise, the SRAS curve will shift to the left, the price level will fall, and Real GDP will rise.
    e. none of the above

5. Long-run equilibrium exists at
    a. the intersection of the AD curve and the SRAS curve.
    b. the intersection of the SRAS curve and the SRAS curve.
    c. the intersection of the LRAS curve and the AD curve.
    d. an output level less than Natural Real GDP.
    e. c and d

6. According to a Say's law, in a money economy a reduction in consumption spending causes a _____ shift of the saving curve and therefore a _____ in the interest rate.
    a. leftward; rise
    b. leftward; fall
    c. rightward; rise
    d. rightward; fall

7. According to Say's law, there can be
    a. neither a general overproduction nor a general underproduction of goods.
    b. a general overproduction, but not a general underproduction, of goods.
    c. a general underproduction, but not a general overproduction, of goods.
    d. both a general overproduction and a general underproduction of goods.

8. The classical economists argued that
    a. supply today creates supply tomorrow.
    b. wages are inflexible.
    c. interest rates are inflexible.
    d. saving is always greater than investment.
    e. wages and prices are flexible.

9. According to classical economists,
   a. total expenditures rise if consumption falls.
   b. total expenditures fall if consumption rises.
   c. Say's law holds in both a barter economy and in a money economy.
   d. total expenditures remain constant if consumption falls.
   e. c and d

10. The economy is in long-run equilibrium. Then, aggregate demand rises. In the short run,
    a. the price level is higher and Real GDP is lower.
    b. the price level is lower and Real GDP is higher.
    c. both the price level and Real GDP are lower.
    d. both the price level and Real GDP are higher.
    e. There is not enough information to answer the question.

True-False
Write a "T" or "F" after each statement.

11. According to classical economists, Say's law holds in a barter economy but not in a money economy.
    ____

12. When the economy is in a recessionary gap, there is a shortage in the labor market. ____

13. When the economy is in long-run equilibrium, the unemployment rate is equal to the natural
    unemployment rate and the Real GDP level is the Natural Real GDP. ____

14. According to classical economists, saving equals investment because the interest rate is rigid. ____

15. A self-regulating economy is one that can remove itself from both inflationary and recessionary gaps.
    ____

Fill in the Blank
Write the correct word in the blank.

16. If the economy is operating below its institutional PPF, it is in a(an) _____ gap.

17. If the economy is self regulating and in an inflationary gap, wage rates will _____ and the
    SRAS curve will shift _____.

18. If the economy is self regulating and in a recessionary gap, wage rates will _____ and the
    SRAS curve will shift _____.

19. The _____ production possibilities frontier lies further to the right than the
    _____ production possibilities frontier.

20. _____ - _____ is the public policy of not interfering with market activities in the
    economy.

Chapter 9
Economic Instability: A Critique of the Self-Regulating Economy

What This Chapter Is About

In the last chapter we discussed the self-regulating economy. Not all economists believe the economy is self regulating. Some economists believe that the economy can sometimes be given to instability. In other words, the economy may not remove itself from, say, a recessionary gap. We discuss this position in this chapter.

Key Concepts in the Chapter
   a.   efficiency wages
   b.   consumption function
   c.   autonomous spending
   d.   multiplier
   e.   Keynesian aggregate supply curve

- **Efficiency wages** refer to wage rates above equilibrium levels. For example, if the equilibrium wage rate is $30 an hour, an efficiency wage rate might be $35 an hour. Some economists believe there are solid microeconomic reasons for efficiency wages.
- The **consumption function** (in this chapter) relates consumption spending to disposable income.
- **Autonomous spending** is spending independent of income. For example, if investment spending rises from $40 million to $50 million even if income (in the economy) is constant, this $10 million change in investment spending is referred to as change in autonomous investment spending.
- The **multiplier** is the number that is multiplied by the change in autonomous spending to obtain the change in Real GDP.
- The **Keynesian aggregate supply (AS) curve** in the simple Keynesian model is horizontal.

Review Questions

1.   Does Keynes believe in Say's law in a money economy? Explain your answer.

2.   According to Keynesians, the economy can get stuck in a recessionary gap. According to them, why might the economy get stuck in a recessionary gap?

3.   What is the Keynesian position on wages and prices?

4. What are the three simplifying assumptions in the simple Keynesia

5. Write the Keynesian consumption function.

6. Using the Keynesian consumption function, what will lead to a rise in consumption?

7. How is the marginal propensity to consume computed?

8. What is the difference between the average propensity to consume (APC) and the marginal propensity to consume (MPC)?

9. Explain how the total expenditures (TE) curve is derived?

92

10. What role

...oes *optimum inventory* play in the Keynesian analysis of the economy?

11. What happens in the economy if TE > TP (TE = total expenditures; TP = total production).

12. According to Keynesians, can the economy be in equilibrium and in a recessionary gap, too? Explain your answer.

13. What does the multiplier equal?

14. What is the Keynesian position on the ability of the private sector to remove the economy from a recessionary gap?

Problems

1. Fill in the blank spaces in the table.

Change in income	Change in consumption	MPC (marginal propensity to consume)
$2,000	$1,000	
$1,000	$800	
$10,000	$9,500	
$3,456	$2,376	

2. Fill in the blank spaces in the table.

If consumption is	And disposable income is	And the marginal propensity to consume is	Then autonomous consumption is
$400	$1,000	0.20	
$1,600	$1,900	0.80	
$1,700	$2,000	0.75	

3. Fill in the blank spaces in the table.

Consumption	Investment	Net Exports	Total expenditure curve shifts (up, down)
rises	falls by less than consumption rises	rises	
falls	rises by more than consumption falls	falls by more than investment rises	
rises	rises	falls by more than investment rises, but falls by less than consumption rises	

4. Fill in the blank spaces in the table.

MPC	Multiplier
0.75	
0.80	
0.60	

5. Fill in the blank spaces in the table. The consumption function is C = Co + MPC ($\bullet$Yd), where Co = $200 and MPC = 0.80.

Disposable income	Change in disposable income	Consumption	Change in consumption	Saving
$10,000	$0	$8,200	$0	
$12,000				
$14,000				

6. Diagrammatically represent an economy stuck in a recessionary gap (within the AD-AS framework).

Price
Level
|
|
|
|
|
|_____ Real GDP

7. Diagrammatically represent an economy stuck in a recessionary gap (within the income-expenditure framework).

TE
|
|
|
|
|
|_____ Real GDP

8. What is the relationship between TE and TP at Q_1? At Q_2? At Q_3?

TE
| 45° line
| TE
|_____ Real GDP
     Q_1 Q_2 Q_3

9. Explain what will happen in the economy if it is at Q_1 in the exhibit in question 8.

10. Explain what will happen in the economy if it is at Q_3 in the exhibit in question 8.

What is the Question?
Identify the question for each of the answers that follow.

1. Wages and prices may be inflexible.

2. Autonomous consumption.

3. $1 \div (1 - MPC)$

4. Consumption divided by disposable income.

5. Inventories rise above optimum levels.

6. It must be horizontal so that changes in aggregate demand change only Real GDP and not the price level, too.

What Is Wrong?
In each of the statements that follow, there is something wrong. Identify what is wrong in the space provided.

1. If the AS curve is horizontal, then an increase in aggregate demand will raise Real GDP, but a decrease in aggregate demand will lower Real GDP and the price level, too.

2. According to Keynes, saving is more responsive to changes in interest rates than to changes in income.

3. Keynes's major work was titled *The General Theory of Employment, Income and Prices,* and it was published in 1937.

4. When TE is greater than TP, inventories rise above the optimum inventory level.

5. When the economy is in disequilibrium, inventories are at their optimum levels.

Multiple Choice
Circle the correct answer.

1. If total production is less than total expenditures, then business firms
    a. have underproduced.
    b. will increase production.
    c. have overproduced.
    d. b and c
    e. a and b

2. Consumption is _____ related to disposable income, according to the consumption function discussed in the text.
    a. inversely
    b. directly
    c. inversely at times, directly at other times
    d. not
    e. There is not enough information to answer the question.

3. Less is produced than households want to buy. This holds when
    a. TE = TP.
    b. TP > TE.
    c. TE > TP.
    d. the multiplier is greater than 1.
    e. none of the above

4. The efficiency wage model is an explanation of wage _____ and therefore provides support for _____ economics.
    a. rigidity; classical
    b. flexibility; Keynesian
    c. rigidity; Keynesian
    d. flexibility; classical
    e. flexibility; monetarist

5. Which of the following statements is true?
    a. Keynes believed that monopolistic elements in the economy will prevent immediate price declines.
    b. Keynes believed that during periods of high unemployment, labor unions will prevent wages from falling fast enough to restore full employment.
    c. Keynes believed in Say's law in a barter economy.
    d. all of the above
    e. none of the above

6. Keynes did not believe that interest rate flexibility would ensure that _____ equals saving.
    a. consumption
    b. investment
    c. the multiplier
    d. marginal propensity to consume
    e. net exports

7. Which of the following is an aspect of Keynesian economics?
    a. Wages and prices are flexible.
    b. The economy can exhibit instability.
    c. The private sector can always remove the economy from a recessionary gap.
    d. The economy cannot get stuck in a recessionary gap.
    e. c and d

8. If income rises from $600 to $700 and consumption rises from $300 to $380, the marginal propensity to consume is _____.
    a. 0.54
    b. 0.80
    c. 1.00
    d. 0.65
    e. none of the above

9. If autonomous consumption rises by $600 and as a result real national income rises by $3,000, then the marginal propensity to consume is _____.
    a. 0.90
    b. 0.80
    c. 0.70
    d. 0.60
    e. 0.40

10. According to efficiency wage models,
    a. labor productivity depends on the wage rate the firm pays employees.
    b. labor productivity depends on environmental conditions.
    c. labor specificity is a function of the wage rate.
    d. efficiency is a result of seven production factors.
    e. none of the above

11. In the real world, we should expect the multiplier process to work itself out
    a. almost instantly.
    b. within a few days.
    c. only if the SRAS curve is upward sloping.
    d. only over many months.
    e. c and d

12. In the TE-TP (Keynesian) model, the price level is assumed to be _____, so any changes in TE will bring about a multiplier effect in _____.
    a. rising; consumption
    b. constant; Real GDP
    c. rising; Real GDP
    d. falling; investment
    e. rising; government purchases

13. If investment and government purchases are independent of income, and consumption rises as income rises, then the TE curve will intersect the vertical axis at some point above the origin. The distance between the origin and the point of intersection is equal to
    a. autonomous investment.
    b. autonomous consumption.
    c. autonomous government spending.
    d. net exports.
    e. the multiplier.

14. The ratio of consumption to income is called the
    a. marginal propensity to save.
    b. average propensity to save.
    c. average propensity to consume.
    d. marginal propensity to consume.
    e. There is not enough information to answer the question.

15. If Keynesians believe that the economy can get stuck in a recessionary gap, then they probably don't always hold that _____ is the best policy.
    a. raising consumption
    b. laissez faire
    c. increasing the money supply
    d. a and b
    e. none of the above

True-False
Write a "T" or "F" after each statement.

16. Keynes believed that an increase in saving would not necessarily stimulate an equal amount of added investment spending. ____

17. According to the Keynesian consumption function, consumption spending can be some positive amount even when disposable income is zero. ____

18. When TE > TP, the inventories of firms are rising above their optimum levels. ____

19. According to Keynesians, the economy can be in a recessionary gap and in equilibrium, too. ____

20. According to Keynes, the private sector could not always remove the economy from a recessionary gap. ____

Fill in the Blank
Write the correct word in the blank.

21. _____ _____ models hold that it is sometimes in the best interest of business firms to pay their employees higher-than-equilibrium wage rates.

22. If wages are _____ in the downward direction, it is possible for an economy to get stuck in a recessionary gap.

23. If the _____ _____ is horizontal, then any change in aggregate demand will change Real GDP, but not the price level.

24. If the marginal propensity to consume is _____, then the multiplier is 2.5.

25. If people save for a certain dollar goal ($50,000), then it is possible for saving to _____ as interest rates rise.

Chapter 10
Fiscal Policy

What This Chapter Is About

In Chapter 8 you learned that some economists believe the economy is self regulating. In Chapter 9, you learned that some economists believe the economy is inherently unstable. If the economy is inherently unstable, if it can't remove itself from recessionary and inflationary gaps, then what is to be done? Some economists propose using fiscal policy to stabilize the economy. Fiscal policy deals with changes in taxes and government expenditures.

Key Concepts in the Chapter

    a.   fiscal policy
    b.   crowding out
    c.   fiscal policy lags
    d.   marginal tax rate
    e.   Laffer curve

- **Fiscal policy** deals with changes in government expenditures and/or taxes to achieve particular economic goals, such as low unemployment, stable prices, and economic growth.
- **Crowding out** refers to the decrease in private expenditures that occurs as a consequence of increased government spending or the financing needs of a budget deficit. Crowding out can be complete, incomplete, or zero (no crowding out).
- **Fiscal policy lags** refer to the time it takes to notice and implement certain measures relevant to fiscal policy. There are five fiscal policy lags: data lag, wait-and-see lag, legislative lag, transmission lag, and effectiveness lag.
- The **marginal tax rate** is the ratio of the additional tax paid on the additional income. For example, if one's income rises by $100, and, as a result, one's income tax rises by $35, then the marginal tax rate is 35 percent.
- The **Laffer curve** plots tax revenues against tax rates. It shows that as tax rates initially rise, tax revenues rise, too. However, after some tax rate, further increases in tax rates lower tax revenues.

Review Questions

1.   What is the difference between automatic and discretionary fiscal policy?

2.   What type of fiscal policy would you propose if the economy were in a recessionary gap? Explain your answer.

3. Give an example of incomplete crowding out.

4. If the government spends more on libraries, does it necessarily follow that private spending on books will fall? Explain your answer.

5. Suppose the federal budget is balanced. Then, government spending rises. How might a rise in government spending impact the value of the dollar on foreign currency markets?

6. Suppose that the budget deficit in country A rises. Does it necessarily follow that interest rates will rise? Explain your answer.

7. What is the legislative lag?

8. How can fiscal policy destabilize the economy?

9. Give a numerical example to illustrate the difference between the average tax rate and the marginal tax rate.

10. Will an increase in the average income tax rate bring about greater income tax revenues? Explain your answer.

Problems

1. Fill in the blank spaces of the table.

If the objective is to raise Real GDP by…	And the MPC is…	Then autonomous government spending should be increased by…
$400 billion	0.80	
$500 billion	0.75	
$100 billion	0.60	

2. Fill in the blank spaces of the table.

If the objective is to raise Real GDP by…	And the MPC is…	Then taxes should be cut by…
$400 billion	0.80	
$500 billion	0.75	
$100 billion	0.60	

3. There is incomplete crowding out and the economy is in a recessionary gap. Is it possible for expansionary fiscal policy to stabilize the economy shown in the diagram? Explain your answer.

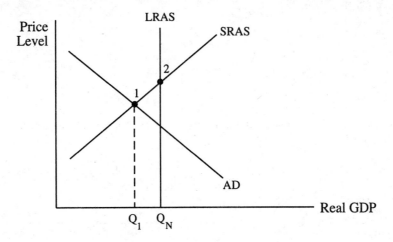

4. Using the diagram that follows, explain how fiscal policy can destabilize the economy.

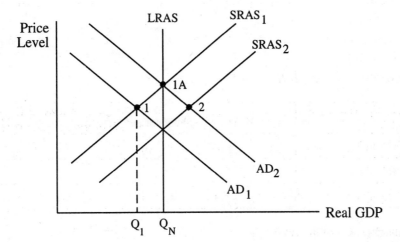

5. Diagrammatically represent the effect on the SRAS and LRAS curves of a permanent marginal tax rate cut.

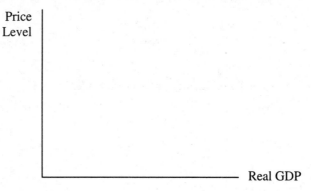

6. Fill in the blank spaces in the table.

Income	Taxes Paid	Marginal tax rate	Average tax rate
$10,000	$2,200	22 percent	22 percent
$11,000	$2,900		
$12,000	$3,700		

7. Fill in the blank spaces in the table.

Taxable income	Tax rate	Tax revenue
$100 million	12.3 percent	
	10.0 percent	$19 million
$200 million		$18 million

What Is the Question?
Identify the question for each of the answers that follow.

1. Changes in government expenditures and/or taxes that occur automatically without (additional) congressional action.

2. Saving increases as a result of the higher future taxes implied by the deficit.

3. Deficits do not necessarily bring higher interest rates.

4. The time it takes before policymakers know of a change in the economy.

5. The change in the tax payment divided by the change in taxable income.

6. The downward-sloping part of the Laffer curve.

Multiple Choice
Circle the correct answer.

1. Which of the following is an example of discretionary fiscal policy?
   a. Congress raises taxes.
   b. Congress lowers taxes.
   c. Congress increases spending.
   d. Congress decreases spending.
   e. all of the above

2. Unemployment compensation benefits is an example of
   a. expansionary discretionary fiscal policy.
   b. automatic fiscal policy.
   c. contractionary fiscal policy.
   d. discretionary fiscal policy.
   e. b and d

3. Suppose that the income tax rate rises as taxable income rises. If taxable income rises in the economy, the "higher tax rate at a higher taxable income" is an example of
   a. discretionary fiscal policy.
   b. automatic fiscal policy.
   c. expansionary discretionary fiscal policy.
   d. contractionary discretionary fiscal policy.
   e. There is not enough information to answer the question.

4. In the simple Keynesian model, Real GDP will rise by $600 billion if the multiplier is _____ and the increase in autonomous spending equals _____ billion.
   a. 2; $250
   b. 1; $1,000
   c. 3; $200
   d. 2; $1,000
   e. There is not enough information to answer the question.

5. In the simple Keynesian model, a rise in autonomous spending of _____ billion is consistent with a MPC of _____ and a desired rise in Real GDP of _____ billion.
    a. $400; 0.90; $2,000
    b. $200; 0.60; $2,000
    c. $800; 0.80; $2,500
    d. $230; 0.75; $7,500
    e. none of the above

6. According to the text, the average American worker worked _____ days in 1999 to pay all his or her taxes.
    a. 93
    b. 200
    c. 132
    d. 216
    e. 199

7. Suppose government believes the simple Keynesian model is descriptive of the current economy. Congress wants to raise Real GDP by $500 billion. The marginal propensity to consume is 0.80. Congress should lower taxes by _____ billion.
    a. $200
    b. $50
    c. $100
    d. $125
    e. none of the above

8. Keynesians would propose discretionary contractionary fiscal policy if
    a. the economy was in a recessionary gap.
    b. the economy was in an inflationary gap.
    c. as a stabilizing measure if the economy was in long-run equilibrium.
    d. the economy was stuck below Natural Real GDP.
    e. none of the above

9. Which of the following economists is known for arguing that current taxpayers will likely leave bequests to their heirs for the purpose of paying higher future taxes?
    a. John Maynard Keynes
    b. Robert Barro
    c. Irving Fisher
    d. Robert Solow
    e. Milton Friedman

10. The Laffer curve shows that
    a. as tax rates rise, tax revenues rise.
    b. as tax rates fall, tax revenues fall.
    c. as tax rates fall, tax revenues rise.
    d. as tax rates rise, tax revenues fall.
    e. all of the above

11. Suppose the government attempts to stimulate the economy by increasing purchases without increasing taxes. Which of the following statements is most likely to be accepted by someone who believes in crowding out?
    a. The government's actions will have their intended effect.
    b. The government's actions will cause businesses to become more optimistic about the economy, and they will increase their output even more than the government had intended.
    c. The government's actions will raise interest rates, causing decreased investment and consumption, and the economy will not expand as much as the government had intended.
    d. The government's actions will cause households to increase their spending.
    e. none of the above

12. Fiscal policy is likely to be ineffective at removing the economy from a recessionary gap if
    a. there is complete crowding out.
    b. there is zero crowding out.
    c. there are no fiscal policy lags.
    d. the data lag is longer than the legislative lag.
    e. none of the above

13. According to _____ economists, current consumption may fall as a result of _____ fiscal policy.
    a. Keynesian; discretionary
    b. new classical; expansionary
    c. new classical; contractionary
    d. Keynesian; contractionary
    e. monetarist; contractionary

14. Who said, "High tax rates are followed by attempts of ingenious men to beat them as surely as snow is followed by little boys on sleds"?
    a. John Maynard Keynes
    b. Arthur Laffer
    c. Arthur Okun
    d. Robert Barro
    e. none of the above

15. If the percentage decrease in the tax rate is greater than the percentage increase in taxable income, then
    a. the Laffer curve does not hold.
    b. tax revenues will decrease.
    c. tax revenues will increase.
    d. the economy is on the downward-sloping portion of the Laffer curve.
    e. b and d

True-False
Write "T" or "F" after each statement.

16. Fiscal policy can be effective at removing the economy from a recessionary gap. ____

17. If there is complete crowding out, fiscal policy is likely to be ineffective at removing the economy from a recessionary gap. ____

18. New classical economists argue that individuals will link expansionary fiscal policy to higher future taxes and decrease their current consumption and increase saving as a result. ____

19. The effectiveness lag refers to the fact that policymakers are usually not aware of changes in the economy as soon as they happen. ____

20. The change in Real GDP equals the multiplier multiplied by the change in autonomous spending. ____

Fill in the Blank
Write the correct word in the blank.

21. In 1999, the average American worked _____ days to pay all federal, state, and local taxes.

22. The _____ tax rate is equal to the change in one's tax payment divided by the change in one's taxable income.

23. On the _____ - _____ portion of the Laffer curve, a cut in tax rates will raise tax revenue.

24. Tax revenues are equal to the tax base multiplied by the average _____ _____.

25. _____ _____ refers to the decrease in private expenditures that occurs as a consequence of increased government spending and/or the greater financing needs of a budget deficit.

Chapter 11
Taxes, Deficits, Surpluses, and the Public Debt

What This Chapter Is About

The last chapter discussed fiscal policy, which dealt with government spending and taxes. We continue the discussion of taxes and government spending in this chapter. We discuss different types of taxes, budget deficits and surpluses, government spending, and the public debt.

Key Concepts in the Chapter

    a.   progressive income tax
    b.   proportional income tax
    c.   regressive income tax
    d.   mandatory spending
    e.   discretionary spending
    f.   public debt

- A **progressive income tax** refers to an income tax system in which one's tax rate rises as one's taxable income rises (up to some point).
- A **proportional income tax** refers to an income tax system in which one's tax rate is the same no matter what one's taxable income.
- A **regressive income tax** refers to an income tax system in which one's tax rate declines as one's taxable income rises.
- **Mandatory spending** refers to spending that is not subject to annual review. Mandatory spending occurs automatically.
- **Discretionary spending** refers to spending that is subject to annual review.
- The **public debt** refers to the total amount that the federal government owes its creditors.

Review Questions

1. Give a numerical example that illustrates a progressive income tax structure.

2. Explain why progressive income taxes may not be consistent with after-tax pay for equal work.

3. What did the average taxpayer pay in federal income taxes in 1995?

4. Describe how a national consumption tax would work.

5. What is the difference between a cyclical deficit and a structural deficit?

6. What is the difference between a nominal budget deficit and a real budget deficit?

7. What is the difference between the public debt and the net public debt?

8. Outline the "current generation bears the burden of the debt" argument.

9. Outline the "future generation bears the burden of the debt" argument.

What Are the Facts?

1. What was the average income tax rate in 1995? _____

2. What percentage of all federal income taxes did the top 1 percent income group pay in 1995?

   _____

3. What percentage of all federal income taxes did the top 5 percent income group pay in 1995?

   _____

4. What percentage of all federal income taxes did the bottom 50 percent income group pay in 1995?

   _____

5. For each dollar the federal government raised in 1999, what percentage came from the personal income tax? _____

6. For each dollar the federal government raised in 1999, what percentage came from the Social Security tax? _____

7. What was the average federal income tax rate of the bottom 50 percent income group in 1995?

   _____

8. What did President Clinton pay in federal income taxes in 1997? _____

9. For each dollar the federal government spent in 1999, what percentage went for national defense?

   _____

10. For each dollar the federal government spent in 1999, what percentage went for Social Security?

    _____

11. In 1999, what percentage of federal government spending went for net interest on the public debt?

    _____

12. What was the public debt equal to in 1999? _____

13. In what year was the public debt the lowest? _____

14. The combined (Social Security) tax rate was what percentage in 1999?

15. In 1995, how many workers contributed Social Security taxes for every one Social Security beneficiary? _____

16. In 1999, what percentage of all government spending was mandatory spending? _____

17. In what recent year did (nearly) three decades of federal budget deficits come to an end? _____

Problems

Using the following table, answer questions 1-5.

Taxable income	Tax rate
$10,000 – $20,000	10 percent
$20,001 – 30,000	$2,000 + 12 percent of everything over $20,000
$30,001 – 40,000	$3,000 + 14 percent of everything over $30,000

1. If a person earns $15,000, what does she pay in taxes?

2. If a person earns $23,100, what does he pay in taxes?

3. If a person earns $33,988, what does she pay in taxes?

4. What is the marginal tax rate of the person who earns $25,000?

5. What is the marginal tax rate of the person who earns $37,000? What is the person's average tax rate?

6. Fill in the blank spaces in the table.

Total budget deficit	Structural deficit	Cyclical deficit
$250 billion	$100 billion	
$100 billion		$75 billion
	$100 billion	$50 billion

7. Fill in the blank spaces in the table.

Nominal budget deficit	Public debt	Inflation rate	Real budget deficit
$200 billion	$4,000 billion	2 percent	
$200 billion	$2,000 billion	8 percent	
$250 billion	$4,000 billion	5 percent	

What is the Question?
Identify the question for each of the answers that follow.

1. Half of the tax is imposed on the employer and half is imposed on the employee.

2. The same tax rate is used for all income levels.

3. A multistage tax that is collected from firms at each state in the production and distribution process.

4. One of the arguments in its favor is that it would encourage saving, thus permitting more investment.

5. It is equal to the total budget deficit minus the cyclical deficit.

Multiple Choice
Circle the correct answer.

1. Suppose the public debt is currently $2,000 billion, and that during the course of the next year the government incurs a budget deficit of $100 billion. Also, assume that during the next year the inflation rate is 5 percent. The nominal public debt will increase by _____, the real value of the public debt will decrease by _____, and the real deficit will be _____.
    a. $100 billion; $100 billion; $0
    b. $100 billion; $0; $50 billion
    c. $50 billion; $100 billion; $50 billion
    d. $100 billion; $200 billion; $100 billion
    e. There is not enough information to answer the question.

2. A value-added tax (VAT) is
    a. assessed against individuals.
    b. collected from firms.
    c. a multistage sales tax.
    d. b and c
    e. all of the above

3. With a progressive income tax, the tax rate
    a. falls as income rises.
    b. is constant as income falls.
    c. rises as income falls.
    d. falls as income falls.
    e. none of the above

4. Which tax brings in the most revenue to the federal government?
    a. personal income tax
    b. corporate income tax
    c. payroll (Social Security) tax
    d. federal inheritance tax
    e. national sales tax

5. If an economy has a structural deficit and a cyclical deficit, one may conclude that
    a. fiscal policy is contractionary.
    b. fiscal policy is expansionary.
    c. the public debt is rising.
    d. the public debt is falling.
    e. b and c

6. The economist whose name is connected with the argument that the public debt is paid for by the current generation is
    a. Abba Lerner.
    b. James Buchanan.
    c. Robert Barro.
    d. Robert Eisner.
    e. none of the above

7. Social Security taxes are placed on
    a. employees only.
    b. employers only.
    c. both employees and employers.
    d. state governments.
    e. c and d

8. In 2030, it is predicted that there will only be _____ workers for every Social Security beneficiary.
    a. 3
    b. 2.5
    c. 4
    d. 1
    e. 4.5

9. Taxable income is
    a. a person's gross income minus sales taxes.
    b. gross income minus any exemptions and deductions.
    c. always higher than a person's gross income.
    d. equal to wages plus interest.
    e. none of the above

10. A person earns $50,000 income this year and ends up spending $40,000. If there were a national consumption tax, the person would be taxed on
    a. $50,000.
    b. $40,000.
    c. $10,000.
    d. $90,000.
    e. There is not enough information to answer the question.

True-False
Write "T" or "F" after each statement.

11. The tax base of a value-added tax is the same as a retail sales tax. ____

12. The cyclical deficit is that part of the budget deficit that would exist even if the economy were operating at full employment. ____

13. The real budget deficit is less than the nominal budget deficit if the inflation rate is greater than zero percent. ____

14. The real budget deficit is greater than the nominal budget deficit if there is a negative inflation rate. ____

15. Economist James Buchanan has argued that although resources are drawn from the private sector when debt-financed public expenditures are made, the people who give up these resources do not pay for, or bear the burden of, the public expenditures secured. ____

16. The federal government ran a budget surplus in 1999 and in 2000. ____

Fill in the Blank
Write the correct word in the blank.

17. Of the major federal spending programs in 1999, the largest percentage of spending went for

    _____ _____.

18. A proportional income tax is sometimes referred to as a _____ tax.

19. The total budget deficit is equal to the structural deficit plus the _____ _____.

20. If people translate budget deficits into higher future taxes, then they may translate budget surpluses into _____ _____ _____.

Chapter 12
Money and Banking

What This Chapter Is About
The money supply has not played a role in our discussion of macroeconomics until this point. With this chapter, we begin to talk about money. In fact, this chapter begins a discussion of money that will carry through the rest of our discussion of macroeconomics. In this chapter, we discuss how money came to exist, the money supply, and the money creation process.

Key Concepts in the Chapter
   a.   money
   b.   barter
   c.   Gresham's law
   d.   fractional reserve banking

- **Money** is any good that is widely accepted for purposes of exchange in the repayment of debts.
- **Barter** refers to exchanging goods and services for other goods and services without the use of money.
- **Gresham's law** states that "bad money drives good money out of circulation."
- **Fractional reserve banking** is a banking arrangement that allows banks to hold reserves equal to only a fraction of their deposit liabilities.

Review Questions

1. Give an example of two people who have a double coincidence of wants.

2. What does it mean to say that money is a unit of account?

3. Explain the part that self interest plays in the story of money emerging from a barter economy.

4. The use of money makes the consumption of additional leisure possible. Explain.

5. What gives money value?

6. Bad money drives good money out of circulation if three conditions hold. What are the three conditions?

7. What does the M1 money supply equal?

8. What does the M2 money supply equal?

9. Since credit cards are widely accepted for purposes of exchange, why aren't they considered money?

10. What do a bank's reserves consist of?

11. If checkable deposits in Bank A go from $400 million to $450 million, will Bank A have to hold more reserves? Explain your answer.

12. Give an example of a cash leakage.

13. What is the difference between the required-reserve ratio and the simple deposit multiplier?

Problems

1. Fill in the blanks in the table.

Required-reserve ratio	Simple deposit multiplier
0.10	
0.12	
0.09	

2. Fill in the blanks in the table.

Currency	Checkable deposits	Traveler's checks	M_1 money supply
$200 billion	$500 billion	$8 billion	
$100 billion		$9 billion	$700 billion
	$300 billion	$10 billion	$500 billion

3. Fill in the blanks in the table.

Checkable deposits	Required-reserve ratio	Required reserves
$400 million	0.10	
$300 million	0.12	
$1,000 million	0.15	

4. Fill in the blanks in the table.

Checkable deposits	Required-reserve ratio	Required reserves	Reserves	Excess reserves
$400 million	0.10		$60 million	
$500 million	0.15		$80 million	
$872 million	0.12		$200 million	

5. Fill in the blanks in the table.

Checkable deposits	Required-reserve ratio	Required reserves	Vault cash	Bank deposits at the Fed	Excess reserves
$230 million	0.13		$10 million	$30 million	
$367 million	0.10		$1 million	$43 million	
$657 million	0.12		$23 million	$60 million	

6. Fill in the blanks in the table.

Change in reserves	Required-reserve ratio	Maximum change in the money supply
+ $4 million	0.10	
+ $50 million	0.12	
- $41 million	0.10	

7. Fill in the blanks in the table.

Checkable deposits	Required-reserve ratio	Required reserves	Vault cash	Bank deposits at the Fed	Excess reserves
$1,000 million	0.10		$50 million		$0
$230 million	0.12		$20 million		$0
$498 million	0.10		$10 million		$0

What is the Question?
Identify the question for each of the answers that follow.

1. Medium of exchange, unit of account, and store of value.

2. Exchanging goods and services for other goods and services.

3. The least exclusive function of money.

4. General acceptability.

5. Deposits on which checks can be written.

6. An asset that can easily and quickly be turned into cash.

7. The central bank of the United States.

8. Bank deposits at the Fed plus vault cash.

9. The difference between reserves and required reserves.

10. 1 divided by the required-reserve ratio.

What Is Wrong?
In each of the statements that follow, something is wrong. Identify what is wrong in the space provided.

1. How much money did you earn last week?

2. A double coincidence of wants is not a necessary condition for trade to take place.

3. Gresham's law states that bad money drives good money out of circulation if the bad money and the good money have different face values, the same intrinsic values, and are fixed at a ratio of 1 for 1.

4. The largest component of M1 is currency.

5. M1 is the broad definition of the money supply.

6. Excess reserves equal reserves plus required reserves.

7. The maximum change in checkable deposits = $r \times \Delta R$.

8. The greater the cash leakages, the larger the increase in the money supply for a given positive change in reserves.

9. Our money today has value because it is backed by gold.

Multiple Choice
Circle the correct answer.

1. If chalk is widely accepted for purposes of exchange, then
    a. chalk is money.
    b. chalk is less valuable than it was before it was widely accepted for purposes of exchange.
    c. we would observe people using chalk to buy their weekly groceries.
    d. a and b
    e. a and c

2. Money is valuable because
    a. it is backed by gold.
    b. the government says it is valuable.
    c. people are willing to accept it in payment for goods and services.
    d. it is backed by silver.
    e. none of the above

3. A common measurement in which values are expressed is referred to as a
    a. medium of exchange.
    b. store of value.
    c. unit of account.
    d. barter payment.
    e. none of the above

4. M1 is comprised of
    a. currency, checkable deposits, Visa and MasterCard.
    b. currency, checkable deposits, traveler's checks.
    c. currency, and checkable deposits.
    d. currency, checkable deposits, savings deposits.

5. A credit card is
    a. considered money.
    b. not considered money.
    c. under certain circumstances considered money.
    d. the same as a repurchase agreement.
    e. none of the above

6. Reserves equal
    a. demand deposits + vault cast – traveler's checks.
    b. currency + savings deposits – vault cash.
    c. bank deposits at the Fed + vault cash + currency.
    d. bank depostis at the Fed + vault cash.

7. If deposits in Bank A total $15 million and the required-reserve ratio is 10 percent, then excess reserves equal _____.
    a. $13.5 million.
    b. $1.5 million.
    c. $10.5 million.
    d. $2.5 million.
    e. none of the above

8. Which of the following required-reserve rations would allow a bank the least amount of loanable funds?
    a. 5 percent
    b. 10 percent
    c. 12 percent
    d. 15 percent

9. The banking system increases the money supply by
    a. printing its own currency.
    b. creating checkable deposits.
    c. creating demand deposits and currency.
    d. creating Federal Reserve Notes.
    e. none of the above

10. Suppose that the excess reserves in Bank A increase by $3,000. If the required-reserve ratio is 20 percent, what is the maximum change in demand deposits brought about by the banking system?
    a. $15,000
    b. $12,000
    c. $10,000
    d. $8,500
    e. none of the above

11. Which of the following statements is false?
    a. A change in the composition of the money supply always decreases the money supply.
    b. If Smith takes $1,000 out of her wallet and deposits it in a bank, the composition of the money supply changes.
    c. If Jones takes $1,000 out of his checking account in the bank and puts it in his wallet, the composition of the money supply changes.
    d. A change in the composition of the money supply can change the size of the money supply.
    e. a and c

12. The simple deposit multiplier is
    a. the required-reserve ratio.
    b. always 1.
    c. the reciprocal of the required-reserve ratio.
    d. different from bank to bank even if the required-reserve ratio is the same for all banks.

13. If there is a change in the composition of the money supply such that there is more currency outside banks and less checkable deposts, the money supply
    a. falls.
    b. rises.
    c. stays constant.
    d. first falls and then sharply rises.

14. If the required-reserve ratio is 20 percent, the simple deposit multiplier is _____.
    a. 3
    b. 4
    c. 5
    d. 6
    e. none of the above

15. Bank A has depostis of $10,000 and reserves of $3,600. If the required-reserve ratio is 0.20 (20%), the bank has excess reserves of _____.
    a. $2,000
    b. $3,600
    c. $1,200
    d. $1,600
    e. none of the above

True-False
Write a "T" or "F" after each statement.

16. A unit of account is a common measurement in which values are expressed. ____

17. Money is unique in that it is the only good that serves as a store of value. ____

18. Money market mutual funds invest in short-term, highly illiquid assets. ____

19. The more new reserves that enter the banking system, the greater the money supply will be, *ceteris paribus*. ____

20. Money did not exist before formal governments existed. ____

Fill in the Blank
Write the correct word in the blank.

21. Two people have a _____ _____ _____ _____ if what the first

     person wants is what the second person has, and what the second person wants is what the first person

     has.

22. About 99 percent of the paper money in circulation is _____ _____

     _____.

23. Under a _____ _____ banking system, banks create money by holding on

     reserve only a fraction of the money deposited with them and lending the remainder.

24. If the required-reserve ratio is 10 percent, the simple deposit multiplier is _____.

25. Money has value because of its _____ _____.

Chapter 13
The Federal Reserve System

What This Chapter Is About
The last chapter briefly mentioned the Federal Reserve System. In this chapter the Fed is discussed at some length. A brief history of the Fed is presented, the functions of the Fed discussed, and the tools the Fed uses to change the money supply are explained.

Key Concepts in the Chapter
    a.   open market operations
    b.   monetary base
    c.   money multiplier
    d.   federal funds rate
    e.   discount rate

- **Open market operations** refer to the buying and selling of government securities by the Fed. When the Fed buys government securities, it is conducting an open market purchase; when it sells government securities, it is conducting an open market sale.
- The **monetary base** is the sum of reserves and currency (held outside banks).
- The **money multiplier** measures the actual change in the money supply for a dollar change in the monetary base. For example, if for every $1 rise in the monetary base, the money supply rises by $5, the money multiplier is 5.
- The **federal funds rate** is the interest rate one bank charges another to borrow reserves. Stated differently, it is the interest rate one bank charges another for a loan.
- The **discount rate** is the interest rate the Fed charges depository institutions that borrow reserves from it. Stated differently, it is the interest rate the Fed charges depository institutions for a loan.

Review Questions

1. How many people sit on the Board of Governors of the Federal Reserve System?

2. How many Federal Reserve districts exist?

3. Identify the locations of the Federal Reserve District Banks.

4. What is the most important responsibility of the Fed?

5. What is the composition of the Federal Open Market Committee (FOMC)?

6. Explain how a check is cleared.

7. What is the difference between the Treasury and the Fed?

8. What does the monetary base equal?

9. Prove that when the Fed buys or sells anything, the dollar value of the purchase or sale will end up changing the monetary base.

10. Explain how an open market purchase increases the money supply.

11. Explain how lowering the discount rate (relative to the funds rate) increases the money supply.

12. Give a numerical example that shows how lowering the required-reserve ratio can increase the money supply.

13. Is the federal funds rate determined in a different way than the discount rate? Explain your answer.

Problems

1. Fill in the blanks in the table.

Change in the monetary base	Money multiplier	Change in the money supply
$300 million	2.5	
	4.1	$600 million
$530 million		$1,749 million

2. Fill in the blanks in the table.

Vault cash	Bank deposits at the Fed	Currency (held outside banks)	Monetary base
$30 billion	$70 billion	$200 billion	
	$420 billion	$400 billion	$1,000 billion
$37 billion		$210 billion	$347 billion

3. Here are some data for Bank A:
        Checkable deposits = $400 million
        Required-reserve ratio = 10 percent
        Required reserves = $40 million
        Reserves = $40 million
        Excess reserves = 0

    Suppose now the required-reserve ratio is lowered to 5 percent. What do the following equal?

        Checkable deposits = _____ million
        Required-reserve ratio = _____ percent
        Required reserves = _____ million
        Reserves = _____ million
        Excess reserves = _____ million

4. Here are some data for Bank B:
        Checkable deposits = $500 million
        Required-reserve ratio = 12 percent
        Required reserves = $60 million
        Reserves = $60 million
        Excess reserves = 0

    Suppose now the Fed buys $10 million worth of securities from Bank B. What do the following equal?

        Checkable deposits = _____ million
        Required-reserve ratio = _____ percent
        Required reserves = _____ million
        Reserves = _____ million
        Excess reserves = _____ million

5. Here are some data for Bank C:
        Checkable deposits = $600 million
        Required-reserve ratio = 10 percent
        Required reserves = $60 million
        Reserves = $60 million
        Excess reserves = 0

    Suppose now Fed buys $10 million worth of securities from Jane, who does her banking at Bank C. The Fed writes a check to Jane for $10 million. Jane deposits the entire check in her account with Bank C. What do the following equal?

        Checkable deposits = _____ million
        Required-reserve ratio = _____ percent
        Required reserves = _____ million
        Reserves = _____ million
        Excess reserves = _____ million

6. Here are some data for Bank D:
        Checkable deposits = $600 million
        Required-reserve ratio = 10 percent
        Required reserves = $60 million
        Reserves = $60 million
        Excess reserves = 0

    Suppose now that the Fed gives a $10 million discount loan to Bank D. What do the following equal?

        Checkable deposits = _____ million
        Required-reserve ratio = _____ percent
        Required reserves = _____ million
        Reserves = _____ million
        Excess reserves = _____ million

7. Fill in the blanks in the table.

Fed action...	Money supply (rises, falls, remains unchanged)
Conducts an open market purchase	
Lowers required-reserve ratio	
Raises the discount rate to a level higher than the federal funds rate	
Conducts an open market sale	
Lowers the discount rate to a level substantially lower than the federal funds rate	
Raises the required-reserve ratio	

8. Fill in the blanks in the table. Assume that the required-reserve ratio is 10 percent.

Fed action...	Maximum change in the money supply
Buys $100 million worth of government securities from Bank A	
Gives a $10 million discount loan to Bank B	
Sells $20 million worth of government securities to Bank C	

What Is the Question?
Identify the question for each of the answers that follow.

1. Any of these changes in Fed policy tools will cause the money supply to rise.

2. This group conducts open market operations.

3. These are sold to raise funds to pay the government's bills.

4. Bank deposits at the Fed plus vault cash plus currency held outside banks.

5. The money supply divided by the monetary base.

6. The Fed buys and sells government securities.

7. Either to the federal funds market or to the Fed for a discount loan.

What Is Wrong?
In each of the statements that follow, something is wrong. Identify what is wrong in the space provided.

1. The president of the St. Louis Fed holds a permanent seat on the FOMC.

2. The Fed is a budgetary and monetary agency and the Treasury is a budgetary agency only.

3. If the monetary base rises by $400 million and the money supply rises by $1,200 million dollars, the multiplier is 4.

4. An open market purchase refers to a commercial bank buying government securities from the Fed.

5. An increase in the discount rate is likely to raise the money supply.

6. Open market operations are flexible, can easily be reversed, but can only be implemented over a substantial period of time.

7. Every time the Fed buys or sells something, reserves change.

8. The simple deposit multiplier is likely to be smaller than the money multiplier.

9. The major responsibility of the Fed is to clear checks.

Multiple Choice
Circle the correct answer.

1. _____ persons sit on the FOMC.
   a. 12
   b. 7
   c. 15
   d. 10
   e. 13

2. When a check is written on an account at Bank C and is deposited in Bank D, the reserve account of _____ will fall while reserves of the entire banking system _____.
   a. Bank C; rise
   b. Bank C; remain unchanged
   c. Bank D; rise
   d. Bank D; remain unchanged

3. Tim removes $5,000 from his checking account. As a result, reserves in the banking system _____ and the monetary base _____.
   a. rise; remains unchanged
   b. fall; rises
   c. rise; rises
   d. fall; falls
   e. fall; remains unchanged

4. Tim takes $400 out of a shoebox (that he keeps under his bed) and deposits it in Bank A. As a result, reserves in the banking system _____ and the monetary base _____.
   a. fall; falls
   b. rise; remains unchanged
   c. fall; remains unchanged
   d. rise; rises
   e. There is not enough information to answer the question.

5. The monetary base is equal to
   a. money supply ÷ money multiplier.
   b. money supply ÷ (1 − money multiplier).
   c. money supply x money multiplier.
   d. money supply x (1 − money multiplier).
   e. none of the above

6. Suppose the public begins to withdraw a lot of currency from the banking system. The Fed could offset the effect on the money supply by
   a. buying government securities.
   b. raising the required-reserve ratio.
   c. raising the discount rate.
   d. selling government securities.
   e. none of the above

7. A bank is less likely to borrow reserves from the Fed when the _____ rises relative to the _____.
   a. discount rate; required-reserve ratio
   b. federal funds rate; discount rate
   c. required-reserve ratio; discount rate
   d. discount rate; federal funds rate
   e. federal funds rate; required-reserve ratio

8. Bank A borrows $10 million from the Fed. As a result,
   a. the monetary base falls by $10 million.
   b. reserves rise by $10 million.
   c. the monetary base rises by $10 million.
   d. the monetary base remains unchanged.
   e. b and c

9. The Fed writes a $10,000 check to Yvonne, who deposits the check with Bank A and receives $10,000 in currency from Bank A. As a result,
   a. the monetary base rises by $10,000.
   b. reserves rise by $10,000.
   c. reserves remain unchanged.
   d. a and b
   e. a and c

10. Suppose there is a cash leakage in the banking system. When the required-reserve ratio is 0.10, the money multiplier is
    a. greater than 10.
    b. less than 10 (but positive).
    c. equal to 10.
    d. negative.
    e. There is not enough information to answer the question.

11. Every time the Fed _____, the monetary base rises.
    a. buys something
    b. sells something
    c. raises the required-reserve ratio
    d. lowers the required-reserve ratio
    e. a and b

12. An open market purchase occurs when
    a. one bank buys government securities from another bank.
    b. a bank buys government securities from the Fed.
    c. the Fed buys government securities from a bank.
    d. the Fed raises the discount rate.
    e. none of the above

13. The Fed
    a. serves as a fiscal agent for the Treasury.
    b. is a lender of last resort.
    c. is a borrower of last resort.
    d. a and b
    e. a, b, and c

14. If the Fed buys $5 billion of government securities and the money multiplier is 3.5, the money supply will
    a. fall by $17.5 billion.
    b. rise by $5 billion.
    c. rise by $1.5 billion.
    d. rise by $17.5 billion.
    e. There is not enough information to answer the question.

15. The Fed began operation in
    a. 1913.
    b. 1914.
    c. 1915.
    d. 1929.
    e. none of the above.

True-False
Write "T" or "F" after each statement.

16. The money multiplier is equal to 1/r, where r is the required-reserve ratio. _____

17. A decrease in the required-reserve ratio will increase the money supply. _____

18. When a bank with a cash management problem turns to the Fed, the Fed functions as a bank supervisor. _____

19. Reserves can increase while the monetary base remains unchanged. _____

20. The monetary base can change while reserves remain unchanged. _____

Fill in the Blank
Write the correct word in the blank.

21. The _____ _____ measures the actual change in the money supply for a dollar change in the monetary base.

22. The interest rate that one bank charges another bank for a loan is called the _____

    _____ _____.

23. A(an) _____ in the discount rate will lower the money supply and a(an)

    _____ in the required-reserve ratio will raise the money supply.

24. The money supply is equal the money multiplier times the _____ _____.

25. Another name for the monetary base is _____ money.

Chapter 14
Money and the Economy

What This Chapter Is About
Earlier chapters discussed a few of the technical details of money—how money came to exist, what the money supply is, how the money supply is increased and decreased. This chapter deals with how money affects the economy.

Key Concepts in the Chapter
   a. equation of exchange
   b. simple quantity theory of money
   c. one-shot inflation
   d. continued inflation
   e. deflation
   f. velocity

   • The **equation of exchange** is an identify stating that the money supply multiplied by velocity is equal to the price level multiplied by Real GDP.
   • The **simple quantity theory of money** predicts that changes in the price level are strictly proportional to changes in the money supply.
   • **One-shot inflation** is a one-time increase in the money supply.
   • **Continued inflation** is a continued, or sustained, increase in the money supply.
   • **Deflation** is a decrease in the price level.
   • **Velocity** is the average number of times a dollar is spent to buy final goods and services in a year.

Review Questions

1. Give an example to illustrate velocity.

2. What is the difference between the equation of exchange and the simple quantity theory of money.

3. What does the simple quantity theory of money predict?

4. What does the aggregate supply curve look like in the simple quantity theory of money? Explain your answer.

5. Use the equation of exchange to explain inflation and deflation.

6. What is the monetarist position on the following:

    a. the shape of the SRAS curve

    b. the factors that change AD in the economy

    c. velocity

    d. the issue of a self-regulating economy

7. One-shot inflation can be caused by a change in a factor on the demand-side of the economy or on the supply-side of the economy. Do you agree or disagree? Explain your answer.

8. Is continued inflation a demand-side (of the economy) or supply-side phenomenon? Explain your answer.

9. What is the liquidity effect?

10. What is the expectations, or Fisher, effect?

11. Explain how a change in the money supply can affect the interest rate.

12. What is the difference between the nominal interest rate and the real interest rate?

13. What is the difference between the *ex ante* real interest rate and the *ex post* real interest rate?

Problems

1. Fill in the blanks in the table. Assume that velocity and Real GDP are constant.

Percentage change in the money supply	Percentage change in the price level
+ 25	
− 10	
+ 9	

2. Fill in the blanks in the table.

Money supply	Velocity	Real GDP	Will there be inflation or deflation?
rises	rises	stays constant	
falls	stays constant	rises	
falls	falls	rises	

3. Fill in the blanks in the table.

Expected inflation rate	Actual inflation rate	Nominal interest rate	*Ex ante* real interest rate	*Ex post* real interest rate
3 percent	2 percent	6 percent		
1 percent	1 percent	5 percent		
2 percent	4 percent	7 percent		

4. The economy is initially in long-run equilibrium. Then, the money supply rises. According to monetarists, what will happen to the price level and to Real GDP in the short run and in the long run?

5. The economy is initially in long-run equilibrium. Then, velocity falls. According to monetarists, what will happen to the price level and to Real GDP in the short run and in the long run.

6. The economy is initially in long-run equilibrium. Diagrammatically represent one-shot inflation that is demand induced.

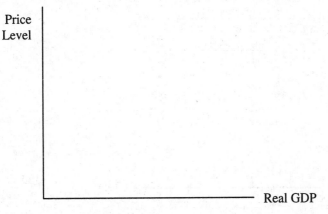

7. The economy is initially in long-run equilibrium. Diagrammatically represent one-shot inflation that is supply induced.

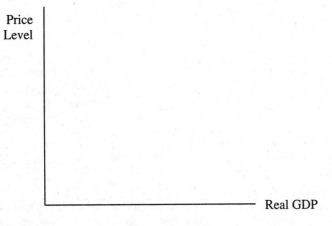

8. What would you see in the world if continued inflation were supply induced? Explain your answer.

9. Diagrammatically represent the liquidity effect. Assume the money supply falls.

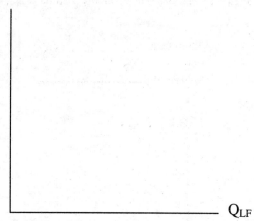

10. Diagrammatically represent the expectations effect. Assume the money supply rises.

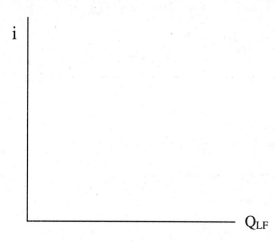

11. Using the figure, identify the route a monetarist would predict the economy would take in the short run and in the long run due to an increase in the money supply. The economy is initially in long-run equilibrium, at point A.

                 Short run: _____

                 Long run :   _____

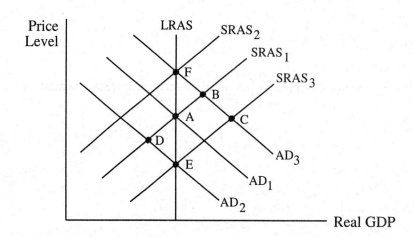

12. Using the figure, identify the route a monetarist would predict the economy would take in the short run and in the long run due to an increase in velocity. The economy is initially in long-run equilibrium, at point A.

Short run: _____

Long run: _____

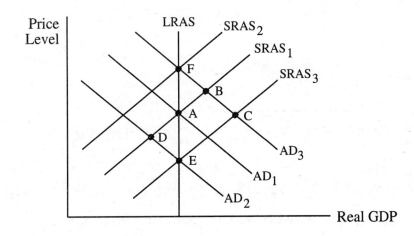

What Is the Question?
Identify the question for each of the answers that follow.

1. In the theory, velocity is assumed constant.

2. In the theory, the AS curve is vertical.

3. This can happen if the money supply rises, velocity rises, or if Real GDP falls.

4. According to these economists, changes in velocity can change aggregate demand.

5. The change in the interest rate due to a change in the expected inflation rate.

6. The change in the interest rate due to a change in the price level.

7. The real interest rate plus the expected inflation rate.

What Is Wrong?

In each of the statements that follow, something is wrong. Identify what is wrong in the space provided.

1. An increase in velocity and a decrease in Real GDP will lead to a decline in the price level.

2. In both the simple quantity theory of money and the monetarist theory, the aggregate demand curve will shift right or left if either the money supply or interest rates change.

3. According to monetarists, prices are flexible but wages are inflexible.

4. The CPI rises from 100 to 120, to 130, to 135, to 145, and so on. This is indicative of one-shot inflation.

5.   Continued decreases in short-run aggregate supply can lead to continued deflation.

Multiple Choice
Circle the correct answer.

1.   The velocity of money can be expressed as
     a.   GDP/M.
     b.   PQ/M.
     c.   M x P/GDP.
     d.   Q/M.
     e.   a and b

2.   The money supply is $700 billion, velocity is 2, and Real GDP is 300 units of goods and services.
     According to the simple quantity theory of money, if the money supply rises to $800, the average price
     in the economy will rise to _____.
     a. $4.25
     b. $5.33
     c. $10.00
     d. $2.50
     e.   There is not enough information to answer the question.

3.   According to the simple quantity theory of money, which of the following will lead to a change in
     aggregate demand?
     a.   a change in velocity
     b.   a change in wage rates
     c.   a change in interest rates
     d.   a change in the money supply
     e.   a and d

4.   According to monetarists, which of the following will lead to a change in aggregate demand?
     a.   a change in velocity
     b.   a change in wage rates
     c.   a change in interest rates
     d.   a change in the money supply
     e.   a and d

5.   Which of the following describes the monetarist view of the economy?
     a.   The economy is self regulating, wages are rigid, and velocity is unpredictable.
     b.   The economy is self regulating, wages are flexible, prices are flexible.
     c.   Velocity changes in a predictable way.
     d.   The SRAS curve is vertical at the existing Real GDP level.
     e.   b and c

6.   Monetarists believe that changes in velocity and the money supply will change _____ in the short
     run, but only _____ in the long run.
     a.   the price level and Real GDP; Real GDP
     b.   interest rates and Real GDP; the price level
     c.   the price level and Real GDP; the price level
     d.   only interest rates; the price level
     e.   none of the above

7. Which of the following will lead to one-shot inflation?
    a. continued increases in the money supply
    b. continued decreases in SRAS
    c. continued increases in the nominal interest rate
    d. b and c
    e. none of the above

8. Which of the following can turn one-shot inflation into continued inflation?
    a. continued increases in long-run aggregate supply
    b. continued decreases in real interest rates
    c. continued increases in aggregate demand
    d. continued increases in short-run aggregate supply
    e. c and d

9. For the *ex post* real interest rate to be less than the *ex ante* real interest rate,
    a. the inflation rate has to turn out to be less than the expected inflation rate.
    b. the inflation rate has to turn out to be greater than the expected inflation rate.
    c. the inflation rate has to turn out to be equal to the expected inflation rate.
    d. individuals have to borrow more at lower interest rates than at higher interest rates.
    e. individuals have to borrow less at lower interest rates than at higher interest rates.

10. The change in the interest rate brought on by a change in Real GDP is referred to as the
    a. liquidity effect.
    b. income effect.
    c. price-level effect.
    d. expectations effect.
    e. Fisher effect.

11. If the simple quantity theory of money predicts well, what would we expect to see (in the real world)?
    a. changes in the money supply strongly correlated with changes in interest rates
    b. changes in the money supply strongly correlated with changes in inflation rates
    c. changes in Real GDP strongly correlated with changes in the money supply
    d. changes in velocity strongly correlated with changes in the money supply
    e. none of the above

12. The economy is initially in long-run equilibrium. The short-run aggregate supply (SRAS) curve shifts to the left. As the result, there is _____. Assuming the economy is self-regulating, the price level will soon _____, unless either the _____ curve shifts to the left or the _____ curve shifts to the _____.
    a. one-shot inflation; rise; SRAS; AD; left
    b. continued inflation; fall; SRAS; AD; right
    c. one-shot inflation; rise; AD; SRAS; right
    d. one-shot inflation; fall; SRAS; AD; right
    e. none of the above

13. According to Milton Friedman, continued inflation is always and everywhere
    a. a supply-side phenomenon.
    b. caused by continued decreases in aggregate supply.
    c. caused by continued increases in the budget deficit.
    d. a monetary phenomenon.
    e. none of the above

14. Wages begin to rise, the SRAS curve shifts to the left, and the price level rises. Under what condition(s) is the increase in the price level (one-shot inflation) demand induced?
    a. Under no condition.
    b. Under the conditions that the economy was initially in long-run equilibrium, that it is self-regulating, and that the AD curve initially shifted to the right.
    c. Under the conditions that the economy was initially in long-run equilibrium, that it is self-regulating, and that the AD curve initially shifted to the left.
    d. Under the conditions that the economy was initially in long-run equilibrium, that it is not self-regulating, and that the AD curve shifted neither to the right nor to the left.

15. If GDP is $8,420 billion and the money supply is $1,010 billion, velocity is _____.
    a. 2.21
    b. 4.19
    c. 4.31
    d. 6.31
    e. none of the above

True-False
Write "T" of "F" at the end of each statement.

16. An increase in velocity and an increase in the money supply will shift the AD curve to the left. _____

17. Total spending or expenditures (measured by MV) must equal the total sales revenues of business firms (measured by PV). _____

18. The monetarist theory of the economy holds that velocity is constant and Real GDP rises by a small percentage on an annual basis. _____

19. The California gold rush led to a decrease in the amount of money in circulation. _____

20. A decrease in the money supply and a decrease in velocity will cause the price level to fall, *ceteris paribus*. _____

Fill in the Blank
Write the correct word in the blank.

21. The AD curve shifts rightward and the price level rises. This is an example of _____ – _____ inflation.

22. The SRAS curve shifts leftward and the price level rises. This is an example of _____ – _____ inflation.

23. The _____ _____ is the only factor that can continually increase without causing a reduction in one of the four components of total expenditures.

24. A change in the expected inflation rate affects both the _____ _____ and _____ _____ loanable funds.

25. The _____ _____ _____ is equal to the nominal interest rate minus the expected inflation rate.

Chapter 15
Monetary Policy

What This Chapter Is About

There are two types of economic policy the government can use to affect the economy. One is fiscal policy, the other is monetary policy. Fiscal policy was discussed in an earlier chapter. In this chapter, monetary policy is discussed.

Key Concepts in the Chapter
    a.   monetary policy
    b.   transmission mechanism
    c.   fine-tuning

- **Monetary policy** deals with changes in the money supply or with changes in the rate of growth of the money supply.
- The **transmission mechanism** refers to the routes or channels that ripple effects created in the money market travel to affect the goods and services market.
- **Fine-tuning** refers to the usually frequent use of monetary and fiscal policies to counteract even small undesirable movements in economic activity.

Review Questions

1. What does the demand for money have to do with the opportunity cost of holding money?

2. Explain how the Keynesian transmission mechanism works.

3. How does the money market equilibrate? In short, what happens if there is either a surplus or shortage of money?

4. What does it mean if investment is interest insensitive? How will interest-insensitive investment affect the Keynesian transmission mechanism?

5. Explain why bond prices and interest rates move in opposite directions.

6. Explain how the monetarist transmission mechanism works.

7. What is expansionary monetary policy? What is contractionary monetary policy?

8. Explain how expansionary monetary policy is supposed to remove an economy from a recessionary gap.

9. Explain how contractionary monetary policy is supposed to remove an economy from a contractionary gap.

10. What are the three points activists make as to why activist monetary policy is preferred to a monetary rule?

11. Use the exhibit to explain how expansionary monetary policy can destabilize the economy.

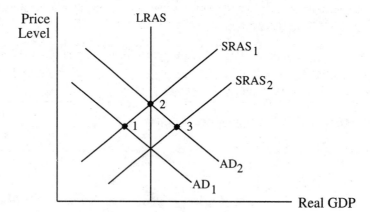

12. Explain how the gold standard (discussed in the text) would work.

Problems

1. Assume the Keynesian transmission mechanism is operational. Fill in the blank spaces in the table.

If the money supply...	And the demand for money curve is...	And investment is...	Then Real GDP will (rise, fall, remain unchanged)
rises	downward sloping	interest sensitive	
falls	horizontal	interest sensitive	
rises	downward sloping	interest insensitive	
falls	downward sloping	interest sensitive	
rises	horizontal	interest sensitive	

2. Assume the Monetarist transmission mechanism is operational. Fill in the blank spaces in the table.

If the money supply…	And the demand for money curve is…	And investment is…	Then Real GDP will (rise, fall, remain unchanged)
rises	downward sloping	interest sensitive	
falls	downward sloping	interest sensitive	
rises	downward sloping	interest insensitive	
falls	downward sloping	interest sensitive	

3. Assume the Keynesian transmission mechanism is operational and that the aggregate supply curve is horizontal. Fill in the blanks in the table.

If the money supply…	And the demand for money curve is…	And investment is…	Then the price level will (rise, fall, remain unchanged)
rises	downward sloping	interest sensitive	
falls	horizontal	interest sensitive	
rises	downward sloping	interest insensitive	
falls	downward sloping	interest sensitive	
rises	horizontal	interest sensitive	

4. There is a surplus of money in the money market. According to a monetarist, how will this affect the goods and services market? Diagrammatically represent your answer.

Price Level

Real GDP

5. There is a surplus of money in the money market. Also, investment is sensitive to changes in interest rates. According to a Keynesian, how will this affect the goods and services market? Diagrammatically represent your answer.

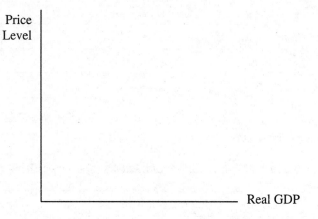

6. The economy is self regulating and in a recessionary gap. If expansionary monetary policy is used to remove the economy from a recessionary gap, will the price level end up higher or lower than it would have had nothing been done?

7. The economy is self regulating and in an inflationary gap. If contractionary monetary policy is used to remove the economy from an inflationary gap, will the price level end up higher or lower than it would have had nothing been done?

8. Assume the monetary rule (discussed in the text) is operational. The objective is to keep prices stable. Fill in the blank spaces in the table.

Percentage change in velocity	Percentage change in Real GDP	Percentage change in the money supply
+ 2 percent	+ 3 percent	
− 1 percent	+ 2 percent	
+ 2 percent	− 3 percent	

9. Suppose the gold standard discussed in the text is operational. Fill in the blank spaces in the table.

Market price of gold (per ounce)	Official price of gold	Will the public buy gold from the government or sell gold to the government? (buy, sell)	The supply of gold in the market will (rise, fall)	The money supply will (rise, fall)	The price level will (rise, fall)
$300	$280				
$259	$280				

10. Diagrammatically represent a liquidity trap.

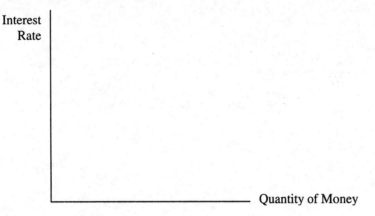

11. Diagrammatically represent interest-insensitive investment.

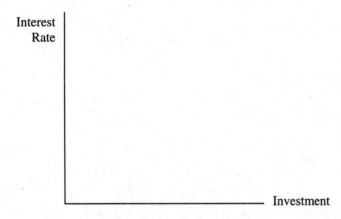

12. Diagrammatically represent a surplus in the money market.

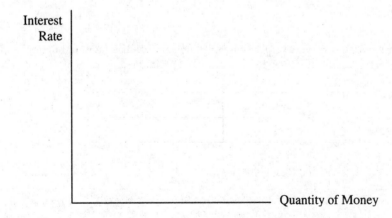

13. Diagrammatically represent how expansionary monetary policy ideally works if the economy is in a recessionary gap.

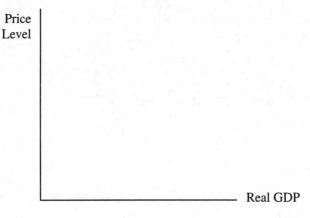

What Is the Question?
Identify the question for each of the answers that follow.

1. The money supply rises but the interest rate does not fall.

2. The interest rate falls, but investment does not increase.

3. A change in the money supply directly leads to a change in aggregate demand.

4. Activist monetary policy may not work, activist monetary policy may be destabilizing, and wages and prices are sufficiently flexible to allow the economy to equilibrate at reasonable speed at Natural Real GDP.

5. If velocity rises by 2 percent, and Real GDP rises by 3 percent, then increase the money supply by 1 percent.

Multiple Choice
Circle the correct answer.

1. The demand curve for money is the graphical representation of the _____ relationship between the quantity demanded of money and the interest rate.
    a. direct
    b. rising
    c. constant
    d. inverse

2. The opportunity cost of holding money is the
    a. interest rate.
    b. price of gold.
    c. inverse of the price of gold.
    d. inverse of the interest rate minus 1.

3. Equilibrium in the money market occurs when the
    a. quantity demanded of money equals the quantity wanted of money.
    b. quantity demanded of money equals the quantity supplied of money divided by the appropriate interest rate.
    c. quantity supplied of money equals the quantity demanded of money.
    d. b or c
    e. none of the above

4. As the interest rate rises, the quantity demanded of money
    a. rises.
    b. falls.
    c. usually does not change.
    d. There is not enough information to answer the question.

5. Which scenario best explains the Keynesian transmission mechanism if the money market is in the liquidity trap?
    a. The money market is initially in equilibrium; the money supply rises; there is an excess demand for money; the interest rate rises; investment falls.
    b. The money market is initially in equilibrium; the money supply rises; there is an excess supply of money that puts downward pressure on interest rates; investment rises.
    c. The money market is initially in equilibrium; the money supply rises; there is an excess supply of money that puts downward pressure on interest rates; investment is unresponsive to the lower interest rate.
    d. The money market is initially in equilibrium; the money supply rises; there is no excess supply of money; the interest rate does not drop; investment does not change.

6. Suppose the price of old and existing bonds are falling. This means that you can expect to see market interest rates
    a. on the decline.
    b. on the rise.
    c. first going up and then coming down.
    d. first coming down and then going up.

7. Compared to the Keynesian transmission mechanism, the monetarist transmission mechanism is
    a. indirect and long.
    b. direct and long.
    c. direct and short.
    d. indirect and short.

8. Which of the following statements is false?
    a. In the monetarist transmission mechanism, changes in the money market only indirectly affect aggregate demand.
    b. In the monetarist transmission mechanism, there is need for the money market to affect the loanable funds market or the investment market before aggregate demand is affected.
    c. In the monetarist transmission mechanism, if individuals are faced with an excess supply of money they spend that money on a wide variety of goods.
    d. a and b
    e. a, b, and c

9. Keynesians would not be likely to advocate expansionary monetary policy to eliminate a recessionary gap if they believed
    a. the liquidity trap exists.
    b. investment spending is interest sensitive.
    c. monetarists were in favor of such a policy.
    d. a and b
    e. a, b, and c

10. Read the following statements:
    (1) The more closely monetary policy can be designed to meet the particulars of a given economic environment, the better.
    (2) Because of long and uncertain time lags, activist monetary policy may be destabilizing rather than stabilizing.
    (3) There is sufficient flexibility in wages and prices in modern economies to allow the economy to equilibrate in reasonable speed at the natural level of Real GNP.
    (4) The "same-for-all-seasons" monetary policy is the way to proceed.

    Which of the statements is likely to be made by an economist who believes in activist monetary policy?
    a. statements 1, 2 and 3
    b. statements 1 and 4
    c. statements 1 and 3
    d. statement 1
    e. statements 1, 3 and 4

11. An economist who proposes a money growth rule (and assumes velocity does not change) will often argue that setting the annual growth rate in the money supply equal to the average annual growth rate in Real GDP
    a. maintains price level stability over time.
    b. is a way to raise investment.
    c. will cause the price level to fall over time and interest rates to stabilize.
    d. a and b
    e. a, b, and c

12. The quantity demanded of money rises as the
    a. interest rate rises.
    b. interest rate falls.
    c. supply of money falls.
    d. none of the above, since the quantity demanded of money is unrelated to the interest rate.

13. What does it mean if the investment demand curve is completely insensitive to changes in interest rates?
    a. Changes in the interest rates will lower but not raise investment spending.
    b. Changes in the interest rates will raise but not lower investment spending.
    c. Changes in the interest rates will not change investment spending.
    d. Changes in the interest rates within a certain range will not change investment spending.

14. When is it best to buy bonds?
    a. When interest rates are expected to rise, because this means bond prices will rise.
    b. When interest rates are expected to fall, because this means bond prices will fall.
    c. When interest rates are expected to rise, because this means bond prices will fall.
    d. When interest rates are expected to fall, because this means bond prices will rise.

True-False
Write a "T" or "F" after each statement.

16. Most Keynesians believe that the natural forces of the market economy work much more quickly and assuredly at eliminating an inflationary gap than a recessionary gap. ____

17. The price of old or existing bonds is directly related to the market interest rate. ____

18. Activists are less likely to advocate fine-tuning the economy than nonactivists. ____

19. The demand curve for money is usually vertical. ____

20. It has been argued that Keynesian monetary policy has a deflationary bias to it. ____

Fill in the Blank
Write the correct word in the blank.

21. Keynesians would not likely propose expansionary monetary policy to cure a recessionary gap if investment was interest _____ or the money market was in the _____

    _____.

22. In the monetarist transmission mechanism, changes in the money market _____ affect aggregate demand.

23. Keynesians are less likely to propose _____ monetary policy to eliminate an inflationary gap than _____ monetary policy to eliminate a recessionary gap.

24. The monetary rule for price stability (described in the text) sets the annual growth rate in the money supply equal to the average annual growth rate in _____ _____ minus the growth rate in

    _____.

25. A gold standard is an example of _____ monetary policy.

Chapter 16
Expectations Theory and the Economy

What This Chapter Is About
Until this chapter, expectations have been absent from the story of macroeconomics. In this chapter, they occupy center stage. Two expectations theories are discussed in this chapter—adaptive and rational. Often, peoples' expectations can influence macroeconomic outcomes.

Key Concepts in the Chapter
    a. Phillips curve
    b. adaptive expectations
    c. rational expectations
    d. policy ineffectiveness proposition

- The **Phillips curve** shows the historical relationship between price inflation and unemployment.
- **Adaptive expectations** are expectations that individuals form based on past experience.
- **Rational expectations** are expectations that individuals form based on past experience and also on their predictions about the effects of present and future policy actions and events.
- According to the **policy ineffectiveness proposition** (PIP), if (1) a policy change is correctly anticipated, (2) individuals form their expectations rationally, and (3) wages and prices are flexible, then neither fiscal policy nor monetary policy is effective at meeting macroeconomic goals.

Review Questions

1. What is the difference between the Phillips curve constructed by A.W. Phillips and the one constructed by Samuelson and Solow?

2. What is the relationship between a downward-sloping Phillips curve and stagflation?

3. According to Milton Friedman, there are two (not one) Phillips curves. How does Friedman come to this conclusion?

4. Give an example to illustrate the difference between adaptive and rational expectations.

5. Why is the Friedman natural rate theory sometimes referred to as the fooling theory?

6. If policy is unanticipated, does it matter to the economic outcome whether or not people hold adaptive or rational expectations? Explain your answer.

7. If policy is correctly anticipated, does it matter to the economic outcome whether or not people hold adaptive or rational expectations? Explain your answer.

8. What is the essence of real business cycle theory?

9. What is the policy ineffectiveness proposition?

10. What are two assumptions in New Keynesian theory?

11. Is it possible that changes in Real GDP can originate on either the demand-side or supply-side of the economy? Explain your answer.

Problems

1. Fill in the blank spaces in the table.

Starting point	People hold	Change in the economy	Change is	Prices and wages are	Short run change in Real GDP (rise, fall, remain unchanged)	Long run change in the price level (rise, fall, remain unchanged)
Long-run equilibrium	adaptive expectations	AD rises	unanticipated	flexible		
Long-run equilibrium	rational expectations	AD rises	correctly anticipated	flexible		
Long-run equilibrium	rational expectations	AD rises	unanticipated	flexible		

2. The economy is on the long-run Phillips curve when aggregate demand rises. If people hold adaptive expectations, draw the point the economy will move to on the short-run Phillips curve.

Inflation
Rate

— Unemployment Rate

3. The economy is on the long-run Phillips curve when aggregate demand rises. If expectations are rational, and wages and prices are flexible, show where the economy will move to on either the short-run or long-run Phillips curve.

Inflation
Rate

— Unemployment Rate

4. The economy is initially in long-run equilibrium when aggregate demand rises. Expectations are rational, the change in aggregate demand is correctly anticipated, but some wages and prices are inflexible. Diagrammatically represent where the economy will move to in the short run (in terms of the AD-AS diagram) and contrast this position with where the economy would move to if wages and prices were flexible.

Price
Level

— Real GDP

5. Real GDP is lower in Year 2 than in Year 1. Is this because the aggregate demand curve has fallen between Year 1 and Year 2? As an aside, there is evidence that the money supply has fallen between Year 1 and Year 2.

6. The economy is in long-run equilibrium. Prices and wages are flexible. Aggregate demand increases by more than people think it will increase. Expectations are rational. Diagrammatically represent the short-run change in the economy.

Price
Level

Unemployment Rate

7. The economy is in long-run equilibrium. Prices and wages are flexible. Expectations are rational. Aggregate demand unexpectedly rises. Diagrammatically represent the short-run change in the economy.

Price
Level

Unemployment Rate

8. The economy is in long-run equilibrium. Prices are wages are flexible. Expectations are adaptive. Aggregate demand increases. Diagrammatically represent the short-run change in the economy.

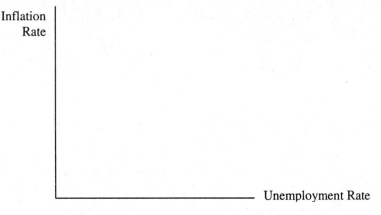

9. Diagrammatically represent the Phillips curve if there is no tradeoff between inflation and unemployment.

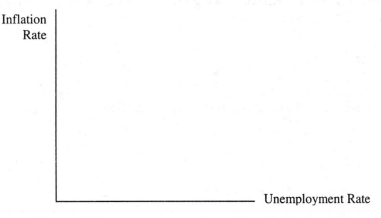

10. If there is only one Phillips curve, and it is always vertical, what does this say about the policy ineffectiveness proposition? Explain your answer.

11. If there is only one Phillips curve, and it is always vertical, what does this say about the issue of flexible wages and prices? What does it say about rational expectations? What does it say about correctly or incorrectly anticipating policy changes? Explain your answers.

What is the Question?
Identify the question for each of the answers that follow.

1. It posited an inverse relationship between wage inflation and unemployment.

2. In the short run, the economy moves away from its natural unemployment rate, but in the long run, the economy operates at its natural unemployment rate.

3. The expected inflation rate changes faster in this theory.

4. Expectations are rational and some prices and wages are inflexible.

5. Stagflation is precluded.

6. According to this theory, there is a tradeoff between inflation and unemployment—but only in the short run.

7. Initially, both Real GDP and the price level fall. Later, the money supply may decline.

What Is Wrong?

In each of the statements that follow, something is wrong. Identify what is wrong in the space provided.

1. Stagflation over time is consistent with a short-run Phillips curve that continually shifts to the left.

2. If the economy is in long-run equilibrium, then it is not on the long-run vertical Phillips curve.

3. Rational expectations theory assumes that people are smarter today than they were yesterday, but not as smart as they will be tomorrow.

4. In real business cycle theory, LRAS shifts to the left after the money supply has fallen.

5. New Keynesian theory holds that wages are not completely flexible because of things such as rational expectations.

6. The policy ineffectiveness proposition holds under the conditions that (1) policy changes are anticipated correctly, (2) wages and prices are flexible, and (3) expectations are adaptive.

Multiple Choice
Circle the correct answer.

1. Starting from long-run equilibrium, if the public anticipates that policymakers will increase aggregate demand by less than in fact policymakers do increase aggregate demand, and if the short-run aggregate supply curve adjusts to the incorrectly anticipated increase in the aggregate demand, then
    a.   Real GDP will rise and the price level will rise.
    b.   Real GDP will decline and the price level will fall.
    c.   Real GDP will stay constant and the price level will rise.
    d.   Real GDP will fall and the price level will rise.
    e.   none of the above

2. The SRAS curve will shift leftward at the same time the AD curve shifts rightward, so that there will be no change in Real GDP. This is a point that would be made by
    a.   new classical economists, assuming SRAS is correctly anticipated.
    b.   new classical economists, assuming AD is correctly anticipated.
    c.   economists that believe in adaptive expectations theory.
    d.   economists that believe that wages are inflexible in the downward direction.
    e.   a and d

3. The simultaneous occurrence of high inflation and high unemployment is called
    a.   reflation.
    b.   stagflation.
    c.   the Phillips curve dilemma.
    d.   the horizontal SRAS curve paradox.
    e.   none of the above

4. According to Milton Friedman, if the expected inflation rate is less than the actual inflation rate, the economy is
    a.   not in long-run equilibrium.
    b.   in long-run equilibrium.
    c.   definitely in short-run equilibrium.
    d.   a and c
    e.   none of the above

5. According to the Friedman natural rate theory, there is
    a.   no short-run tradeoff between inflation and unemployment.
    b.   a short-run tradeoff between inflation and unemployment.
    c.   no long-run tradeoff between inflation and unemployment.
    d.   a and b
    e.   b and c

6. According to the short-run Phillips curve,
    a.   high inflation and low inflation can occur together.
    b.   low unemployment and high inflation can occur together.
    c.   high unemployment and high inflation can occur together.
    d.   low unemployment and low inflation can occur together.
    e.   a and b

7. The Phillips curve Samuelson and Solow fitted to the data was
    a.   upward-sloping.
    b.   vertical.
    c.   downward-sloping.
    d.   horizontal.
    e.   none of the above

8. What is Milton Friedman's view of the Phillips curve?
    a. There is one Phillips curve and it is downward sloping.
    b. There are two Phillips curve, a vertical short-run Phillips curve and a vertical long-run Phillips curve.
    c. There is no Phillips curve.
    d. There are two Phillips curve, a short-run Phillips curve that is downward sloping and a long-run Phillips curve that is downward-sloping.
    e. none of the above

9. Which of the following would cause the economy to move from one point on the long-run Phillips curve to another point on the long-run Phillips curve?
    a. Starting from long-run equilibrium, an increase in AD, rational expectations, flexible wages and prices, and correctly anticipated changes in SRAS.
    b. Starting from long-run equilibrium, a decrease in AD, adaptive expectations, rigid wages and prices, and correctly anticipated changes in AD.
    c. Starting from long-run equilibrium, a correctly anticipated increase in AD, rigid prices and wages, and rational expectations.
    d. Starting from long-run equilibrium, a correctly anticipated increase in AD, flexible prices and wages, and rational expectations.
    e. There is not enough information to answer the question.

10. In the Friedman natural rate theory,
    a. the economy is self regulating.
    b. the economy is not self regulating.
    c. wages and prices are inflexible.
    d. rational expectations hold.
    e. a and c

11. People look to the past, present, and the future. This is most nearly consistent with
    a. adaptive expectations in the New Keynesian theory.
    b. business cycle theory.
    c. the Friedman "fooling" theory.
    d. rational expectations.
    e. the fact that Real GDP rises in the long run.

12. What will happen if wages and prices are flexible, people form their expectations rationally, and they anticipate policy incorrectly?
    a. Real GDP will change in the short run.
    b. The price level will fall in the long run.
    c. Real GDP will not change in the short run.
    d. The price level will not change in the long run.
    e. There is not enough information to answer the question.

13. New classical economists believe that when policy is unanticipated, there is a tradeoff between inflation and unemployment in
    a. the long run, but not the short run.
    b. neither the long run nor the short run.
    c. in the short run, but not the long run.
    d. both in the short run and the long run.
    e. There is not enough information to answer the question.

14. In the 1960s,
    a.   there was a tradeoff between inflation and unemployment.
    b.   there was no tradeoff between inflation and unemployment.
    c.   stagflation existed.
    d.   there was no inflation.
    e.   none of the above

15. Under New Keynesian theory, a fully anticipated increase in aggregate demand will lead to _____ in Real GDP and _____ in the price level in the short run.
    a.   a decrease; a decrease
    b.   no change; an increase
    c.   no change; no change
    d.   an increase; an increase
    e.   an increase; no change

True-False
Write "T" or "F" after each statement.

16. If the Phillips curve is upward-sloping, stagflation is not a possibility. _____

17. Policy is likely to be ineffective (PIP exists) if wages are inflexible in the downward direction. _____

18. Under some conditions, a rise in aggregate demand can throw the economy into a recessionary gap. _____

19. In real business cycle theory, a decrease in Real GDP is prompted by a decrease in investment. _____

20. What to some people looks like a demand-induced decrease in Real GDP and rise in unemployment could be a supply-induced decrease in Real GDP and rise in the unemployment rate. _____

Fill in the Blank
Write the correct word in the blank.

21. According to Milton Friedman, if the expected inflation rate equals the actual inflation rate, the economy is in _____ – _____ _____.

22. _____ is the simultaneous occurrence of high rates of inflation and unemployment.

23. _____ _____ economists argue that if policy is correctly anticipated, individuals form their expectations rationally, and wages and prices are flexible, then neither expansionary fiscal or monetary policy will be able to change the unemployment rate in the short run.

24. Real business cycle contractions originate on the _____ – _____ of the economy.

25. According to _____ _____ _____ theory, individuals form their expectations rationally and wages and prices are flexible.

Chapter 17
Economic Growth

What This Chapter Is About

This chapter is about economic growth, one of the most important topics in the study of macroeconomics. This chapter discusses economic growth, per capital economic growth, and the causes and effects of economic growth.

Key Concepts in the Chapter

    a.   absolute real economic growth

    b.   per capita real economic growth

- **Absolute real economic growth** refers to an increase in Real GDP from one period to the next.
- **Per capita real economic growth** refers to an increase in per capita Real GDP from one period to the next. Per capita Real GDP is Real GDP divided by population.

Review Questions

1. What is the difference between absolute and per capita real economic growth?

2. What does it mean if economic growth occurs from an inefficient level of production?

3. What does it mean if economic growth occurs from an efficient level of production?

4. What does it mean to say "natural resources are neither a sufficient nor a necessary factor for growth"?

5.   What is human capital?

6.   How can capital investment lead to increases in labor productivity?

7.   What do property rights refer to?

8.   What is industrial policy?

9.   What do the critics of industrial policy say about it?

10. What two resources did neoclassical growth theory emphasize?

11. New growth theory holds that technology is endogenous. What does this mean?

12. What role do ideas play in new growth theory?

13. Paul Romer said "economic growth occurs whenever people take resources and rearrange them in ways that are more valuable." What does this mean?

14. Can economic growth affect the price level? Explain your answer.

Problems

1. Fill in the blanks in the table.

If the annual growth rate in Real GDP is	then it will take _____ years for the economy to double in size.
3 percent	
4 percent	
5 percent	

2. Diagrammatically represent economic growth from an inefficient level of production (within the PPF framework).

Capital
Goods |

                                          Consumer Goods

3. Diagrammatically represent economic growth from an efficient level of production (within the PPF framework).

Capital
Goods |

                                          Consumer Goods

4. Diagrammatically represent economic growth from an efficient level of production (within the AD-AS framework).

Price
Level |

                                          Real GDP

5. Diagrammatically represent economic growth from an inefficient level of production (within the AD-AS framework).

Price
Level

Real GDP

6. Country X has experienced both a constant price level and absolute real economic growth (from an efficient level of production). Show this diagrammatically.

Price
Level

Real GDP

7. Country Y has experienced both a rising price level and absolute real economic growth (from an efficient level of production). Show this diagrammatically.

Price
Level

Real GDP

What is the Question?
Identify the question for each of the answers that follow.

1. Real GDP divided by population.

2. This type of economic growth shifts the LRAS curve rightward.

3. It makes it possible to obtain more output from the same amount of resources.

4. It emphasized both capital and labor.

5. According to this theory, technology is endogenous.

6. He asks us to think about technology the way we think about prospecting for gold.

What Is Wrong?
In each of the statements that follow, something is wrong. Identify what is wrong in the space provided.

1. Absolute real economic growth refers to an increase in per capita GDP from one period to the next.

2. Economic growth can occur from below, on, or beyond the production possibilities frontier.

3. Economic growth that occurs from an inefficient level of production shifts the LRAS curve to the right.

4. Countries rich in natural resources will grow faster than countries poor in natural resources.

5. According to neoclassical growth theory, technology is endogenous; according to new growth theory, technology is exogenous.

Multiple Choice
Circle the correct answer.

1. Economic growth occurring from an efficient level of production is usually portrayed as a
    a. rightward shift in the PPF.
    b. rightward shift in the LRAS curve.
    c. movement from one point below the PPF to a point on the PPF.
    d. a and b
    e. b and c

2. If an economy's Real GDP grows at 2.4 percent annually, then Real GDP will double in how many years?
    a. 30 years
    b. 15 years
    c. 10 years
    d. 8 years
    e. There is not enough information to answer the question.

3. How is per capita Real GDP computed?
    a. Real GDP multiplied by population.
    b. Real GDP adjusted for prices.
    c. Real GDP divided by population.
    d. Real GDP multiplied by GDP.
    e. none of the above

4. If the rate of economic growth slowed from 6 percent to 3 percent per year, how many additional years would it take for Real GDP to double?
    a. 12 years
    b. 24 years
    c. 8 years
    d. 5 years
    e. There is not enough information to answer the question.

5. If the economy is operating below its PPF, then any economic growth that takes place is said to occur from
   a. an efficient level of production.
   b. an inefficient level or production.
   c. a decrease in population.
   d. an increase in labor productivity.
   e. b and d

6. Which of the following will contribute to economic growth?
   a. technological advance
   b. increase in labor productivity
   c. increase in the labor force
   d. increase in capital
   e. all of the above

7. Total output is $4,000 billion worth of goods and services and total labor hours equal 200 billion. Average productivity (per hour) equals
   a. $20
   b. $80
   c. $2
   d. $4
   e. There is not enough information to answer the question.

8. Meta-ideas relate to
   a. the methods of producing ideas.
   b. persuading people that some ideas are more important than other ideas.
   c. quantifying ideas for economic use.
   d. simplying ideas.
   e. none of the above

9. Suppose an economy produces $6,000 billion worth of output using 300 billion labor hours. If an additional person enters the economy and produces $30 worth of output, she causes _____ real economic growth.
   a. absolute, but not per capita,
   b. per capital, but not absolute,
   c. absolute and per capita
   d. neither absolute nor per capita

10. Some economists have argued that per capita real economic growth first appeared in areas where
    a. credit did not exist.
    b. property rights were established.
    c. resources were used as means instead of ends.
    d. b and c
    e. none of the above

11. An intangible factor in producing economic growth is
    a. money.
    b. capital.
    c. property rights.
    d. labor.
    e. b and c

12. The economist credited with pioneering new growth theory is
    a. Milton Friedman.
    b. John Maynard Keynes.
    c. Robert Solow.
    d. Robert Barro.
    e. Paul Romer.

13. Paul Romer would probably agree with which of the following statements?
    a. The two most important factors in economic growth are capital and labor.
    b. Economic growth is affected by the number and quality of ideas.
    c. Technology does not influence economic growth.
    d. Labor is more important than capital when it comes to economic growth.
    e. b and d

14. Economic growth can be promoted by
    a. demand-side policies, but not supply-side policies.
    b. supply-side policies, but not demand-side policies.
    c. both supply-side policies and demand-side policies.
    d. neither supply-side policies nor demand-side policies.

15. Countries rich in natural resources are
    a. guaranteed economic growth.
    b. likely to grow slower than countries poor in natural resources, *ceteris paribus*.
    c. likely to grow faster than countries poor in natural resources, *ceteris paribus*.
    d. not guaranteed economic growth.
    e. c and d

True-False
Write a "T" or "F" after each statement.

16. Absolute real economic growth refers to an increase in Real GDP from one period to the next.

17. Economic growth can occur from an inefficient level of production, but not from an efficient level of production.

18. Industrial policy is a deliberate government policy of "watering the green spots," or aiding those industries that are most likely to be successful in the world marketplace.

19. New growth theory holds that technology is exogenous.

20. According to Paul Romer, discovering and implementing new ideas is what causes economic growth.

Fill in the Blank
Write the correct word in the blank.

21. The price level will _____ if economic growth occurs from an efficient level of production and the AD curve shifts rightward more than the LRAS curve shifts rightward.

22. The price level will _____ if economic growth occurs from an inefficient level of production and the AD curve shifts rightward.

23. To calculate the time required for any variable to double, simply divide its percentage growth rate into 72. This is called the _____ _____ _____.

24. Per capita Real GDP is Real GDP divided by _____.

25. A movement from the area below the PPF to a point on the PPF represents economic growth from an _____ level of production.

Chapter 18
Elasticity

What This Chapter Is About

Elasticity is one of the most important topics in economics. There are different types of elasticity—price elasticity of demand, cross elasticity of demand, income elasticity of demand, and price elasticity of supply. All four of these concepts are discussed in this chapter.

Key Concepts in the Chapter

    a.   price elasticity of demand
    b.   cross elasticity of demand
    c.   income elasticity of demand
    d.   price elasticity of supply

- **Price elasticity of demand** measures the responsiveness in quantity demanded to a change in price.
- **Cross elasticity of demand** measures the responsiveness in quantity demanded of one good to a change in price of another good.
- **Income elasticity of demand** measures the responsiveness in quantity demanded to a change in income.
- **Price elasticity of supply** measures the responsiveness in quantity supplied to a change in price.

Review Questions

1.   What is price elasticity of demand?

2.   What is the relationship between price elasticity of demand and the number of substitutes for a good?

3.   If a good has many substitutes, does it follow that demand for the good is elastic?

4. What is the relationship between time (since a change in price) and price elasticity of demand?

5. What is the relationship between the percentage of one's budget spent on a good and price elasticity of demand?

6. What does cross elasticity of demand measure?

7. What does it mean if a good is income inelastic?

8. What is price elasticity of supply?

Problems

1. Fill in the blanks in the table.

Price and quantity demanded at point A	Price and quantity demanded at point B	Price elasticity of demand is equal to	Is demand (elastic, unit elastic, or inelastic)?
$10 100	$8 140		
$8 200	$15 120		
$7 40	$10 33		

2. Fill in the blanks in the table.

Price elasticity of demand is	Change	Price elasticity of demand (rises, falls, remains unchanged)
0.34	more substitutes for the good	
1.99	more time passes since change in price	
2.20	smaller percentage of one's budget spent on the good	

3. Fill in the blanks in the table.

Demand is	Price (rises, falls)	Total revenue (rises, falls, remains unchanged)
elastic	falls	
inelastic	rises	
unit elastic	rises	
inelastic	falls	
elastic	rises	

4. Fill in the blanks in the table.

Price of good X (rises, falls)	Quantity demanded of good Y (rises, falls)	Cross elasticity of demand is	The two goods, X and Y, are (substitutes, complements)
rises by 10 percent	falls by 5 percent		
falls by 20 percent	rises by 4 percent		
rises by 8 percent	rises by 5 percent		

5. Fill in the blanks in the table.

Income (rises, falls)	Quantity demanded (rises, falls)	Income elasticity of demand is
rises by 20 percent	rises by 10 percent	
falls by 10 percent	falls by 15 percent	
rises by 5 percent	rises by 20 percent	

6. Fill in the blanks in the table.

Price (rises, falls)	Quantity supplied (rises, falls)	Is supply (elastic, inelastic, unit elastic)?
rises 3 percent	rises 4 percent	
rises 1 percent	rises 6 percent	
falls 20 percent	falls 10 percent	

7. Fill in the blanks in the table.

Initial equilibrium price and quantity	New equilibrium price and quantity (after $1 tax has been placed on supplier)	Percentage of the tax paid by the seller in terms of a higher price	Percentage of the tax paid by the seller in terms of a lower price kept
$40 100	$40.44 90		
$9 87	$9.57 80		
$10 200	$10.76 150		

8. Diagrammatically prove that the more inelastic the demand curve, the larger the percentage of a tax (placed on a the seller) that is paid for by the buyer.

Price

Quantity

What Is the Question?
Identify the question for each of the answers that follow.

1. Measures the responsiveness of quantity demanded given a change in price.

2. Price and total revenue are directly related.

3. Quantity demanded changes by 20 percent if price changes by 10 percent.

4. There is no change in quantity demanded as price changes.

5. The number of substitutes, the percentage of one's budget spent on the good, and time (since the change in price).

6. Price of one good rises and quantity demanded for another good rises.

7. In either of these cases, the tax placed on the seller is fully paid by the buyer.

What Is Wrong?
In each of the statements that follow, something is wrong. Identify what is wrong in the space provided.

1. If price rises, and total revenue falls, then demand is inelastic.

2. The elasticity coefficient is greater than 1 for a good that is income inelastic.

3. Cars have more substitutes than Ford cars.

4. As we move down a demand curve, price elasticity of demand rises.

5. For inelastic demand, quantity demanded changes proportionately more than price changes.

6. A perfectly inelastic demand curve can be downward-sloping.

7. The elasticity coefficient is greater than zero for goods that are complements.

8. If demand is inelastic, buyers pay the full tax that is placed on sellers.

9. If income elasticity of demand is 1.24, it means that for every 1 percent change in income there is a 1.24 percent change in price.

10. Price elasticity of supply measures the responsiveness of quantity supplied to changes in income.

Multiple Choice
Circle the correct answer.

1. In general, elasticity deals with
    a. the responsiveness in one variable to a change in another variable.
    b. price and quantity demanded.
    c. income and quantity demanded.
    d. supply and demand.
    e. b and c

2. Price elasticity of demand is a measure of the responsiveness of quantity demanded to changes in
    a. interest rates.
    b. supply.
    c. price.
    d. demand.

3. If quantity demanded rises by 27 percent as price falls by 30 percent, price elasticity of demand equals
    a. 2.4.
    b. 0.9.
    c. 1.1.
    d. 1.7.
    e. none of the above.

4. Price rises from $12 to $14 and the quantity demanded falls from 80 units to 60 units. What is the price elasticity of demand between the two prices?
    a. approximately 1.86
    b. approximately 0.80
    c. approximately 0.53
    d. 1.00
    e. none of the above

5. If the percentage change in quantity demanded is greater than the percentage change in price, demand is
    a. inelastic.
    b. unit elastic.
    c. elastic.
    d. perfectly elastic.
    e. perfectly inelastic.

6. If quantity demanded is completely unresponsive to changes in price, demand is
    a. inelastic.
    b. unit elastic.
    c. elastic.
    d. perfectly inelastic.
    e. perfectly elastic.

7. If the price of good X falls and the demand for good X is elastic, then
   a. the percentage rise in quantity demanded is greater than the percentage fall in price and total revenue rises.
   b. the percentage rise in quantity demanded is less than the percentage fall in price and total revenue falls.
   c. the percentage rise in quantity demanded is greater than the percentage fall in price and total revenue falls.
   d. the percentage fall in quantity demanded is greater than the percentage fall in price and total revenue rises.
   e. the percentage rise in quantity demanded is equal to the percentage fall in price and total revenue remains constant

8. The more substitutes a good has, *ceteris paribus*,
   a. the higher its price elasticity of demand.
   b. the lower its price elasticity of demand.
   c. the less elastic the demand for the good.
   d. the more inelastic the demand for the good.

9. *Ceteris paribus*, the price elasticity of demand is lowest for which of the following goods?
   a. McDonald's hamburgers
   b. hamburgers
   c. Wendy's hamburgers
   d. Burger King hamburgers
   e. it is between a, c, and d

10. _____ measures the responsiveness of changes in the quantity demanded of one good to changes in the price of another good.
    a. Price elasticity of demand
    b. Income elasticity of demand
    c. Price elasticity of supply
    d. Cross elasticity of demand

11. _____ measures the responsiveness of changes in the quantity demanded of a good to changes in income.
    a. Price elasticity of demand
    b. Price elasticity of supply
    c. Income elasticity of demand
    d. Cross elasticity of demand

12. Income elasticity of demand for an inferior good is
    a. less than zero.
    b. greater than zero.
    c. equal to zero.
    d. none of the above.

13. Suppose someone says that because of the per-unit tax being placed on the producers of good Y, the producers of good Y will end up paying the full tax. This person assumes that the demand curve for good Y is
    a. elastic.
    b. perfectly inelastic.
    c. inelastic.
    d. perfectly elastic.
    e. unit elastic.

14. If price and total revenue move in the opposite direction, then
    a. demand is elastic.
    b. demand is inelastic.
    c. demand is unit elastic.
    d. supply is elastic.
    e. supply is inelastic.

15. If price and total revenue move in the same direction, then
    a. demand is elastic.
    b. demand is inelastic.
    c. demand is unit elastic.
    d. supply is elastic.
    e. supply is inelastic.

True-False
Write "T" of "F" after each statement.

16. The greater the percentage of one's budget spend on a good, the higher the price elasticity of demand.
    ____

17. The less time that passes (after a change in price), the lower the price elasticity of demand. ____

18. A normal good can be income inelastic but not income elastic. ____

19. Supply is elastic if price changes by a greater percent than quantity supplied.

20. Total revenue always rises when price rises. ____

Fill in the Blank
Write the correct word in the blank.

21. If the percentage in quantity demanded is greater than the percentage change in price, the
    _____ _____ is greater than 1, and demand is _____.

22. If price rises and total revenue rises, too, demand is _____.

23. As we move up a straight-line downward-sloping demand curve from lower to higher prices, price
    elasticity of demand _____.

24. The short-run price elasticity of demand for gasoline is likely to be _____ than the long-
    run price elasticity of demand for gasoline.

25. If price falls and total revenue rises, then demand is _____.

Chapter 19
The Logic of Consumer Choice

What This Chapter Is About

How do consumers make decisions? How do they decide how many units of a good to buy? This chapter answers these questions and more. In a way, this chapter gives you a deeper understanding of demand, discussed in an earlier chapter. It also introduces you to the marginal benefits-marginal costs framework of analysis, which is used extensively in economics.

Key Concepts in the Chapter

a. utility
b. total utility
c. marginal utility
d. law of diminishing marginal utility
e. consumer equilibrium
f. substitution effect
g. income effect
h. efficiency

- **Utility** is a measure of satisfaction, happiness, or benefit that results from the consumption of a good.
- **Total utility** is the total satisfaction a person receives from consuming a particular quantity of a good.
- **Marginal utility** is the additional utility a person receives from consuming an additional unit of a particular good.
- The **law of diminishing marginal utility** states that the marginal utility gained by consuming equal successive units of a good will decline as the amount consumed increases.
- **Consumer equilibrium** exists when the consumer has spent all income and the marginal utility-price ratios (MU/P ratios) are the same.
- The **substitution effect** refers to that portion of the change in the quantity demanded of a good that is attributable to a change in its relative price.
- The **income effect** refers to that portion of the change in the quantity demanded of a good that is attributable to a change in real income (brought about by a change in absolute price).
- **Efficiency** has been achieved at the point at which marginal benefits equal marginal costs.

Review Questions

1. Give an example to illustrate the difference between total utility and marginal utility.

2. Give an example to illustrate the law of diminishing marginal utility.

3. Give an example of a person making an interpersonal utility comparison. Define what it means to make an interpersonal utility comparison.

4. What is the diamond-water paradox?

5. What is the solution to the diamond-water paradox?

6. What does this say: $MU_a/P_a > MU_b/P_b$? Of what significance is this condition to a buyer?

7. Explain how consumers achieve consumer equilibrium.

8. Give an example to illustrate what the substitution effect is.

188

9. Give an example to illustrate what the income effect is.

10. What is marginal cost?

11. Is there an efficient amount of time to exercise? Explain your answer.

Problems

1. Fill in the blank spaces in the table.

Unit	Total utility (utils)	Marginal utility (utils)
1st	100	
2nd	146	
3rd		28

2. At what quantity of X and Y is the consumer in equilibrium if the price of X is $2, the price of Y is $1, and the consumer has $7?

Good X (units)	Total utility (utils)	Good Y (units)	Total utility (utils)
1	60	1	80
2	110	2	100
3	150	3	110

3. Fill in the blank spaces in the table.

Price falls by	Change in quantity demanded	Additional units consumer would buy due to higher real income	Additional units purchased due to the substitution effect
$2	133	60	
$4	187	85	
$3	222	125	

4. Fill in the blank spaces in the table.

Units of good X	Total cost	Marginal cost
1	$40	
2	$89	
3	$149	

5. Fill in the blank spaces in the table.

Number of hours playing baseball	Total benefits (in utils)	Marginal benefits (in utils)
1	100	
2	178	
3	210	

6. Diagrammatically represent and explain efficiency. (You will need to label both the horizontal and vertical axes on the diagram.)

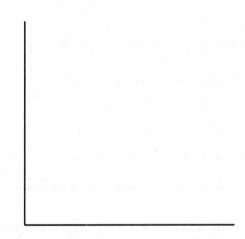

What Is the Question?
Identify the question for each of the answers that follow.

1. The additional utility gained from consuming an additional unit of good X.

2. Marginal utility turns negative.

3. The consumer will buy more of good X and less of good Y.

4. That portion of the change in the quantity demanded of a good that is attributable to a change in its relative price.

5. The change in total cost divided by the change in quantity of output.

6. It slopes downward (left to right) because of the law of diminishing marginal utility.

7. The point at which marginal benefits equal marginal costs.

What Is Wrong?
In each of the statements that follow, something is wrong. Identify what is wrong in the space provided.

1. If total utility is falling, then marginal utility is greater than zero.

2. A millionaire gets less utility from an additional $100 than a poor person receives from an additional $100.

3. The income effect refers to that portion of the change in the quantity demanded of a good that is attributable to a change in its relative price.

4. If total cost rises, marginal cost must rise, too.

5. If total benefits rise, then marginal benefits must rise, too.

6. If the marginal utility-price ratio for good A is greater than the marginal utility-price ratio for good B, then a consumer will buy more of both good A and B.

Multiple Choice
Circle the correct answer.

1. If Fiona says that drinking soda gives her utility, what specifically does she mean?
    a. That there are things worse than drinking soda.
    b. That drinking soda is tasty.
    c. That drinking soda is something that gives her satisfaction or pleasure.
    d. That there is nothing better than drinking soda.
    e. b and d

2. Suppose Will consumes 5 units of good X and receives 20 utils from the first unit, 18 from the second, 12 from the third, 7 from the fourth, and 1 from the fifth. The total utility Will receives from consuming 5 units is
    a. 50 utils.
    b. 58 utils.
    c. 40 utils.
    d. 45 utils.
    e. none of the above

3. Suppose Bob received 123 utils from consuming one banana and 159 utils from consuming two
    bananas. What is the marginal utility of the second banana?
    a.   282 utils.
    b.   30 utils.
    c.   0 utils.
    d.   36 utils.
    e.   none of the above.

4. The law of diminishing marginal utility says that the marginal utility gained by consuming equal
    _____ units of a good will _____ as the amount consumed _____.
    a.   successive; decline; decreases
    b.   successive; decline; increases
    c.   large; decline; decreases
    d.   small; decline; increases
    e.   none of the above

5. Which of the following is false?
    a.   It is impossible for total utility to rise as marginal utility falls.
    b.   Marginal utility is the same as average utility.
    c.   Marginal utility is greater than total utility for the first unit of a good consumed.
    d.   a and c
    e.   a, b, and c

6. In which of the following settings is an interpersonal utility comparison not being made?
    a.   Brady says to Armand, "I get a lot more satisfaction from eating hamburgers than you do."
    b.   Francis says, "I don't know what he is feeling or thinking; I can't read a person's heart or mind."
    c.   Ida ways to Lucy, "I know you like this course a lot more than I do."
    d.   a and b
    e.   a, b, and c

7. Suppose for a consumer the marginal utility of pickles is 50 utils and the MU of milk is 30 utils; the
    price of pickles is $1.00 and the price of milk is $1.25. Given this,
    a.   the same amount of utility is gained from consuming milk as pickles, per penny.
    b.   more utility is gained from consuming milk than pickles, per penny.
    c.   more utility is gained from consuming pickles than milk, per penny.
    d.   the consumer is in consumer equilibrium.

8. The price of good Y, a normal good, falls from $10 to $8. As a result, the quantity demanded of good
    Y rises from 125 units to 155 units. Holding real income constant, the quantity demanded of good Y
    rises 20 units. Which of the following is true?
    a.   The consumer consumes 20 more units of Y because it has become relatively cheaper; therefore
         this is the income effect.
    b.   The consumer consumes 10 more units of Y because he or she has more real income; therefore
         this is the income effect.
    c.   The consumer consumes 20 more units of Y because it has become relatively cheaper; therefore
         this is the substitution effect.
    d.   The consumer consumes 10 more units of Y because it has become relatively more expensive;
         therefore this is the income effect.

9. In the study of the "buying" behavior of two white rats, as the "relative price" of one beverage was raised,
    a. one white rat began to consume more of the higher priced beverage and the other began to consume less.
    b. both white rats began to consume less of the higher priced beverage.
    c. both white rats began to consume more of the higher priced beverage.
    d. both white rats continued consuming the same amount of the beverage as before its price was raised.

10. Which of the following statements is false?
    a. If Tracy receives 30 utils from consuming one hamburger and 55 utils from consuming two hamburgers, the marginal utility of the second hamburger is 25 utils.
    b. The law of diminishing marginal utility says that the more of a particular good one consumes, the more utility one receives from the consumption of that good.
    c. The consumption of gold probably takes place at relative high marginal utility, since there is little gold in the world.
    d. b and c
    e. none of the above

11. We would expect the total utility of diamonds to be _____ than the total utility of water, and the marginal utility of diamonds to be _____ than the marginal utility of water.
    a. higher; higher
    b. lower; lower
    c. higher; lower
    d. lower; higher

12. In order for an individual to achieve consumer equilibrium through the consumption of two goods, A and B, that individual must fulfill the condition
    a. $TU_A = TU_B$
    b. $TU_A/P_A = TU_B/P_B$
    c. $MU_A = MU_B$
    d. $MU_A/P_A = MU_B/P_B$
    e. $MU_B/P_A = MU_A/P_B$

13. If the marginal utility of a good is negative, then consumers
    a. should buy less of it.
    b. will only consume it if it is free.
    c. should buy more of it to make its marginal utility rise.
    d. either b or c
    e. none of the above

14. If total utility of a good is high while the price of the good is low, it is likely that the good
    a. is plentiful.
    b. is inferior.
    c. is rare.
    d. has high marginal utility.

15. Real income is
    a. income adjusted for price changes.
    b. the amount of money a person earns in a year.
    c. income after taxes.
    d. the amount of money a person spends in a year.
    e. none of the above

True-False
Write "T" or "F" after each statement.

16. One makes an interpersonal utility comparison if he or she compares the utility one person receives from a good with the utility another person receives from the same good. ____

17. That portion of the change in quantity demanded of a good that is attributable to a change in its relative price is called the substitution effect. ____

18. A consumer is in disequilibrium if she receives different marginal utility per dollar for different goods she purchases. ____

19. Total utility may increase as marginal utility decreases. ____

20. The law of diminishing marginal utility can be used to make interpersonal utility comparisons. ____

Fill in the Blank
Write the correct word in the blank.

21. The _____ – _____ _____ states that that which sometimes has great value in use has little value in exchange, and that which has little value in use sometimes has great value in exchange.

22. When the consumer has spent all this income, and the marginal utilities per dollar spent on each good purchased are equal, the consumer is said to be in _____.

23. That portion of the change in the quantity demanded of a good that is attributable to a change in real income (brought about by a change in absolute price) is called the _____ _____.

24. Prices reflect _____ _____.

25. If total utility for two units of a good is more than double what it is for one unit, then the marginal utility of the second unit is _____ than the marginal utility of the first unit.

Chapter 20
The Firm

What This Chapter Is About
This chapter is about the firm—why the firm exists, different types of firms, how firms finance their activities, and more.

Key Concepts in the Chapter
    a.   market coordination
    b.   managerial coordination
    c.   shirking
    d.   separation of ownership from control

- **Market coordination** is the process in which individuals perform tasks, such as producing certain quantities of goods, based on changes in market forces.
- **Managerial coordination** is the process in which managers direct employees to perform certain tasks.
- **Shirking** refers to the behavior of a worker who is putting forth less than the agreed-effort.
- **Separation of ownership from control** refers to the division of interests between owners and managers that may occur in large business firms.

Review Questions

1.   Give an example of market coordination.

2.   Give an example of managerial coordination.

3.   According to Alchian and Demsetz, what condition is necessary before teams (firms) are formed?

4. What affects how much a person shirks?

5. What is a residual claimant?

6. How might above-market wages influence shirking?

7. There are markets inside and outside the firm. Explain.

8. What is the difference between satisficing behavior and trying to maximize profits?

9. What does it mean to say a sole proprietor has unlimited liability?

10. What are the disadvantages of a partnership?

11. What are the disadvantages of a corporation?

12. What is the difference between limited liability and unlimited liability?

13. What does the net worth of a firm equal?

14. What is the difference between a person that buys a bond issued by Corporation X and a person who buys shares of stock in Corporation X?

15. What is the difference between a nonprofit firm and a business firm?

Problems

1. Fill in the blank spaces in the table.

Type of firm	Example
Proprietorship	
Partnership	
Corporation	

2. Fill in the blank spaces in the table.

Advantages of proprietorships	Disadvantages of proprietorships
1.	1.
2.	2.
3.	3.

3. Fill in the blank spaces in the table.

Assets ($ millions)	Liabilities ($ millions)	Net worth ($ millions)
10	7	
100	65	
198	77	

4. Fill in the blank spaces in the table.

Face value of bond	Coupon rate	Annual coupon payments
$10,000	5.0 percent	
$20,000	7.5 percent	
$10,000	6.5 percent	

What Is the Question?
Identify the question for each of the answers that follow.

1. These economists suggest that firms are formed when benefits can be obtained from individuals working as a team.

2. The process in which managers direct employees to perform certain tasks.

3. This rises as the cost of shirking falls.

4. This is the person in a business firm who coordinates team production and reduces shirking.

5. Persons who share in the profits of a business firm.

6. Richard Cyert, James March, and Herbert Simon.

7. This type of business firm generated the largest percentage of total business receipts.

8. One advantage is that they are easy to form and to dissolve.

9. One disadvantage is that profits are taxed twice.

10. It is also known as equity.

11. Assets minus liabilities.

What Is Wrong ?
In each of the statements that follow, something is wrong. Identify what is wrong in the space provided.

1. Alchian and Demsetz argue that firms are formed when there are benefits to forming firms.

2. Five people form a firm and decide to equally split the proceeds of what they produce and sell. The individual costs of shirking are lower in this setting than in a setting where ten people form a firm and decide to equally split the proceeds of what they produce and sell.

3. Economists who advance the efficiency wage theory argue that paying employees above-market wage rates will cause them to shirk more than if they were simply paid market wage rates.

4. Partnerships are the most common form of business organization in the United States.

5. Assets plus liabilities equal net worth.

6. Total liabilities plus net worth equal accounts payable.

7. When a person buys a share of stock issued by a firm, the person effectively grants a loan to the firm.

8. There are fewer residual claimants in a business firm than in a nonprofit firm.

9. In private and public nonprofit firms, taxpayers pay the costs of the firm.

Multiple Choice
Circle the correct answer.

1. "The market guides and coordinates individuals' actions." Which of the following is an example of this happening?
   a. An employer tells an employee to come to work on Saturday instead of Friday.
   b. The manager of a plant issues a directive that there will be no more smoking inside or outside the plant.
   c. The price of computers rises, the profits from producing computers rises, and more firms end up producing computers.
   d. a and c
   e. a, b, and c

2. Economists Alchian and Demsetz suggest that firms are formed when
   a. people demand goods.
   b. the sum of what individuals can produce alone is greater than what they can produce as a team.
   c. capital gains taxes are lowered.
   d. the sum of what individuals can produce as a team is greater than what they can produce alone.
   e. c and d

3. In which setting is there likely to be the least amount of shirking?
   a. Fifty individuals decide to work together to produce shoes; they decide to split the proceeds equally.
   b. Harrison works for himself producing watches.
   c. Nineteen individuals decide to work together to produce book covers; they decide to split the proceeds equally.
   d. a and c, since the costs of shirking are equally low in these two settings.

4. Some persons argue that the monitor-employee relationship is one of the monitor exploiting the employee. The "theory of the firm" proposed in the text, however, comes closer to being one where the monitor-employee relationship is one of
   a. shared residual claimant status.
   b. mutual trust.
   c. mutual benefit.
   d. shared decision-making.

5. Economist _____ has argued that firms seek to maximize sales.
   a. Richard Cyert
   b. William Baumol
   c. James March
   d. Herbert Simon

6. As a percentage of U.S. firms, which type of business firm is least common?
   a. proprietorships
   b. partnerships
   c. corporations
   d. nonprofit corporations

7. Which of the following is not an advantage of the partnership form of organization?
   a. ease of organization
   b. benefits of specialization
   c. unlimited life
   d. absence of double taxation of profits

8. Limited liability is one of the advantages of a
   a. proprietorship.
   b. partnership.
   c. corporation.
   d. b and c
   e. none of the above

9. What does "separation of ownership from control" refer to?
   a. It refers to the unlimited liability provision of proprietorships.
   b. It refers to some persons in a firm having more decision-making authority than others; for
      example, the president has more decision-making authority than the vice president of finance.
   c. It refers to the owners of the corporation being different persons from the managers who control it
      on a day-to-day basis.
   d. It refers to the fact that many firms are physically so large that they are impossible to control on a
      day-to-day basis.

10. Which of the following statements is true?
    a. A person who buys a bond always pays more than the face value for the bond.
    b. If a corporation issues a bond and you purchase it, you become one of the owners of the
       corporation.
    c. A stockholder of Firm X does not have an ownership right in Firm X.
    d. If the coupon rate on a bond is 11 percent, this means the owner of the bond receives periodic
       payments equal to the coupon rate times the price he paid for the bond (whether or not the price he
       paid for the bond equals the face value of the bond).
    e. none of the above.

11. Which of the following is true?
    a. There are residual claimants in nonprofit firms.
    b. A police force that receives state-appropriated funds is a private nonprofit firm.
    c. A charitable organization is considered a profit firm.
    d. a and b
    c. none of the above.

12. A partnership is a form of business that is owned by
    a. two or more co-owners, who share any profits the business earns and who are legally responsible
       for any debts incurred by the firm.
    b. a single owner, who keeps all the profits and incurs all the losses.
    c. five or more equal shareholders who have unlimited responsibility.
    d. a group of proprietors who act in their mutual best interest before worker union groups.
    e. none of the above.

13. Assets minus liabilities equals net
    a. worth.
    b. margin.
    c. product.
    d. profit.

14. A thing of value to which a firm has a legal claim is called
    a. an estate.
    b. a factor.
    c. a resource.
    d. an asset.

15. The major disadvantage of a corporation is
    a. the double taxation of corporate income or profits.
    b. its large size.
    c. the social pressures placed upon it.
    d. the government regulations it must submit to.

True-False
Write "T" or "F" at the end of each statement.

16. The invisible hand of the marketplace refers to market coordination and not managerial coordination.
    ____

17. The lower the cost of shirking, the more shirking, *ceteris paribus*. ____

18. A residual claimant receives the excess of revenues over costs as his or her income. ____

19. Herbert Simon has argued that firms do not try to maximize profits, but instead try to achieve some satisfactory target profit level. ____

20. One of the disadvantages of corporations is that their profits are taxed twice. ____

Fill in the Blank
Write the correct word in the blank.

21. _____ _____ is a legal term that signifies that the personal assets of the owners(s) of a firm may be used to pay off the debts of the firm.

22. A _____ is a legal entity that can conduct business in its own name the way an individual does.

23. Nonprofit firms are firms in which there are no _____ _____.

24. In a _____ _____ there are usually general partners and limited partners.

25. _____ _____ assures the owners that if the corporation should incur debts that it cannot pay, creditors do not have recourse to the owners' personal property for payment.

Chapter 21
Production and Costs

What This Chapter Is About
This chapter deals with the production and cost side of the firm. In later chapters, the revenue side of the firm will be discussed.

Key Concepts in the Chapter
    a.   explicit cost
    b.   implicit cost
    c.   normal profit
    d.   sunk cost
    e.   fixed costs
    f.   variable costs
    g.   marginal cost
    h.   law of diminishing marginal returns
    i.   average-marginal rule

- An **explicit cost** is a cost that is incurred when an actual monetary payment is made.
- An **implicit cost** is a cost that represents the value of resources used in production for which no actual monetary payment is made.
- **Normal profit** is zero economic profit. A firm that earns normal profit is earning revenues equal to its total opportunity costs.
- **Sunk cost** is a cost incurred in the past that cannot be changed by current decisions and therefore cannot be recovered.
- **Fixed costs** are costs that do not vary with output.
- **Variable costs** are costs that vary with output.
- **Marginal cost** is the change in total cost that results from a change in output. It is the additional cost of producing additional output.
- The **law of diminishing marginal returns** states that as ever larger amounts of a variable input are combined with fixed inputs, eventually the marginal physical product of the variable input will decline.
- The **average-marginal rule** states that if the marginal magnitude is below the average magnitude, the average magnitude is declining; if the marginal magnitude is above the average magnitude, the average magnitude is rising.

Review Questions

1.   Give an example of an explicit cost.

2.   Give an example of an implicit cost.

3. Why is economic profit smaller than accounting profit?

4. A firm that earns zero economic profit is likely to stay in business. Why?

5. Give an example of sunk cost.

6. When making decisions, economists say it is better to ignore sunk cost. Give an example that illustrates why it would be better to ignore sunk cost than not to ignore it.

7. Give an example of a fixed input.

8. Give an example of a variable input.

9. What is the difference between average total cost and marginal cost?

10. Give an example that illustrates the law of diminishing marginal returns.

11. How are diminishing marginal returns related to rising marginal cost?

12. What is the difference between marginal productivity and average productivity?

13. What do diminishing marginal returns (in production) have to do with rising average total costs?

14. Give an example that illustrates the average-marginal rule.

15. What is the long-run average total cost (LRATC) curve?

16. What does it mean if a firm experiences economies of scale?

17. Explain how a change in taxes can affect a firm's cost curves.

18. Why does the AFC curve continually decline over output?

Problems
1. Fill in the blanks in the table.

Explicit costs	Implicit costs	Total revenue	Economic profit	Accounting profit
$40,000		$100,000	$20,000	$60,000
	$30,000	$230,000	$50,000	
$30,000	$40,000	$300,000		

2. Fill in the blank spaces in the table.

Variable cost	Fixed cost	Units of output produced	Average variable cost	Average fixed cost
$500	$1,000	100		
$400	$500	200		
$1,000	$200	400		

3. Fill in the blank spaces in the table.

Variable cost	Fixed cost	Units of output produced	Average total cost
$500	$200	100	
$300	$400	50	
$400	$1,000	75	

4. Fill in the blank spaces in the table.

Average total cost is	Marginal cost is	Average total cost is (rising, fall, remaining unchanged)
$40	$45	
$30	$20	
$20	$37	

5. Fill in the blank spaces in the table.

Variable input (units)	Fixed input (units)	Quantity of output	Marginal physical product of variable input
0	1	0	0
1	1	20	
2	1	45	

6. Fill in the blank spaces in the table.

Marginal physical product (units)	Variable cost	Marginal cost
20	$400	
18	$360	
33	$660	

7. Diagrammatically represent a TFC curve. Explain why you drew the curve the way you did.

8. Diagrammatically represent an AFC curve. Explain why you drew the curve the way you did.

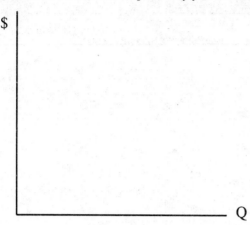

9. In the following diagram the ATC curve is drawn. Draw the MC curve in relation to the ATC curve. Why did you draw the MC curve the way you did?

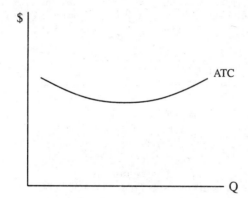

10. A firm initially faces increasing marginal returns, then constant marginal returns, and finally diminishing marginal returns. Draw the marginal cost curve that would reflect these changes in production. Explain why you drew the MC curve the way you did.

What Is the Question?
Identify the question for each of the answers that follow.

1. A cost that is incurred when an actual monetary payment is made.

2. It is a cost that cannot be recovered.

3. When marginal physical product is rising, this cost is declining.

4. These costs do not vary with output.

5. Total cost divided by output.

6. When this cost is above average total cost, average total cost is rising.

7. As output increases, the difference between average variable cost and this cost becomes smaller.

8. The lowest output level at which average total costs are minimized.

9. This exists when inputs are increased by some percentage and output increases by a smaller percentage, causing unit costs to rise.

What Is Wrong?
In each of the statements or diagrams that follow, something is wrong. Identify what is wrong in the space provided.

1. Economic profit is the difference between total revenue and explicit costs.

2. When a firm earns zero economic profit it has not covered its total opportunity costs.

3. The difference between the ATC curve and the AVC curve gets larger as output rises.

4. Marginal physical product is equal to output divided by units of the variable input.

5. When marginal physical product falls, marginal cost falls, too.

6.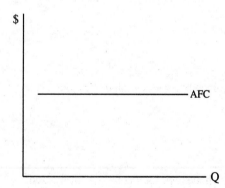

7.

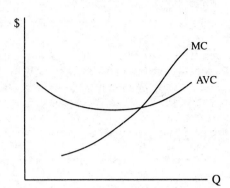

8.

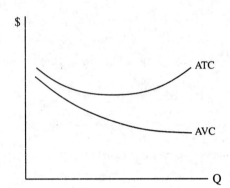

9.

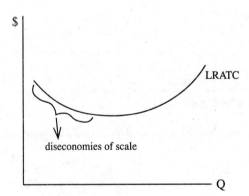

Multiple Choice
Circle the correct answer.

1. Which of the following statements is true?
    a. Implicit costs are necessarily higher than explicit costs.
    b. Explicit costs are necessarily higher than implicit costs.
    c. Tammy owns a restaurant; she paid Jack $15,000 for the curtains he installed in the restaurant. The $15,000 for curtains is an explicit cost.
    d. An implicit cost is a cost that represents actual monetary payment.
    e. none of the above

2.   Which of the following is false?
    a. Economic profit is always higher than accounting profit.
    b. Accounting profit is the difference between total revenue and explicit costs.
    c. Economic profit is the difference between total revenue and implicit costs.
    d. a and c
    e. a, b, and c

3. Here is some information that relates to a business Max opened last year (all data relate to a year): price = $5; quantity sold = 15,000; implicit cost = $4,500; explicit cost = $8,500. What did economic profits equal for the year?
    a. $66,500
    b. $62,000
    c. $52,000
    d. $70,500

4. You purchased a lamb chop from the grocery store yesterday for $5. The store has a no-return policy. The $5 purchase of the lamb chop is best described as
    a. an average cost.
    b. a normal cost.
    c. a sunk cost.
    d. a low fixed cost.

5. Evie recently went into the business of producing and selling greeting cards. For this business, which of the following is likely to be a fixed cost?
    a. paper costs
    b. labor costs
    c. the six-month lease for the factory
    d. long distance telephone costs
    e. a, b, and d

6. Which of the following statements is true?
    a. Since fixed costs are constant as output changes in the short run, it follows that average fixed cost is constant in the short run, too.
    b. Marginal cost is the additional cost of producing an additional unit of output.
    c. Changes in variable costs are reflected dollar-for-dollar in total cost.
    d. b and c
    e. a and b

7. The law of diminishing marginal returns states that
   a. as ever larger amounts of a variable input are combined with fixed inputs, eventually the marginal physical product of the variable input will increase.
   b. as ever smaller amounts of a variable input are combined with fixed inputs, eventually the marginal pysical product of the variable input will increase.
   c. as ever larger amounts of a fixed input are combined with a variable input, eventually the marginal physical product of the fixed input will decline.
   d. as ever larger amounts of a variable input are combined with a fixed input, eventually the marginal physical product of the variable input will decline.

8. The production of a good usually requires two types of inputs,
   a. variable and fixed.
   b. long-run and short-run.
   c. total and unit.
   d. sunk and fixed.
   e. none of the above

Exhibit A

(1) Variable input	(2) Fixed input	(3) Quantity of output	(4) MPP of variable input
0	1	0	
1	1	40	A
2	1	62	B
3	1	80	C
4	1	96	D
5	1	106	E
6	1	114	F

Note: MPP = marginal physical product

9. In Exhibit A above, the numbers that go in blanks A and B are, respectively,
   a. 40; 22
   b. 0; 22
   c. 20; 20
   d. 1; 2
   e. 20; 22

10. In Exhibit A above, the numbers that go in blanks C and D are, respectively,
    a. 18; 16
    b. 20; 16
    c. 40; 184
    d. 20; 22
    e. none of the above

11. If the average variable cost curve is falling,
    a. the marginal cost (MC) curve must be above it.
    b. MC must be less than AVC.
    c. the MC curve is necessarily rising.
    d. the MC curve is horizontal (neither rising nor falling).

Exhibit B

(1) Variable input	(2) Price per variable input	(3) Fixed cost	(4) Output	(5) Marginal cost
1	$15	$100	30	
2	$15	$100	31	A
3	$15	$100	33	B
4	$15	$100	36	C
5	$15	$100	38	D

12. In Exhibit B above, the dollar amounts that go in blanks A and B are, respectively,
    a. $10.00; $7.50
    b. $10.00; $5.00
    c. $15.00; $7.50
    d. $5.00; $5.00
    e. $2.00; $12.00

13. In Exhibit B above, the dollar amounts that go in blanks C and D are, respectively,
    a. $5.00; $7.50
    b. $10.00; $3.33
    c. $5.00; $10.00
    d. $10.00; $10.00
    e. $9.33; $10.00

14. If, in the production process, inputs are increased by 18 percent and output increases by more than 18 percent, _____ are said to exist.
    a. economies of scale
    b. diminishing marginal returns
    c. diseconomies of scale
    d. constant returns to scale
    e. none of the above

15. If, in the production process, inputs are increased by 10 percent and output increases by less than 10 percent, _____ are said to exist.
    a. economies of scale
    b. diminishing marginal returns
    c. diseconomies of scale
    d. constant returns to scale
    e. none of the above

True-False
Write "T" or "F" at the end of each statement.

16. It is impossible for the marginal cost curve to be rising if it is below the average variable cost curve.
    ____

17. Accounting profit is the difference between total revenue and explicit costs. ____

18. A firm that earns zero economic profit is earning a normal profit. ____

19. In the long run, there are only fixed costs. ____

20. The average-marginal rule states that if the marginal magnitude is below the average magnitude, the average magnitude rises. ____

Fill in the Blank
Write the correct word in the blank.

21. The _____ – _____ _____ _____ _____
    curve shows the lowest unit cost at which the firm can produce any given level of output.

22. The _____ _____ _____ is the lowest output level at which
    average total costs are minimized.

23. If inputs are increased by some percentage and output increases by a smaller percentage, unit costs
    _____, and _____ _____ _____ are said to exist.

24. Assume labor and some fixed input are used to produce good X. As the marginal physical product of
    labor increases, marginal cost _____.

25. The _____ _____ _____ of the variable input is equal to the
    change in output that results from changing the variable input by one unit, holding all other inputs
    fixed.

Chapter 22
Perfect Competition

What This Chapter Is About

Beginning in this chapter, and continuing for the next two chapters, market structures are discussed. Think of a market structure as the setting in which a firm finds itself. That setting relates to the number of buyers and sellers in the market, the good being produced, whether or not there is easy entry into the market, and more.

Key Concepts in the Chapter

    a.   price taker
    b.   marginal revenue
    c.   profit-maximization rule
    d.   resource allocative efficiency

- A **price taker** is a seller that does not have the ability to control the price of the product it sells; it takes the price determined in the market.
- **Marginal revenue** is the change in total revenue that results from selling one additional unit of output.
- The **profit-maximization rule** states that profit is maximized by producing the quantity at which $MR = MC$.
- **Resource allocative efficiency** exists when the firm produces the quantity of output at which price equals marginal cost, $P = MC$.

Review Questions

1. What are the four assumptions in the theory of perfect competition?

2. Firm A is a price taker when it comes to selling its good. What does this mean?

3. Why are the demand curve and marginal revenue curve the same curve for the perfectly competitive firm?

4. Explain why a perfectly competitive firm is resource-allocative efficient.

5. The MR curve is downward sloping and the MC curve is upward sloping. Why will a profit-maximizing firm produce the quantity of output at which MR = MC instead of producing the quantity of output at which there is the greatest difference between MR and MC?

6. What does a firm consider when deciding whether or not to shut down (its operation) in the short run?

7. If a firm produces the quantity of output at which MR = MC, is it guaranteed to earn profit? Explain your answer.

8. The firm's supply curve is that portion of its MC curve that is above its AVC curve. Why isn't the entire MC curve the firm's supply curve instead of only a portion of it?

9. How is the market supply curve derived?

10. What is the link between the market supply curve and the law of diminishing marginal returns?

11. What conditions does a perfectly competitive firm satisfy when it is in long-run equilibrium?

12. If price is above short-run average total cost, the perfectly competitive firm is not in long-run equilibrium. Why?

13. If SRATC is greater than LRATC, the perfectly competitive firm is not in long-run equilibrium. Why?

14. What is a constant cost industry?

15. There are positive economic profits in a perfectly competitive market. Explain what happens as a result.

16. Will a perfectly competitive firm advertise its product? Why or why not?

17. Firm X is not productive efficient. What does this mean?

Problems

1. Fill in the blank spaces in the table.

Price	Quantity	Total revenue	Marginal revenue
$10	1		
$10	2		
$10	3		

2. Assuming the firm is a perfectly competitive firm, fill in the blank spaces in the table.

Price	Quantity	Total revenue
$40		$4,000
	50	
	80	

3. Assuming the firm is a perfectly competitive firm, fill in the blank spaces in the table.

Price	Quantity	Marginal revenue
$15	1	
	2	
	3	

4. Fill in the blank spaces in the table.

Price	Quantity	Average variable cost	Average total cost	Total variable cost	Will the firm (continue to produce, shut down)
$10	100	$7	$9		
$15	50	$13	$16		
$23	1,000	$24	$26		

5. Fill in the blank spaces in the table.

Price	Quantity	Average variable cost	Average total cost	Average fixed cost	Total cost
$10	100	$4	$6		
$40	2,000	$45	$46		
$25	198	$21	$23		

6. Fill in the blank spaces in the table.

Price	Marginal cost	ATC	Is the perfectly competitive firm earning profits? (yes, no)	Is the perfectly competitive firm in long-run equilibrium? (yes, no)
$40	$40	$30		
$30	$30	$35		
$25	$25	$23		

7. Fill in the blank spaces in the table.

Price	Quantity	ATC	AVC	Profit (+) or Loss (−)
$33	1,234	$31	$30	
$55	2,436	$25	$20	
$100	1,000	$110	$99	

What Is the Question?

1. A seller that does not have the ability to control the price of the product it sells.

2. The firm sells its good at market equilibrium price.

3. When price is below average variable cost.

4. That portion of its MC curve above its AVC curve.

5. The horizontal summation of the individual firms' supply curves.

6. There is no incentive for firms to enter or exit the industry, there is no incentive for firms to produce more or less output, and there is no incentive for firms to change plant size.

7. P = SRATC, P = MC, and SRATC = LRATC.

8. The long-run supply curve is upward sloping.

9. The long-run supply curve is downward-sloping.

10. P = MC.

11. The firm produces its output at the lowest possible per-unit cost.

What Is Wrong?
In each of the statements that follow, something is wrong. Identify what is wrong in the space provided.

1. Firms in a perfectly competitive market have easy entry into the market and costly exit from the market.

2. In long-run competitive equilibrium, the average or representative firm may earn positive economic profit.

3. Price is greater than marginal revenue for a perfectly competitive firm.

4. A perfectly competitive firm will shut down in the short run if its price is below average total cost.

5. If a firm produces the quantity of output at which MR = MC, it is guaranteed to earn profits.

6. The market supply curve is the vertical summation of the individual firms' supply curves.

7. If SRATC = LRATC for a firm, there is no incentive for the firm to enter or exit the industry.

8. The long-run supply curve is downward-sloping for an increasing cost industry.

9. When average fixed cost is positive, average total cost is usually, but not always, greater than average variable cost.

10. A firm that produces its output at the lowest possible per unit cost is said to exhibit resource-allocative efficiency.

Multiple Choice
Circle the correct answer.

1. Which of the following is one of the assumptions upon which the theory of perfect competition is built?
    a. there are few buyers and few sellers
    b. there are many buyers and few sellers
    c. there are few buyers and many sellers
    d. there are many buyers and many sellers

2. Which of the following markets comes closest to being a perfectly competitive market?
    a. the corn market
    b. the cigarette market
    c. the insurance market
    d. the soft drink market

3. In a perfectly competitive market there are
    a. neither barriers to entry nor to exit.
    b. barriers to entry, but not to exit.
    c. barriers to exit, but not to entry.
    d. barriers to both entry and exit.

4. A firm that is a price taker is a firm that
    a. has the ability to control the price of the product it sells.
    b. has the ability, albeit limited, to control the price of the product it sells.
    c. can raise the price of the product it sells and still sell some units of its product.
    d. sells a high-quality product.
    e. none of the above

5. Which of the following statements is true?
    a. In the theory of perfect competition, the single firm's demand curve is downward-sloping.
    b. In the theory of perfect competition, the market demand curve is downward-sloping.
    c. In the theory of perfect competition, the single firm's demand curve is horizontal.
    d. In the theory of perfect competition, the market demand curve is horizontal.
    e. b and c

6. If the firm produces the quantity of output at which marginal revenue (MR) equals marginal cost
    (MC), is it guaranteed of maximizing profit?
    a. Yes, when MR=MC, it follows that total revenue (TR) is greater than total cost (TC), and thus the
        firm maximizes profit.
    b. Yes, since it is always the case that if the MC curve is rising, the average variable total cost curve
        lies below it and thus profit is earned.
    c. No, when the firm produces the quantity at which MR = MC, it could be the case that average total
        cost is greater than price. If this is the case, the firm will take a loss, not earn a profit.
    d. No, at the quantity of output at which MR = MC, it could be the case that average total cost is
        greater than price. If this is the case, the firm will take a loss, not earn a profit.

7. Consider the following data: equilibrium price = $12, quantity of output produced = 100 units, average
    total cost = $9, and average variable cost = $6. Given this, total revenue is _____, total cost is
    _____ and fixed cost is _____.
    a. $1,200; $900; $300
    b. $1,200; $700; $100
    c. $1,200; $900; $600
    d. $1,000; $800; $200
    e. none of the above

8. Consider the following data: equilibrium price = $12, quantity of output produced = 50 units, average
    total cost = $9, and average variable cost = $8. What will the firm do, and why?
    a. Shut down in the short run, since it is taking a loss of $150.
    b. Continue to produce in the short run, since firms are always stuck with having to produce in the
        short run.
    c. Shut down in the short run, since average total cost is greater than average variable cost.
    d. Continue to produce in the short run, since price is greater than average total cost and average
        variable cost.

9. The perfectly competitive firm's short-run supply curve is that portion of its
    a. average variable cost curve above its marginal revenue curve.
    b. marginal cost curve above its average total cost curve.
    c. marginal cost curve above its average variable cost curve.
    d. average total cost curve above price.
    e. none of the above

10. Which of the following conditions does not characterize long-run competitive equilibrium?
    a.   Economic profit is positive.
    b.   Firms are producing the quantity of output at which price is greater than marginal cost.
    c.   No firm has an incentive to change its plant size.
    d.   a and b
    e.   a, b and c

11. The following holds: (1) there is no incentive for firms to enter or exit the industry; (2) for some firms
    in the industry short-run average total cost is greater than long-run average total cost at the level of
    output where marginal revenue equals marginal cost; (3) all firms in the industry are currently
    producing the quantity of output at which marginal revenue equals marginal cost; (4) all firms in the
    industry are producing a homogeneous product. Is the industry in long-run competitive equilibrium?
    a.   Yes.
    b.   No, because of numbers 1 and 2.
    c.   No, because of numbers 2 and 3.
    d.   No, because of number 2.
    e.   No, because of numbers 1, 2, 3 and 4.

12. An increasing-cost industry has a long-run (industry) supply curve that is
    a.   upward-sloping
    b.   downward-sloping
    c.   horizontal
    d.   vertical

13. Demand increases in a decreasing-cost industry that is initially in long-run competitive equilibrium.
    After full adjustment, price will be
    a.   equal to its original level.
    b.   below its original level.
    c.   above its original level.
    d.   There is not enough information to answer the question.

14. The change in total revenue which results from selling one additional unit of output is called
    a.   average revenue.
    b.   median revenue.
    c.   marginal revenue.
    d.   standard revenue.

15. Which of the following conditions about a firm in long-run competitive equilibrium is false?
    a. $P = AVC$
    b. $P = MC$
    c. $P = SRATC$
    d. $P = LRATC$

True-False

Write "T" or "F" after each statement.

16. A real-world market has to meet all the assumptions of the theory of perfect competition before the theory predicts well. _____

17. In the theory of perfect competition, price is greater than marginal revenue. _____

18. A perfectly competitive firm is a price searcher. _____

19. A decreasing-cost industry is an industry in which average total costs decrease as industry output increases. _____

20. If price is above average total costs, the firm earns profits and will continue to operate in the short run. _____

Fill in the Blank

Write the correct word in the blank.

21. A firm that produces the quantity of output at which price equals marginal cost is said to exhibit _____ _____ _____.

22. In the long run in perfect competition, profits are _____.

23. Firms attempt to produce that quantity of output at which (the condition) _____ = _____ holds.

24. The firm's _____ – _____ _____ curve is that portion of its marginal cost curve that lies above the average variable cost curve.

25. The greater the fixed cost-total ratio, the _____ likely the firm will operate in the short run.

Chapter 23
Monopoly

What This Chapter Is About
This chapter discusses the theory of monopoly.

Key Concepts in the Chapter
    a.   price searcher
    b.   deadweight loss of monopoly
    c.   rent seeking

- A **price searcher** is a seller that has the ability to control to some degree the price of the product it sells.
- **Deadweight loss of monopoly** refers to the net value of the difference between the monopoly quantity of output and the competitive quantity of output.
- **Rent seeking** refers to the actions of individuals and groups who spend resources to influence public policy in the hope of redistributing (transferring) income to themselves from others.

Review Questions

1.   What are the three assumptions of the theory of monopoly?

2.   What is a natural monopoly?

3.   Why is a monopoly a price searcher?

4. How does the monopoly seller decide what quantity of output to produce?

5. Compared with a perfectly competitive seller, a monopoly seller produces too little output and charges too high a price. Explain.

6. Economist Gordon Tullock has argued that rent-seeking behavior is individually rational but socially wasteful. What does this mean?

7. Identify and define the three types of price discrimination.

8. What are the necessary conditions for price discrimination?

9. Is the perfectly price-discriminating monopolist resource-allocative efficient? Explain your answer.

Problems

1. Fill in the blank spaces in the table.

Price	Quantity	Total revenue	Marginal revenue
$10	1		
$9	2		
$8	3		

2. Using the diagram that follows, identify the consumers' surplus under perfect competition and monopoly.

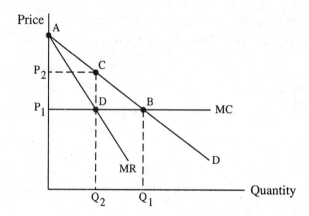

Consumers' surplus under perfect competition = _____

Consumers' surplus under monopoly = _____

3. Using the diagram that follows, identify the deadweight loss triangle of monopoly.

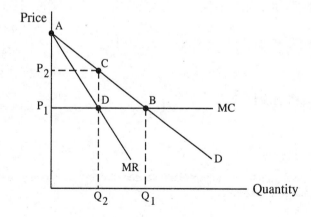

4. Diagrammatically represent the quantity of output the monopolist produces and the price it charges.

Price

Quantity

5. Diagrammatically represent a monopolist that incurs losses.

Price

Quantity

What Is the Question?
Identify the question for each of the answers that follow.

1. A right granted to a firm by government that permits the firm to provide a particular good or service and excludes all others from doing the same.

2. An exclusive right to sell something.

3. Price is greater than marginal revenue.

4. Actions of individuals and groups who spend resources to influence public policy in the hope of redistributing (transferring) income to themselves from others.

5. This occurs when the seller charges a uniform price per unit for one specific quantity, a lower price for an additional quantity, and so on.

6. The increase in costs and organizational slack in a monopoly resulting from the lack of competitive pressure to push costs down to their lowest possible level.

7. Total revenue is greater if the monopolist can do this.

8. If it does this, the monopolist will be resource-allocative efficient.

What Is Wrong?

In each of the statements that follow, something is wrong. Identify what is wrong in the space provided.

1. The single-price monopolist exhibits resource-allocative efficiency.

2. One of the assumptions in the theory of monopoly is that the single seller sells a product for which there are no perfect substitutes.

3. For the monopolist, price is equal to marginal revenue.

4. If fixed costs exist, then a firm that maximizes revenue automatically maximizes profit, too.

5. The monopoly seller produces the quantity of output at which MR = P and charges the highest price per unit for this quantity.

6. A monopoly seller cannot incur losses, since it is the single seller of a good.

7. Perfect price discrimination occurs when the seller charges a uniform price per unit for one specific quantity, a lower price for an additional quantity, and so on.

8. A monopoly seller can charge any price it wants for the good it produces and sells.

Multiple Choice
Circle the correct answer.

1. Which of the following is *not* an assumption of the theory of monopoly?
    a. There is only one seller in the industry.
    b. The seller sells a product for which there are no close substitutes.
    c. The seller has high variable costs.
    d. There are high barriers to entry into the industry.

2.   Which of the following is the best example of a barrier to entry into a monopolistic industry?
    a. diminishing returns
    b. economies of scale
    c. comparative advantage
    d. high elasticity of demand

3. In the United States, patents are granted to inventors of a product or process for a period of
    a. 2 years.
    b. 12 years.
    c. 20 years.
    d. 22 years.
    e. none of the above.

4. A price searcher
   a. faces a horizontal demand curve.
   b. is a seller that searches for good employees and pays them a low wage.
   c. is a seller that searches for the best price at which to buy its nonlabor inputs.
   d. is a seller that has the ability to control, to some degree, the price of the product it sells.
   e. a and c

5. Which of the following statements is true?
   a. A price searcher must raise price to sell an additional unit of its product.
   b. For a price searcher, price equals marginal revenue for all units except the first.
   c. For a price searcher, price is less than marginal revenue for all units except the first.
   d. A price searcher, like a price taker, produces that quantity of output for which marginal revenue equals marginal cost.
   e. c and d

6. The marginal revenue curve lies above the damand curve for a
   a. monopoly firm.
   b. price taker.
   c. price searcher.
   d. a and c
   e. none of the above

7. Economic or monopoly rent is a payment in excess of
   a. price.
   b. average variable cost.
   c. opportunity cost.
   d. explicit cost, but not necessarily a payment in excess of implicit cost.
   e. none of the above

8. When a seller charges different prices for the product he sells and the price differences do not reflect cost differences, the seller is engaging in
   a. rent seeking.
   b. arbitrage.
   c. the capitalization of profits.
   d. price discrimination.

9. A seller who charges the highest price each consumer would be willing to pay for the product rather than go without that product is practicing
   a. perfect price discrimination.
   b. disciplined price discrimination.
   c. ideal price discrimination.
   d. competitive price discrimination.

10. For a firm that perfectly price discriminates,
    a. price equals marginal revenue.
    b. price is less than marginal cost.
    c. price is greater than average total cost.
    d. There is not enough information to answer the question.

11. Which of the following is a rent-seeking activity?
    a. Carol produces shoes that will be purchased by the Army.
    b. Mick produces blankets that are sold in Egypt.
    c. Jackie produces suntan lotion that is sold exclusively in Hawaii.
    d. a and b
    e. none of the above

12. According to Gordon Tullock,
    a. monopoly profits or rents are subject to rent seeking.
    b. the welfare cost triangle is subject to rent seeking.
    c. X-inefficiency is something that differentiates government monopolies from private monopolies.
    d. the theory of monopoly is superior to the theory of perfect competition.

13. (Single-price) monopoly firms produce
    a. the resource-allocative efficient output.
    b. more than the resource-allocative efficient output.
    c. less that the resource-allocative efficient output.
    d. where P = MC.

14. The monopolist will maximize profits at a level of output at which marginal revenue equals
    a. average fixed cost.
    b. average variable cost.
    c. average total cost.
    d. marginal cost.

15. Perfect price discrimination is sometimes called discrimination among
    a. buyers.
    b. sellers
    c. quantities.
    d. units.

True-False
Write "T" or "F" after each statement.

16. If a firm is a price searcher, it necessarily cannot price discriminate. _____

17. The revenue-maximizing price is the profit-maximizing price when there are no variable costs. _____

18. A monopoly firm charges a higher price and produces more output than a perfectly competitive firm with the same cost conditions. _____

19. Monopoly profits can turn out to be zero in the long run through the capitalization of profits. _____

20. In perfect competition, P = MC; in monopoly, P < MC. _____

Fill in the Blank
Write the correct word in the blank.

21. _____ _____ is the condition where economies of scale are so pronounced in an industry that only one firm can survive.

22. _____ _____ is a seller that has the ability to control to some degree the price of the product it sells.

23. Buying a good in a market where its price is low, and selling the good in another where its price is higher, is called _____.

24. _____ – _____ is the increase in costs and organization slack in a monopoly resulting from the lack of competitive pressure to push costs down to their lowest possible level.

25. The major developer of the theory or rent seeking is _____ _____.

Chapter 24
Monopolistic Competition and Oligopoly

What This Chapter Is About
We have discussed two market structures so far—perfect competition (Chapter 21) and monopoly (Chapter 22). In this chapter we discuss two more market structures—monopolistic competition and oligopoly.

Key Concepts in the Chapter
    a.   monopolistic competition
    b.   oligopoly
    c.   game theory

- The theory of **monopolistic competition** is based on three assumptions: (1) many sellers and buyers, (2) firms produce and sell slightly differentiated products, (3) easy entry and exit.
- The theory of **oligopoly** is based on three assumptions: (1) few sellers and many buyers, (2) firms produce either homogeneous of differentiated products, (3) significant barriers to entry.
- **Game theory** is a mathematical technique used to analyze the behavior of decision makers who try to reach an optimal position for themselves through game playing or the use of strategic behavior, are fully aware of the interactive nature of the process at hand, and anticipate the moves of other decision makers.

Review Questions

1. What are the three assumptions of the theory of monopolistic competition?

2. How is a monopolistic competitor like a perfectly competitive firm?

3. How is a monopolistic competitor like a monopoly firm?

4.   What quantity of output will the monopolistic competitor produce?

5.   Is a monopolistic competitor resource-allocative efficient? Explain your answer.

6.   Why does a monopolistic competitor have excess capacity?

7.   What are the three assumptions of the theory of oligopoly?

8.   What is a four-firm concentration ratio?

9. What is the essence of the prisoner's dilemma game? Stated differently, how do we know something is a prisoner's dilemma game?

10. What is the objective of a cartel?

11. Why might cartel members try to cheat on each other (break their agreement not to compete)?

12. What conditions does a contestable market satisfy?

Problems

1. Diagrammatically represent a monopolistic competitive firm incurring losses.

Price

Quantity

2. Diagrammatically represent the excess capacity for a monopolistic competitive firm.

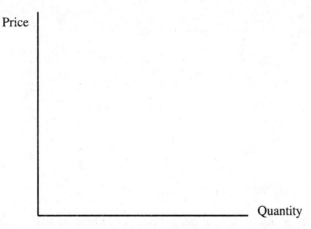

3. Several firms form a cartel. Before the cartel, each firm earns normal profit. As a part of the cartel, each firm charges P_1 in the diagram that follows. What are profits equal to for the firm that holds to the cartel? What are profits equal to for the firm if it cheats on the cartel agreement while no other firms cheat on the cartel agreement.

    Profits if the firm holds to the cartel agreement =

    _____

    Profits if the firm cheats on the cartel agreement while no other firms cheat on the agreement =

    _____

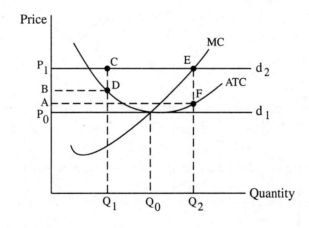

4. Give an example that illustrates how to compute the four-firm concentration ratio.

5. What are the four problems associated with a cartel?

What Is the Question?
Identify the question for each of the answers that follow.

1. States that a monopolistic competitor in equilibrium produces an output smaller than the one that would minimize its costs of production.

2. It does not produce at the lowest point on its ATC curve because the demand curve it faces is downward-sloping.

3. There are significant barriers to entry in this market structure.

4. Individually rational behavior leads to a jointly inefficient outcome.

5. The key behavioral assumption is that oligopolists in an industry act as if there is only one firm in the industry.

6. This is a way out of the prisoner's dilemma for two firms trying to form a cartel.

7. If a single firm lowers price, other firms will do likewise, but if a single firm raises price, other firms will not follow suit.

8. The theory fails to explain how the original price comes about.

9. One firm determines price and the all other firms take this price as given.

10. There is easy entry into the market and costless exit from the market, new firms entering the market can produce the product at the same cost as current firms, and firms exiting the market can easily dispose of their fixed assets by selling them elsewhere.

What Is Wrong?
In each of the statements that follow, something is wrong. Identify what is wrong in the space provided.

1. The monopolistic competitor is a price taker and the oligopolist is a price taker.

2. For the monopolistic competitor, price lies below marginal revenue.

3. When profits are normal, the monopolistic competitor exhibits resource-allocative efficiency.

4. The cartel theory assumes that firms in an oligopolistic industry act in a manner consistent with there being only a few firms in the industry.

5. The kinked demand curve theory assumes that if a single firm raises price, other firms will do likewise, but if a single firm lowers price, other firms will not follow.

6. The price leadership theory assumes that the dominant firm in the industry determines price and all other firms sell below this price.

7. Both monopolistic competitive firms and oligopolistic firms produce the quantity of output at which price equals marginal revenue.

8. A contestable market is one in which there is easy entry into the market and costless exit from the market, new firms entering the market can produce the product at the same costs as current firms, and firms exiting the market only have to suffer the loss of their fixed assets.

Multiple Choice
Circle the correct answer.

1. Which of the following is *not* an assumption of the theory of monopolistic competition?
   a. There are high barriers to entry.
   b. There are many sellers and many buyers.
   c. Each firm in the industry produces and sells a highly differentiated product.
   d. a and c
   e. all of the above

2. The monopolistic competitor
   a. is a price searcher.
   b. is a price taker.
   c. is a mix between a price taker and a price searcher (it has elements of competition and monopoly).
   d. produces that quantity of output at which MR > MC.

3. Total industry sales for Year 1 are $10 million. The top four firms, A, B, C, and D, account for sales of $2 million, $2.5 million, $3.1 million, and $0.5 million, respectively. What is the four-firm concentration ratio?
   a. 0.91
   b. 0.55
   c. 0.69
   d. 0.81
   e. none of the above

4. Concentration ratios are not perfect guides to industry concentration because they do not
    a. take into account foreign competition and competition from substitute goods.
    b. adjust for inflation.
    c. adjust for quality of products.
    d. adjust for price.

5. If a single firm lowers price, other firms will do likewise, but it a single firm raises price, other firms will not necessarily follow suit. This is the behavioral assumption in the
    a. cartel theory.
    b. price leadership theory.
    c. kinked demand curve theory.
    d. price discrimination theory.
    e. none of the above

6. Which of the following statements is true?
    a. According to the kinked demand curve theory, the marginal cost (MC) curve can shift within a certain region and the firm will continue to produce the same quantity but charge a different price.
    b. According to the kinked demand curve theory, the marginal cost (MC) curve can shift within a certain region and the firm will continue to produce the same quantity and charge the same price.
    c. According to the kinked demand curve theory, the demand curve can shift within a certain region and the firm will continue to produce the same quantity and charge the same price.
    c. According to the kinked demand curve theory, the demand curve can shift within a certain region and the firm will continue to produce the same quantity but charge a different price.

7. The top firm in the industry determines price and all other firms take this price as given. This is the behavioral assumption of the
    a. kinked demand curve theory.
    b. price leadership theory.
    c. both the cartel and price leadership theories.
    d. monopolistic competitive theory.

8. In the price leadership theory, at a price of $5 per unit, the fringe firms supply the entire market. At a price of $4, the (market) quantity demanded is 900 units and the quantity supplied by fringe firms is 430. Given this, which of the following quantity-price combinations is represented by a point on the dominant firm's demand curve?
    a. 1,330 units at $5
    b. 230 units at $4
    c. 470 units at $4
    d. 470 units at $5
    e. 1 unit at $5

9. The key behavioral assumption of the cartel theory is that oligopolists in an industry
    a. try to maximize revenue instead of profits.
    b. act as if they are perfect monopolistic competitors.
    c. act in a manner consistent with there being only one firm in the industry.
    d. try to manipulate government into subsidizing their activities.
    e. b and d

10. Which of the following is an example of an oligopoly?
    a. a law partnership
    b. a local gas company
    c. a dental firm
    d. General Motors Company
    e. none of the above

11. Product differentiation is most likely a form of
    a. advertising.
    b. nonprice competition.
    c. lowering variable costs.
    d. lowering the fixed costs to total cost ratio.
    e. none of the above

12. *Ceteris paribus*, the free rider problem is more serious
    a. the smaller the number of potential cartel members.
    b. the larger the number of potential cartel members.
    c. the higher total costs.
    d. the lower total costs.
    e. b and c

13. Which of the following statements is true?
    a. One of the developers of contestable markets theory is William Baldwin.
    b. Orthodox market structure theory places much greater weight than contestable markets theory on
        the number of firms in an industry as a major factor in determining a firm's behavior.
    c. Contestable markets theory emphasizes product differentiation; orthodox market structure theory
        does not.
    d. Contestable markets theory emphasizes nonprice competition; orthodox market structure theory
        does not.
    e. a and b

14. The prisoner's dilemma game illustrates that
    a. what is good for you and me individually may be bad for us collectively.
    b. what is good for me is good for you.
    c. cartels are likely to be stable in the long run.
    d. what is high is low and what is low is high.
    e. none of the above.

15. A monopolistic competitor has a demand curve that is
    a. more elastic than a perfectly competitive firm.
    b. less elastic than a perfectly competitive firm.
    c. less elastic than a monopoly firm.
    d. b and c

True-False
Write "T" or "F" after each statement.

16. There is easy entry but costly exit in monopolistic competition. _____

17. In monopolistic competition, the marginal revenue curve lies below the demand curve. _____

18. In equilibrium a monopolistic competitor produces an output smaller than the one that would minimize
    its costs of production.

19. Third-degree price discrimination is sometimes seen in the form of cents-off coupons. _____

20. There are few sellers and few buyers in oligopoly. _____

Fill in the Blank
Write the correct word in the blank.

21. The economist _____ _____ found no evidence that the oligopolists
he examined were more reluctant to match price increases than price cuts.

22. A _____ is an organization of firms that reduces output and increases price in an effort to
increase joint profits.

23. Once a cartel agreement is made, there is an incentive for cartel members to _____ on the
agreement.

24. The _____ _____ _____ states that a monopolistic
competitor will, in equilibrium, produce an output smaller than the one at which average total costs
(unit costs) are minimized.

25. The tactic of _____ – _____ – _____ is possible in a contestable market.

Chapter 25
Government and Product Markets:
Antitrust and Regulation

What This Chapter Is About
This chapter deals with government involvement in product markets. Essentially, it looks at government's attempts to apply the antitrust laws and to regulate.

Key Concepts in the Chapter
    a.   antitrust law
    b.   network good
    c.   lock-in effect

- **Antitrust law** is legislation passed for the stated purpose of controlling monopoly power and preserving and promoting competition.
- A **network good** is a good whose value increases as the expected number of units sold increases.
- The **lock-in effect** is descriptive of the situation where a particular product or technology becomes settled upon as the standard and is difficult or impossible to dislodge as the standard.

Review Questions

1.   What is exclusive dealing?

2.   Of what relevance to antitrust policy is how broadly or narrowly a market is defined?

3.   Give an example to illustrate how the Herfindahl index is computed.

4.   What is the difference between a vertical merger and a horizontal merger?

5.   What antitrust issue was relevant to the Utah pie case?

6.   What is the relevance of switching costs to a network monopoly?

7.   On May 15, 1998, the U.S. Justice Department issued a civil action complaint against Microsoft, Inc. What did the complaint charge?

8.   Outline the details of the capture theory of regulation.

9.   What is a criticism of profit regulation (with respect to a natural monopolist)?

10. How do economists view regulation? Are they pro-regulation, anti-regulation, or neither pro- nor anti-regulation? Explain your answer.

Problems

1. Fill in the blank spaces in the table.

Provision of the antitrust act	Name of the Act
Every person who shall monopolize, or attempt to monopolize, or combine or conspire with any other person or persons to monopolize any part of the trade or commerce...shall be guilty of a misdemeanor.	
Prohibits suppliers from offering special discounts to large chain stores unless they also offer the discounts to everyone else.	
Empowers the Federal Trade Commission to deal with false and deceptive acts or practices.	
Declares illegal unfair methods of competition in commerce.	
Declares illegal exclusive dealing and tying contracts.	

2. Fill in the blank spaces in the table.

Number of firms in the industry	Market shares of the firms, in order from top to bottom	Herfindahl index
6	20, 20, 20, 20, 10, 10	
10	20, 10, 10, 10, 10, 10, 10, 10, 5, 5	
10	10, 10, 10, 10, 10, 10, 10, 10, 10, 10	

3. Fill in the blank spaces in the table.

Proposed merger	What type of merger? (horizontal, vertical, conglomerate)
Between two firms, each of which produces and sells tires.	
Between two firms, one of which produces and sells houses and the other which produces and sells wood.	
Between two firms, one of which produces and sells books and one of which produces and sells bottled water.	

4. Using the diagram that follows, what price will the natural monopoly charge if it is resource-allocative efficient?

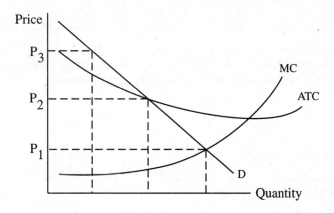

5. Using the diagram in question 4, what price will the natural monopoly charge under profit regulation?

6. Diagrammatically show that price regulation can lead to a natural monopoly incurring losses.

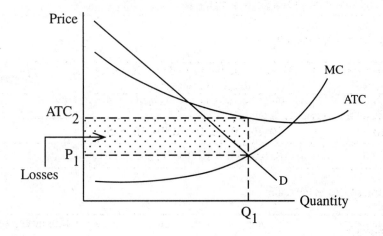

What Is the Question?
Identify the question for each of the answers that follow.

1. This antitrust act made interlocking directorates illegal.

2. One advantage is that it provides information about the dispersion of firm size in an industry.

3. This is descriptive of the situation where a particular product or technology becomes settled upon as the standard and is difficult or impossible to dislodge as the standard.

4. This is the time period between when a natural monopoly's costs change and when the regulatory agency adjusts prices of the natural monopoly.

5. Holds that regulators are seeking to do, and will do through regulation, what is in their best interest.

6. One criticism is that it does not explain which specific acts constitute "restraint of trade."

7. This theory holds that regulators are seeking to do, and will do through regulation, what is in the best interest of the public or society at larger.

What Is Wrong?
In each of the statements that follow, something is wrong. Identify what is wrong in the space provided.

1. The size of the market is irrelevant to whether a firm is a monopolist or not.

2. A conglomerate merger is a merger between companies in the same market.

3.   For a network good, its value increases as the expected number of units bought decreases.

4.   The lock-in effect reduces switching costs.

5.   The more broadly a market is defined, the more likely a firm will be considered a monopolist.

6.   George Stigler and Claire Friedland studied both unregulated and regulated electric utilities and found a small difference in the rates charged by them.

7.   The federal government looks more closely at proposed vertical mergers than horizontal mergers.

8.   A profit-maximizing natural monopoly will produce the quantity of output at which $MR = MC$ and charge the price that equals its ATC.

9.   The capture theory of regulation holds that no matter what the motive for the initial regulation and the establishment of the regulatory agency, eventually the bureaucrats that run the agency will control the industry.

Multiple Choice
Circle the correct answer.

1.   The Clayton Act made
     a.   price discrimination illegal.
     b.   price discrimination legal.
     c.   mergers between companies in the same industry illegal.
     d.   union strikes illegal in certain states.

2. Selling to a retailer on the condition that the seller not carry any rival products is called _____, and it was made illegal by the _____ Act.
    a. exclusive dealing; Robinson-Patman
    b. exclusive dealing; Clayton
    c. a tying contract; Wheeler-Lea
    d. price discrimination; Clayton

3. The piece of antitrust legislation which declares illegal "unfair methods of competition in commerce" is the _____ Act.
    a. Sherman
    b. Federal Trade Commission
    c. Clayton
    d. Robinson-Patman
    e. none of the above

4. Which of the following statements is true?
    a. In the Dupont case in 1956, the market relevant to Dupont was ruled to be the cellophane market, rather than the broader flexible wrapping materials market.
    b. In 1975, a court ruled that Alcoa was a monopoly.
    c. The way a market is defined can have much to say as to whether a firm is viewed as a monopoly or not.
    d. a and c
    e. a, b, and c

5. The advantage of the Herfindahl index over the four-firm and eight-firm concentration ratios is that it provides information about
    a. the dispersion of firm size in an industry.
    b. the price effects of industry concentration.
    c. merger acquisitions.
    d. b and c
    e. none of the above

6. Consider a merger between Firm A, with a market share of 19 percent, and Firm B, with a market share of 16 percent. Will the Antitrust Division of the Justice Department file suit against these two firms if they enter into a merger?
    a. No, because together they have 35 percent of the market.
    b. Yes, because the Herfindahl index is 617 (which is more than 200).
    c. No, because the difference between the Herfindahl index when the two firms are not merged and the Herfindahl index when they are merged is more than 200.
    d. No, because neither firm has a market share under 10 percent.
    e. No, because the Herfindahl index is 139 (which is more than 100).

7. When one firm can supply the entire output demanded at lower cost than two or more firms can, we have a(an)
    a. natural market.
    b. natural monopoly.
    c. regulated firm.
    d. efficient firm.
    e. none of the above

Exhibit A

(1) Firm	(2) Quantity	(3) Average total cost
A	200 units	$5
B	400 units	$4
	600 units	$7

8. In Exhibit A above, the resource-allocative efficient output is 600 units. Currently, Firm B is the only firm supplying the good; it is supplying 400 units. Based on the data presented in Exhibit A, is Firm B a natural monopoly? If so, why?
    a. No, because Firm A can supply 200 units at a lower average total cost than Firm B can supply 400 units.
    b. No, because it is not the only firm that can supply the good.
    c. Yes, because it can supply the entire output.
    d. No, because it cannot supply the entire output (600 units) at lower cost ($4,200) than the two firms together (where Firm A produces 200 units at $5 per unit and Firm B produces 400 units at $4 per unit).

9. In marginal-cost price regulation of the natural monopoly firm, the objective is to set a price
    a. that will guarantee zero economic profit.
    b. equal to average total cost.
    c. consistent with the maximization of profits.
    d. equal to the quantity of output at which demand intersects marginal cost.
    e. none of the above

10. One of the criticisms of average-cost pricing regulation of the natural monopoly firm is:
    a. if the natural monopoly firm knows it is guaranteed a price equal to average total cost, it will cut costs and decrease quality.
    b. the natural monopoly firm is forced into taking a loss.
    c. the natural monopoly is guaranteed a positive economic profit.
    d. none of the above

11. Which of the following is usually noted as a natural monopoly?
    a. a firm that builds houses
    b. a company that sells electricity
    c. a bank
    d. a cruise ship company
    e. none of the above

12. Under Civil Aeronautics Board (CAB) chairman _____, the airline industry began to be deregulated in 1978.
    a. Alfred Kahn
    b. R. T. McClow
    c. Everett George
    d. Michael Kennedy
    e. none of the above

13. George Stigler is closely associated with the _____, which says _____.
    a. public interest theory of regulation; regulators work hard to benefit the public interest
    b. capture hypothesis; regulatory agencies are "captured" by the special interests of the industry that are being regulated
    c. capture hypothesis; eventually the public "captures" the benefits of regulation through lower prices
    d. public interest theory or regulation; the public is dissatisfied with the efforts of the regulatory agencies but can do little about this situation.

14. One of the major criticisms of the antitrust laws is that
    a. certain antitrust acts hinder, rather than promote, competition.
    b. they are too short in length.
    c. they do not all employ the Herfindahl index.
    d. they do not all employ the four-firm concentration ratio.

15. Which of the following is a way of regulating a natural monopoly firm?
    a. output regulation
    b. average-cost regulation
    c. marginal-cost price regulation
    d. a, b, and c
    e. none of the above

True-False
Write "T" or "F" after each statement.

16. A criticism of profit regulation is that firms have no incentive to hold costs down. ____

17. The Herfindahl index is equal to the sum of the squares of the market shares of each firm in the industry divided by two. ____

18. Antitrust law is legislation passed for the stated purpose of increasing monopoly power and reducing competition. ____

19. The Wheeler-Lea Act empowered the Federal Trade Commission to deal with false and deceptive acts or practices. ____

20. The Clayton Act made tying contracts illegal. ____

Fill in the Blank
Write the correct word in the blank.

21. The _____ _____ _____ _____ _____ holds that regulators are seeking to do and will do through regulation what is in the best interest of the public or society at large.

22. The _____ _____ _____ _____ declared illegal "unfair methods of competition in commerce."

23. The local gas company is usually cited as an example of a _____ _____.

24. The way _____ is defined will help determine whether a particular firm is considered a monopoly or not.

25. The Herfindahl index and the four- and eight-firm concentration ratios have been criticized from implicitly arguing from _____ to _____ _____.

Chapter 26
Agriculture: Farmers' Problems, Government Policies, and Unintended Effects

What This Chapter Is About

Various agricultural markets—the corn market, wheat market, and so on—are often put forth as examples of perfectly competitive markets. Do sellers in perfectly competitive markets face any unusual problems? Does government get involved in affecting outcomes in perfectly competitive markets? This chapter answers these questions and more.

Key Concepts in the Chapter
- a. price elasticity of demand
- b. income elasticity of demand
- c. price support

- **Price elasticity of demand** measures the responsiveness of a change in quantity demanded to a change in price.
- **Income elasticity of demand** measures the responsiveness of a change in quantity demanded to changes in income.
- A **price support** is a government-mandated minimum price for agricultural products; it is an example of a price floor.

Review Questions

1. If an increase in the supply of a food item lowers farmers' income, what does this say about the elasticity of demand for the food item? Explain your answer.

2. What do price inelasticity of demand for a food item and major changes in the weather have to do with the fact that farmers may experience large changes in their income from year to year?

3. Why might a farmer want to enter into a futures contract?

4. An individual farmer may prefer 1) good weather for himself and bad weather for all other farmers over 2) good weather for all farmers, including himself. Why?

5. What are the effects of an agricultural price support?

6. Diagrammatically represent and explain how target prices work.

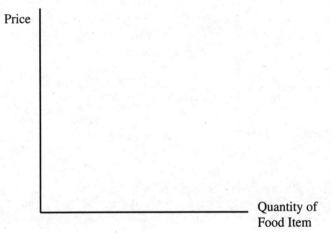

7. What might land prices have to do with an agricultural price-support program?

8. What is a production flexibility contract payment?

9. How did the FAIR Act reform agricultural policy?

10. It's been said that the production flexibility of the FAIR Act should help solve some environmental problems. Explain.

11. It's been said that the FAIR Act stabilizes farm spending instead of farm income. Explain.

12. Explain how a nonrecourse commodity loan works.

Problems

1. Fill in the blank spaces in the table.

If demand for the food item is	And supply of the food item	Then farmers' income (rises, falls, remains unchanged)
elastic	rises	
inelastic	rises	
inelastic	falls	

2. Fill in the blank spaces in the table.

Target price	Market price	Quantity supplied at target price	Deficiency payment
$4	$1	4,000 units	
$5	$5	3,000 units	
$6	$3	10,000 units	

3. Fill in the blank spaces in the table. Assume that the federal government uses 85 percent of the contract acreage to determine the production flexibility contract payment.

Contract acreage (acres)	Yield per acre (bushels)	Crop payment rate (per bushel)	Production flexibility contract payment
1,000	110	$0.33	
2,000	210	$0.54	

4. Diagrammatically represent how a supply-restricting agricultural policy might work.

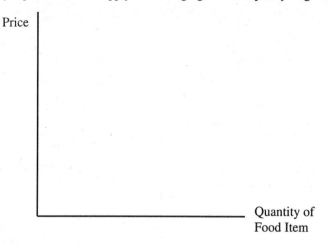

Price

Quantity of Food Item

What Is the Question?
Identify the question for each of the answers that follow.

1. An obligation to make or take delivery of a specified quantity of a good at a particular time in the future at a price agreed on when the contract is signed.

2. A government-mandated minimum price for agricultural products.

3. It restricts output by limiting the number of farm acres that can be used to produce a particular crop.

4. It repealed target prices and deficiency payments.

5. Contract acreage multiplied by 0.85 multiplied by yield per acre multiplied by crop payment rate.

6. April 4, 1996.

What Is Wrong?

In each of the statements that follow, something is wrong. Identify what is wrong in the space provided.

1. When agricultural productivity increases, the supply of food items shifts right, price falls, and total revenue (received by farmers) rises if demand is inelastic.

2. The demand for many farm products is income inelastic, which means that quantity demanded changes by a larger percentage than income changes.

3. In the past, the three major agricultural policies to assist farmers were price supports, which attempted to set the prices of agricultural products indirectly; supply-restricting policies, which attempted to decrease supply and bring about a higher price for agricultural products indirectly; and target prices, which neither tried to set prices directly nor decrease supply, but instead paid farmers a production flexibility contract payment if the market price for their goods did not equal the target price.

4. Under the FAIR Act, farmers have less flexibility to grow crops than they had under the old farm policies.

5.   Today, one farmer in the United States produces enough food to feed 100 people.

Multiple Choice
Circle the correct answer.

1.   At the beginning of the century, a farmer produced enough food to feed
     a.   8 people.
     b.   17 people.
     c.   35 people.
     d.   83 people.

2.   The supply curve of farm products has shifted rightward during much of the 20th century principally because of
     a.   higher prices for food.
     b.   consistently good weather.
     c.   increased productivity in the agricultural sector.
     d.   more people going into farming.

3.   Increased productivity in the agricultural sector is not always a benefit to farmers because with increased productivity comes
     a.   higher prices and if demand is inelastic, and higher prices mean lower revenues.
     b.   higher prices and if demand is elastic, and higher prices mean lower revenues.
     c.   lower prices and if demand is elastic, and lower prices mean lower revenues.
     d.   lower prices and if demand is inelastic, and lower prices mean constant revenues.
     e.   lower prices and if demand is inelastic, and lower prices mean lower revenues.

4.   In the United States, studies show that as real income has been rising, the per capita demand for food has been increasing by
     a.   as much, which means the demand for food is unit elastic.
     b.   much more, which means the demand for food is income elastic.
     c.   much more, which means the demand for food is income inelastic.
     d.   much less, which means the demand for food is income inelastic.
     e.   none of the above

5.   Why is good weather sometimes bad news for farmers?
     a.   Because good weather lowers the demand for, and price of, agricultural products.
     b.   Because good weather shifts the supply curve of agricultural products leftward, driving up price, and lowering total revenue (assuming demand is elastic).
     c.   Because good weather shifts the supply curve of agricultural products rightward, driving down price and total revenue (assuming demand is inelastic).
     d.   Because good weather increases the demand for, and price of, farm inputs.

6.   Suppose there is a target price program. Under this program 500 bushels of X are produced at a target price of $7 per bushel but consumers will only buy 500 bushels at $4 per bushel. What is the total deficiency payment to farmers?
     a. $1,500
     b. $2,000
     c. $3,000
     d. $1,000

7. Which agricultural policy results in the government buying and storing surplus production?
   a. acreage allotments
   b. target prices
   c. support prices
   d. marketing quotas
   e. production flexibility contracts

8. Before the FAIR Act, the pattern of U.S. agricultural subsidization _____ soil conservation by _____ crop rotation.
   a. harmed; encouraging
   b. harmed; discouraging
   c. promoted; encouraging
   d. promoted; discouraging

9. The FAIR Act, by eliminating _____, seeks to stabilize _____.
   a. direct subsidies; federal farm spending
   b. direct subsidies; farm income
   c. deficiency payments; federal farm spending
   d. deficiency payments; farm income

10. If the supply of a crop rises by less than the demand for that crop rises, the price of that crop
   a. rises.
   b. falls.
   c. remains the same.
   d. falls if demand is inelastic.
   e. falls if demand is elastic.

True-False
Write "T" or "F" after each statement.

11. Bad weather may be good for farmers (in that farmers may earn more income with bad weather than good weather). _____

12. The FAIR Act eliminated government intervention in agriculture. _____

13. The FAIR Act eliminated all nonrecourse commodity loans. _____

14. The production flexibility contract payment equals the contract acreage multiplied by 0.85 multiplied by the crop payment rate multiplied by the yield per acre. _____

15. In 1956, the Eisenhower administration initiated the soil bank program. _____

Fill in the Blank

Write the correct word in the blank.

16. The demand for many agricultural products is _____, which means if price falls, total revenue _____.

17. Under the _____ _____ _____, government did not restrict land usage, but instead set a limit on the quantity of a product that a farmer was allowed to bring to market.

18. _____ _____ _____ _____ refers to the responsiveness of a change in quantity demanded to a change income.

19. An agricultural price support is an example of a _____ _____.

20. Under a price support program, consumers end up paying _____ _____.

Chapter 27
Factor Markets:
With Emphasis on the Labor Market

What This Chapter Is About
There are many markets in an economy. This chapter is about a market that most people are particularly interested in—the labor market.

Key Concepts in the Chapter
a. derived demand
b. marginal revenue product
c. factor price taker
d. least-cost rule
e. marginal productivity theory

- **Derived demand** is demand that is the result of some other demand. For example, factor demand is the result of the demand for the products that factors go to produce.
- **Marginal revenue product** is the additional revenue generated by employing an additional factor unit.
- A **factor price taker** is a firm that can buy all of a factor it wants at the equilibrium price.
- The **least-cost rule** specifies the combination of factors that minimizes costs. It requires that the MPP/P ratio for each factor be the same.
- **Marginal productivity theory** states that firms in competitive or perfect product and factor markets pay factors their marginal revenue products.

Review Questions

1. Give an example that illustrates what derived demand is.

2. When is the factor demand curve downward sloping?

3. When is value marginal product the same as marginal revenue product?

4. How many units of a factor should a firm buy? Explain your answer.

5. How are costs minimized if the least-cost rule is observed?

6. What are three main determinants of elasticity of demand for labor?

7. As the wage rate rises, the quantity supplied of labor rises. Does it follow that the income effect does not occur? Explain your answer.

8. What affects the demand for labor?

9. What affects the supply of labor?

10. Explain how what appears to be employer discrimination may be an information problem instead.

Problems

1. Fill in the blank spaces in the table.

Quantity of factor Z	Quantity of output	Product price	Total revenue	Marginal revenue product
1	30	$40		
2	50	$40		
3	60	$40		

2. Fill in the blank spaces in the table.

Quantity of factor Z	Price of factor Z	Total cost	Marginal factor cost
1	$10		
2	$10		
3	$10		

3. Fill in the blank spaces in the table.

MPP of factor X (units)	Price of factor X	MPP of factor Y (units)	Price of factor Y	Should the firm buy more of factor X or factor Y?
30	$2	40	$1.25	
50	$4	100	$5	
100	$30	100	$40	

4. Fill in the blank spaces in the table.

Change	Does this affect the demand for labor (yes, no)?	Does this affect the supply of labor (yes, no)?	Effect on wage (up, down, no change)
product supply falls			
product demand rises			
training costs rise			
positive change in the nonpecuniary aspects of the job			

5. Diagrammatically represent the VMP and MRP curves for a monopolist, monopolistic competitor, and oligopolist.

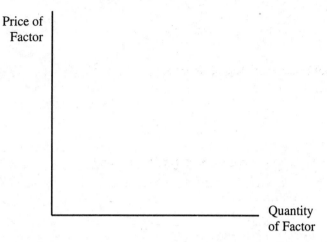

6. Diagrammatically represent the factor supply curve for a factor price taker.

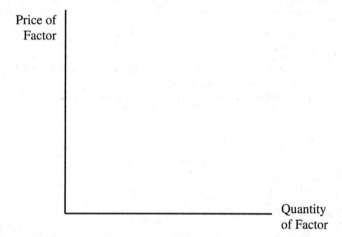

What Is the Question?
Identify the question for each of the answers that follow.

1. The additional revenue generated by employing an additional factor unit.

2. It is also the factor demand curve.

3. It slopes downward because the MPP of the factor eventually declines.

4.   It will buy the number of factor units for which MRP = MFC.

5.   The firm will buy more of factor X and less of factor Y.

6.   It is equal to the MPP of the factor divided by the cost of the factor.

7.   The percentage change in the quantity demanded of labor divided by the percentage change in the wage rate.

8.   It is upward sloping because the substitution effect outweighs the income effect.

9.   One of the reasons is that jobs have different nonpecuniary qualities.

10. States that firms in competitive or perfect product and factor markets pay factors their marginal revenue products.

What Is Wrong?
In each of statements that follow, something is wrong. Identify what is wrong in the space that is provided.

1.   If price equals marginal revenue, then VMP is greater than MRP.

2. The factor demand curve usually lies above the MRP curve.

3. The firm will purchase the quantity of a factor at which the difference between the MRP and MFC of the factor are maximized.

4. An increase in MPP will shift the factor demand curve to the left.

5. If the demand for the product that labor produces is highly elastic, a small percentage increase in price will decrease quantity demanded of the product by a relatively small percentage.

6. The more substitutes for labor, the lower the elasticity of demand for labor; the fewer substitutes for labor, the higher the elasticity of demand for labor.

7. Screening is the process used by employers to increase the probability of choosing good employees (to promote) from within the firm.

8. A firm minimizes costs by buying factors in the combination at which the MPP-to-price ratio for the expensive factors is greater than the MPP-to-price ratio for the less expensive factors.

9. The supply curve is upward-sloping for a factor price taker.

10. The higher the labor cost-total cost ratio, the lower the elasticity of demand for labor.

Multiple Choice
Circle the correct answer.

1. A factor price taker is a firm that
    a. can buy all of a factor it wants at the equilibrium price.
    b. can sell all of a product it wants at the equilibrium price.
    c. must pay a higher price to buy an additional unit of a factor.
    d. must lower price to sell an additional unit of the good it produces.

2. A firm that is a price taker in a factor market faces
    a. an upward-sloping supply curve of factors.
    b. a vertical supply curve of factors.
    c. a downward-sloping supply curve of factors.
    d. a horizontal supply curve of factors.

3. The demand for factors is
    a. a derived demand.
    b. an extra demand.
    c. an indirect demand.
    d. a distinct demand.
    e. none of the above

Exhibit A

(1) Units of Factor X	(2) Quantity of output	(3) Product price	(4) Marginal revenue product
0	10	$12	
1	20	$12	A
2	29	$12	B
3	36	$12	C
4	41	$12	D

4. In Exhibit A, the collar amounts that go in blanks A, B, C, and D are, respectively,
    a. $120; $108; $84; $60
    b. $100; $204; $30; $40
    c. $190; $180; $70; $40
    d. $105; $140; $40; $30

5. Suppose a factor price searcher taker purchases one unit of factor X for $15. What would it purchase the second unit of factor X for, and what would marginal factor cost (MFC) equal?
    a. It would purchase the second unit for $15, and MFC equals $15.
    b. There is not enough information to know what it would purchase the second unit for, and thus we do not know what MFC equals.
    c. It would purchase the second unit for $15, but there is not enough information to know what MFC equals.
    d. There is not enough information to know what it would purchase the second unit for, but MFC equals $15.
    e. none of the above

6. The marginal factor cost (MFC) curve is
    a. vertical for a factor price taker.
    b. horizontal for a factor price taker.
    c. horizontal for a factor price searcher.
    d. upward-sloping for a factor price searcher.
    e. b and d

7. For a product price searcher,
    a. VMP = MRP.
    b. VMP < MRP.
    c. VMP > MRP.
    d. There is not enough information to answer the question.

8. For a price taker in both the product and factor markets, at the profit-maximizing factor quantity,
    a. VMP = MRP > MFC = factor price
    b. VMP < MRP = MFC = factor price
    c. VMP > MRP = MFC = factor price
    d. VMP = MRP = MFC = factor price

9. The wage rate increases 30 percent and the quanitity demanded of labor falls by 90 percent. The elasticity of demand for labor is _____.
    a. 1.33
    b. 2.40
    c. 1.50
    d. 3.00
    e. none of the above

10. The lower the elasticity of demand for a product,
    a. the higher the ratio of labor costs to total costs.
    b. the lower the ratio of labor costs to total costs.
    c. the lower the elasticity of demand for the labor that produces the product.
    d. the higher the elasticity of demand for the labor that produces the product.
    e. none of the above

11. A rise in the wage rate
    a. shifts the supply curve of labor rightward.
    b. increases the quantity supplied of labor.
    c. shifts the supply curve of labor leftward.
    d. decreases the quantity supplied of labor.

12. The supply of labor curve will slope upward if the
    a. substitution effect outweighs the income effect.
    b. income effect outweighs the substitution effect.
    c. wage rises.
    d. wage falls.

13. Marginal factor cost is
    a. the additional cost incurred by employing an additional factor unit.
    b. the additional revenue generated by employing an additional factor unit.
    c. always equal to marginal revenue product.
    d. constant in the long run.
    e. a and d

14. The marginal revenue product (MRP) curve is the firm's
    a. marginal output curve.
    b. factor supply curve.
    c. average revenue curve.
    d. factor demand curve.

15. The more substitutes there are for labor,
    a. the more sensitive buyers of labor will be to a change in the price of labor.
    b. the less sensitive buyers of labor will be to a change in the price of labor.
    c. the higher costs will rise in the short run.
    d. the greater marginal revenue will be in the long run.
    e. none of the above

True-False
Write "T" or "F" after each statement.

16. The firm minimizes costs by buying factors in the combination at which the MPP-price ratio for each
    is the same. _____

17. Marginal productivity theory states that firms in competitive or perfect product and factor markets pay
    factors their marginal revenue products. _____

18. A factor price taker faces a horizontal supply curve of factors. _____

19. A firm can be a product price taker and a factor price searcher, but it cannot be a product price searcher
    and a factor price taker. _____

20. If the demand curve for the product that labor produces shifts rightward, the demand curve for labor
    shifts leftward. _____

Fill in the Blank
Write the correct word in the blank.

21. _____ _____ _____ = P x MPP.

22. The process used by employers to increase the probability of choosing "good" employees based on
    certain criteria is called _____.

23. The elasticity of demand for labor is defined as the percentage change in the _____
    _____ _____ _____ divided by the percentage change in the
    _____ _____.

24. The firm buys and employs the factor quantity at which (the condition) _____ = _____
    holds.

25. The demand for labor is _____.

Chapter 28
Wages, Unions, and Labor

What This Chapter Is About
This chapter discusses the labor union, its practices, and its effects.

Key Concepts in the Chapter
    a.   collective bargaining
    b.   monopsony

- **Collective bargaining** is the process whereby wage rates and other issues are determined by a union bargaining with management on behalf of all union members.
- A **monopsony** is a single buyer in a factor market.

Review Questions

1. What are three possible labor union objectives when it comes to the labor union employment?

2. The labor union faces a wage-employment tradeoff. Explain.

3. How might a labor union try to lower the elasticity of demand for its labor?

4. How might a labor union try to increase the demand for its labor?

5. What is the difference between a union shop and a closed shop?

6. Why is a monopsony sometimes called a buyer's monopoly?

7. What is the relationship between marginal factor cost and the wage rate for a monopsonist?

8. Explain how changes in supply conditions and wage rates in the unionized sector can cause changes in supply and wage rates in the nonunionized sector.

9. What is the traditional (or orthodox) view of labor unions?

10. What quantity of a factor does a monopsonist purchase?

Problems

1. Fill in the blank spaces in the table.

Description	Type of union
A union whose membership is made up of individuals who practice the same craft or trade.	
A union whose membership is made up of individuals who work for the local, state, or federal government.	
A union whose membership is made up of individuals who work in the same firm or industry but do not all practice the same craft or trade.	

2. Fill in the blank spaces in the table.

Action	Effect on elasticity of demand for union labor (rises, falls, remains unchanged)
reduced availability of substitute products	
reduced availability of substitute factors	

3. Fill in the blank spaces in the table.

Action	Effect on demand for union labor (rises, falls, remains unchanged)
MPP of union labor falls	
product demand rises	
substitute factor prices fall	

4. Fill in the blank spaces in the table.

Action	Does it affect the demand for union labor, or the supply of union labor?
MPP of union labor rises	
substitute factor prices rise	
introduction of union shop	

5. Diagrammatically show that a labor union can change the supply of labor through collective bargaining and a strike.

6. Fill in the blank spaces in the table.

Number of workers	Wage rate	Total labor cost	Marginal factor cost
1	$10.00		
2	$10.10		
3	$10.20		
4	$10.30		
5	$10.40		

What Is the Question?
Identify the question for each of the answers that follow.

1. An organization whose members belong to a particular profession.

2. The labor union will want this wage rate to prevail if its objective is to maximize the total wage bill.

3. The wage-employment tradeoff decreases.

4. The purpose is to convince management that the supply curve is what the union says it is.

5. MFC is greater than the wage rate.

6. An organization in which an employee must belong to the union before he or she can be hired.

7. Increasing product demand, increasing substitute factor prices, and increasing marginal physical product.

8. The change in total labor cost divided by the change in the number of workers.

What Is Wrong?
In each of the statements that follow, something is wrong. Identify what is wrong in the space provided.

1. Union membership as a percentage of the labor force was about 25 percent in the United States in the late 1990s.

2. If the objective of the labor union is to maximize the total wage bill, it will want the wage rate that corresponds to the inelastic portion of the labor demand curve.

3. The more substitutes for union labor, the lower the elasticity of demand for union labor.

4. The National Working Rights Act allowed states to pass right-to-work laws.

5. The MFC curve lies below the supply of labor curve for a monopsonist.

6. The percentage of the national income that goes to labor has been rising over the past 30 years.

7. If labor is homogeneous and mobile, an increase in the wage rate in the union sector will bring about an increase in the wage rate in the nonunion sector.

8. An industrial union is a union whose membership is made up of individuals who practice the same craft or trade.

Multiple Choice
Circle the correct answer.

1. Labor Union A faces an inelastic demand curve for its labor. Labor Union B faces an elastic demand curve for its labor. Which of the two labor unions is less likely to push for higher wages, *ceteris paribus*, and why?
   a. Labor Union A, because for A it is more costly (in terms of union members losing jobs) than it is for B to push for higher wages.
   b. Labor Union B, because for B it is more costly (in terms of union members losing jobs) than it is for A to push for higher wages.
   c. Labor Union A, because the members of it work in the manufacturing sector of the economy and not the service sector.
   d. Labor Union B, because the members of it work in the service sector of the economy and not the manufacturing sector.

2. _____, the lower the elasticity of demand for the product, which in turn means the lower the elasticity of demand for union labor, which means the union will have a smaller cutback in employment for higher wages (the wage-employment tradeoff is less pronounced).
   a. The fewer substitutes that exist for the product the labor union produces
   b. The more substitutes that exist for the product the labor union produces
   c. The more workers in the labor union
   d. The higher the profits of the firm the labor union works for

3. Unions may be interested in increasing the productivity of their members because as their productivity rises, _____, and their wages rise.
   a. the demand for their labor falls
   b. the supply of their labor falls
   c. the supply of their labor rises
   d. the demand for their labor rises

4. The _____ Act prohibited the closed shop.
   a. Norris-LaGuardia
   b. Taft-Hartley
   c. Wagner
   d. Bush
   e. none of the above

5. Which of the following comes closest to being a monopsony?
   a. a computer company in California
   b. a Burger King in a big city
   c. a farmer who hires labor
   d. a firm in a small town and there are no other firms for miles around
   e. a and b are equally monopsonistic

6. Which of the following statements is false?
   a. A monopsony cannot buy additional units of a factor without increasing the price it pays for the factor.
   b. A monopsony can buy additional units of a factor without increasing the price it pays for the factor.
   c. The supply curve a monopsony faces is the industry supply of a factor.
   d. a and c.

7. During the time labor unions have been in existence,
   a. there has been almost no change in the fraction of national income that goes to labor.
   b. the fraction of national income that goes to labor has decreased.
   c. the fraction of national income that goes to labor has increased.
   d. the fraction of national income that goes to rent has increased.

8. In a perfectly competitive industry, do higher wages for labor union members diminish profits?
   a. No, higher wage costs can only affect profits if they affect labor morale, and this doesn't happen.
   b. Yes, in the long run, but no in the short run, since in the short run profits are (close to being) fixed.
   c. Yes, in the short run, but not in the long run, since in the long run some firms will exit the industry because of higher costs and losses and price will rise, reestablishing zero economic profit.
   d. No, because higher labor costs usually bring more firms into the industry and this effect dampens price hikes.

9. The traditional or orthodox view of the effects of labor unions is that they
   a. positively impact productivity and efficiency.
   b. negatively impact productivity and efficiency.
   c. do not drive an artificial wedge between the wages of comparable labor in the union and nonunion sectors of the labor market.
   d. a and c
   e. b and c

10. Which of the following is consistent with the view of labor unions as a collective voice?
   a. Job exiting is increased.
   b. Workers feel less secure in their jobs.
   c. The turnover rate is increased.
   d. Labor productivity declines.
   e. none of the above

11. Which of the following is an example of an employee association?
   a. the American Medical Association
   b. the International Brotherhood of the Teamsters
   c. the Letter Carriers Union
   d. a and b
   e. none of the above

12. The act that says "every person who shall monopolize, or attempt to monopolize, or combine or conspire with any other person or persons, to monopolize any part of the trade or commerce among the several States, or with foreign nations, shall be deemed guilty of a midemeanor," is the
    a. McCormick Harvester Act.
    b. Wagner Act.
    c. Sherman Antitrust Act.
    d. Norris-LaGuardia Act.
    e. none of the above

13. Which of the following does not affect the demand for or quantity demanded of labor?
    a. increasing the marginal physical product of labor
    b. rising factor prices for labor
    c. increasing demand for the product that labor produces
    d. a strike

14. Over the past two decades one of the fast growing subsets of the union movement has been
    a. teamster union membership
    b. public employee union membership.
    c. garment workers membership.
    d. postal worker membership.

15. In the late 1990s, approximately _____ percent of the labor force in the United States belonged to labor unions.
    a. 14.1
    b. 12.3
    c. 10.2
    d. 7.5

True-False
Write "T" or "F" at the end of each statement.

16. Less than one out of every five workers in the United States in 1990 was a union member. _____

17. The American Federation of Labor was formed in 1886 under the leadership of Taft Hartley. _____

18. The Landrum-Griffin Act was passed with the expressed intent of policing the internal affairs of labor unions. _____

19. There is evidence that labor unions generally have the effect of increasing their members' wages and lowering the wage rates of nonunion labor. _____

20. Some economists contend that employee associations are a type of labor union. _____

Fill in the Blank
Write the correct word in the blank.

21. Laws that make it illegal to require union membership for purposes of employment are called _____ – _____ – _____ laws.

22. A single buyer in a factor market is called a _____.

23. The total wage bill is maximized at that point where the demand for labor is _____ _____.

24. A _____ occurs when unionized employees refuse to work at a certain wage or under certain conditions.

25. The monopsonist buys the factor quantity at which (the condition) _____ = _____ holds.

Chapter 29
The Distribution of Income and Poverty

What This Chapter Is About
In an earlier chapter we discussed the factors that determine income. In this chapter we discuss the income distribution—specifically, how the income that is earned in society is distributed. We also discuss the issue of poverty. What are its causes? Why are some people poor and other people rich? What are the policies used to deal with poverty?

Key Concepts in the Chapter
a. *ex ante* distribution of income
b. *ex post* distribution of income
c. Lorenz curve
d. Gini coefficient
e. human capital
f. wage discrimination
g. poverty income threshold

- The *ex ante* **distribution of income** is the before-tax-and-transfer payment distribution of income.
- The *ex post* **distribution of income** is the after-tax-and-transfer payment distribution of income.
- The **Lorenz curve** is a graph of the income distribution. It expresses the relationship between cumulative percentage of households and cumulative percentage of income.
- The **Gini coefficient** is a measurement of the degree of inequality in the income distribution.
- **Human capital** refers to education, the development of skills, and anything else that is particular to the individual and increases his or her productivity.
- **Wage discrimination** is the situation that exists when individuals of equal ability and productivity are paid different wage rates.
- The **poverty income threshold** is the income level below which people are considered to be living in poverty.

Review Questions

1. What is the difference between the *ex ante* distribution of income and the *ex post* distribution of income?

2. What are the four components of individual income?

3. Explain how a Lorenz curve is constructed.

4. What is a limitation of the Gini coefficient?

5. Identify the factors that contribute to income inequality.

6. What is the Rawlsian normative standard of the income distribution?

7. What is absolute poverty? What is relative poverty?

8. How does age affect the income distribution?

9. What is the marginal productivity normative standard of income distribution?

10. What is the public good-free rider argument for taxing persons to pay for the welfare assistance of some?

Problems

1. Fill in the blank spaces in the table.

Quintile	Percentage of total income, 1998
Lowest fifth	
Second fifth	
Third fifth	
Fourth fifth	
Highest fifth	

2. Fill in the blank spaces in the table.

Quintile	Income share (percent)	Cumulative percentage of income	Cumulative percentage of households
Lowest fifth	10		
Second fifth	12		
Third fifth	22		
Fourth fifth	25		
Highest fifth	31		

3.   Fill in the blank spaces in the table.

Group	Percent of group in poverty, 1998
Total population	
White	
African-American	
Hispanic	
Under 18 years of age	
18-24 years old	
65 years old and older	

4.   Diagrammatically represent the Lorenz curve if there is a perfectly equal income distribution.

Cumulative
Percentage
of Income

Quantity Percentage
of Households

5.   Use the first table to fill in the blank spaces in the second table.

Cumulative percentage of households	Cumulative percentage of income
20	10
40	30
60	51
80	73
100	100

Quintile	Income share
Lowest fifth	
Second fifth	
Third fifth	
Fourth fifth	
Highest fifth	

What Is the Question?
Identify the question for each of the answers that follow.

1. Payments to persons that are not made in return for goods and services currently supplied.

2. Labor income plus asset income plus transfer payments minus taxes

3. This exists when individuals of equal ability and productivity are paid different wage rates.

4. It is determined in factor markets.

5. The Gini coefficient is 1.

6. The income level below which people are considered to be living in poverty.

7. An example is that everyone who earns less than $5,000 is living in poverty.

8. An example is that the bottom one-tenth of income earners are living in poverty.

9. It holds that individuals currently not receiving welfare think they might one day need welfare assistance and thus are willing to take out a form of insurance for themselves by supporting welfare programs.

What Is Wrong?
In each of the statements that follow, something is wrong. Identify what is wrong in the space provided.

1. The income distribution in the United States in 1998 was more nearly equal than it was in 1967.

2. The government can change the distribution of income through taxes, but not through transfer payments.

3. The Lorenz curve is a measurement of the degree of inequality in the distribution of income.

4. The Rawlsian normative standard of the income distribution holds that there should be complete income equality.

5. Asset income is equal to the wage rate an individual receives multiplied by the number of hours he or she works.

6. In general, human capital refers to the increases in productivity brought about by humans when they use physical capital goods.

7. The Gini coefficient is zero (0) if there is an unequal income distribution.

Multiple Choice
Circle the correct answer.

1. Which of the following statements is true?
    a. Between 1967 and 1998, the income distribution in the United States has become less equal.
    b. In 1967, the lowest 20% of all income earners earned over 10% of the total money income.
    c. The people that make up the highest fifth of all income earners are millionaires.
    d. a and c
    e. a, b, and c

2. The *ex post* income distribution is
    a. less equal then the *ex ante* income distribution.
    b. more equal then the *ex ante* income distribution.
    c. as equal as the *ex ante* income distribution.
    d. not adjusted for taxes and transfer payments.
    e. b and d

3. The smaller the Gini coefficient, the
    a. greater the degree of income inequality.
    b. greater the degree of income equality.
    c. higher the birth rate.
    d. larger the population.
    e. none of the above

4. Which of the following statements is false?
    a. Economists agree that it is better for a country to have a lower Gini coefficient than a higher one.
    b. Economists agree that it is better for a country to have a higher Gini coefficient than a lower one.
    c. There is greater income equality in the United States than Sweden.
    d. Because the Gini coefficient is lower in Country A than Country B, the lowest income group in Country A has a greater percentage of total income than the lowest income group in Country B.
    e. all of the above

5. One way to increase the degree of income inequality is to
    a. decrease transfer payments going to people with low labor and asset incomes and decrease taxes on people with high labor and asset incomes.
    b. increase transfer payments going to people with low labor and asset incomes and decrease taxes on people with high labor and asset incomes.
    c. increase transfer payments going to people with low labor and asset incomes by more than you increase taxes on the same people.
    d. increase transfer payments going to people with high labor and asset incomes by less than you increase taxes on the same people.
    e. a and d

6. Which of the following statements is true?
    a. If people were alike in terms of their marketable innate abilities and attributes, there would be less income inequality.
    b. Some degree of income inequality can be attributed to the fact that some people consume more leisure than others.
    c. Schooling is referred to as human capital.
    d. a and c
    e. a, b, and c

7. Human capital refers to
    a. equal pay.
    b. education and development of skills.
    c. factories and computers.
    d. a and c
    e. none of the above

8. The proponents of absolute income equality sometimes argue that an equal income distribution of income will maximize total utility. Their argument goes like this:
    a. Individuals are alike when it comes to how much satisfaction they receive from an increase in income; receiving additional income is subject to the law of diminishing marginal utility, redistributing income from the rich to the poor helps the poor less than it hurts the rich, so total utility rises.
    b. Individuals are alike when it comes to how much satisfaction they receive from an increase in income; receiving additional income is subject to the law of constant marginal costs, redistributing income from the rich to the poor helps the poor more than it hurts the rich, so total utility rises.
    c. Individuals are not alike when it comes to how much satisfaction they receive from an increase in income; receiving additional income is subject to the law of diminishing marginal utility, redistributing income from the rich to the poor helps the poor less than it hurts the rich, so total utility rises.
    d. Individuals are alike when it comes to how much satisfaction they receive from an increase in income; receiving additional income is subject to the law of diminishing marginal utility, redistributing income from the rich to the poor helps the poor more than it hurts the rich, so total utility rises.

9. Which of the following is a definition of poverty in relative terms?
    a. A family is in poverty if it receives less than $10,000 a year.
    b. A family is in poverty if it receives an income that places it in the lowest 5 percent of family income recipients.
    c. A family is in poverty if the majority of families receive more income than it receives.
    d. b and c
    e. a, b, and c

10. Which of the following leads to an underestimate of the number of persons in poverty?
    a. illegal income
    b. unreported income
    c. some poor persons can't be found, therefore they can't be counted
    d. a and b
    c. a, b, and c

True-False
Write "T" or "F" at the end of each statement.

11. The *ex ante* distribution of income is the before-tax and before-transfer distribution of income. _____

12. The Lorenz curve is a graphical representation of the distribution of income. _____

13. The mean household income of the highest fifth of income earners in 1998 was $127,529. _____

14. John Rawls wrote *A Theory of Justice.* _____

15. The acceptance of the public good-free rider argument leads individuals to conclude that government is justified in taxing all persons to pay for welfare assistance for some. _____

Fill in the Blank
Write the correct word in the blank.

16. _____ _____ are payments to persons that are not made in return for goods and services currently supplied.

17. The _____ _____ is a measurement of the degree of inequality in the income distribution.

18. _____ _____ exists when individuals of equal ability and productivity, as measured by their marginal revenue products, are paid different wage rates.

19. The closer the Gini coefficient is to _____, the greater the degree of income inequality.

20. The _____ _____ distribution of income is the before-tax-and-transfer payment distribution of income.

Chapter 30
Interest, Rent, and Profit

What This Chapter Is About
There are four broad categories of resources—land, labor, capital, and entrepreneurship. In an earlier chapter we discussed the payment to labor—the wage rate. In this chapter we discuss the payments to land, capital, and entrepreneurship.

Key Concepts in the Chapter
   a.   positive rate of time preference
   b.   nominal interest rate
   c.   real interest rate
   d.   present value
   e.   economic rent
   f.   pure economic rent

- A **positive rate of time preference** is a preference for earlier availability of goods over later availability.
- The **nominal interest rate** is the interest rate determined by the forces of supply and demand in the loanable funds market.
- The **real interest rate** is the nominal interest rate adjusted for expected inflation—that is, the nominal interest rate minus the expected inflation rate.
- **Present value** is the current worth of some future dollar amount of income or receipts.
- **Economic rent** is payment in excess of opportunity costs.
- **Pure economic rent** is a category of economic rent where the payment is to a factor that is in fixed supply, implying that it has zero opportunity costs.

Review Questions

1.   Give an example to illustrate the difference between interest and the interest rate.

2.   What does it mean if a person has a low positive rate of time preference?

3. Give an example of a roundabout method of production.

4. What do positive interest rates have to do with roundabout methods of production and positive rates of time preference?

5. Why do interest rates differ?

6. A capital good will cost a firm $5,000. The good will generate $1,200 each year for five years. After five years, the capital good must be scrapped and it has no scrap value. If the interest rate is 7 percent, should the firm buy the capital good? Explain your answer.

7. David Ricardo believed that land rent was price determined, not price determining. What did he mean?

8. Give an example to illustrate the difference between economic rent and pure economic rent.

9. What is the difference between an artificial rent and a real rent?

10. What might profit have to do with uncertainty? With innovation?

11. Profit and loss act as signals. Explain.

Problems

1. Fill in the blank spaces in the table.

Dollar amount received	Number of years before dollar amount is received	Interest rate (percent)	Present value
$1,000	2	5	
$10,000	3	6	
$100	2	7	

2.   Fill in the blank spaces in the table.

Cost of capital good	Life of capital good	Income from capital good each year	Interest rate (percent)	Should the firm buy the capital good? (yes, no)
$4,000	3 years	$1,500	2	
$19,000	5 years	$4,000	5	
$20,000	6 years	$5,000	4	

3.   Diagrammatically represent pure economic rent.

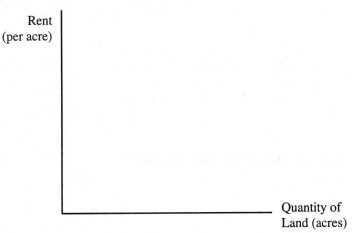

Rent
(per acre)

Quantity of
Land (acres)

4.   Diagrammatically represent economic rent.

Rent
(per acre)

Quantity of
Land (acres)

5.   Fill in the blank spaces in the table.

Wage rate	Next best wage rate	Economic rent
$12	$11	
$10	$10	
$100	$66	

What Is the Question?
Identify the question for each of the answers that follow.

1. The production of capital goods that enhance productive capabilities and ultimately bring about increased consumption.

2. It is composed of the demand for consumption loans and the demand for investment loans.

3. If this is the case, then firms will borrow in the loanable funds market and invest in capital goods.

4. The interest rate determined by the forces of supply and demand in the loanable funds market.

5. They are equal when the expected inflation rate is zero.

6. The current worth of some future dollar amount of income receipts.

7. The supply curve is vertical in this case.

8. Consumers do this because they have a positive rate of time preference.

9. These turn away from losses.

What Is Wrong?
In each of the statements that follow, something is wrong. Identify what is wrong in the space provided.

1. Interest refers to the price paid by borrowers for loanable funds and to the return on cash.

2. Savers supply loanable funds because they have a negative rate of time preference.

3. A person with a high positive rate of time preference is more likely to be a saver than a person with a low positive rate of time preference.

4. David Ricardo argued that high land rents weren't an effect of high interest rates and high grain prices.

5. The present value of $4,000 in three years, if the interest rate is 5 percent, is $3,288.

6. A decreased threat of war would probably raise peoples' rate of time preference.

7. As the interest rate falls, present value falls.

8. Uncertainty exists when a potential occurrence is so unpredictable that the probability of it occurring is less than 1.

9. Economists emphasize accounting profit over economic profit because economic profit determines entry into and exit from an industry.

Multiple Choice
Circle the correct answer.

1. The supply of loanable funds most directly depends on
    a. people's investment activity.
    b. stock market activity.
    c. people's saving and newly created money.
    d. the profits and losses of firms.

2. Which of the following statements is true?
    a. The quantity supplied of loanable funds and the interest rate are inversely related.
    b. The supply curve of loanable funds is horizontal.
    c. One of the reasons the federal government demands loanable funds is that it needs to finance budget surpluses.
    d. Savers are people who consume less than their current income.
    e. none of the above

3. If consumers have a positive rate of time preference, this means they prefer
    a. earlier availability of goods to later availability.
    b. later availability of goods to earlier availability.
    c. goods to services, since services can be delivered more quickly.
    d. goods to services, since goods are more tangible.
    e. none of the above.

4. The people least likely to save are those people with a
    a. low rate of time preference, since they only slightly prefer present consumption to future consumption.
    b. low rate of time preference, since they greatly prefer present consumption to future consumption.
    c. high rate of time preference, since they greatly prefer present consumption to future consumption.
    d. efficient rate of time preference, since they do not prefer consuming luxury goods to necessities.
    e. roundabout rate of time preference, since they don't really care about consuming.

5. If the price for loanable funds is greater than the return on capital, then firms
    a. will borrow in the loanable funds market and invest in capital goods, and as this happens the quantity of capital decreases and its return rises.
    b. will borrow in the loanable funds market and invest in capital goods, and as this happens the quantity of capital increases and its return falls.
    c. do not borrow in the loanable funds market, and over time the capital stock will decrease and the return on capital will fall.
    d. do not borrow in the loanable funds market, and over time the capital stock will decrease and the return on capital will rise.

6. If a 5 percent inflation rate is expected by both the suppliers and demanders of loanable funds, then the
    a. nominal interest rate will rise, *ceteris paribus.*
    b. real interest rate will fall, *ceteris paribus.*
    c. real interest rate will rise.
    d. nominal interest rate will fall, *ceteris paribus.*

7. If the nominal interest rate is 10 percent and the expected inflation rate is 6 percent, the real interest rate equals
    a. 16 percent.
    b. 6 percent.
    c. 10 percent.
    d. 4 percent.
    e. none of the above

8. The present value of $10,000 two years in the futre, at a 5 percent interest rate, is approximately
    _____.
    a. $7,789
    b. $9,260
    c. $8,790
    d. $9,090

9. As interest rates decrease, present values _____, and firms will buy _____ capital goods.
    a. increase; fewer
    b. decrease; fewer
    c. increase; more
    d. decrease; more

10. A payment in excess of opportunity costs is called
    a. price.
    b. implicit price.
    c. economic rent.
    d. excess profits.
    e. none of the above

11. The economist David Ricardo argued that grain prices were _____ because land rents were _____.
    a. high; high
    b. low; high
    c. high; low
    d. low; low
    e. none of the above

12. Uncertainty
    a. is the result of a positive time preferentce.
    b. is the same thing as risk.
    c. exists when the probability of a given event can be estimated.
    d. is the result of a negative time preference.
    e. none of the above

13. Michael can work at job X earning $150,000 a year, or job Y earning $183,000 a year, or job Z earning $195,000 a year. If Michael chooses job Z, then economic rent equals
    a. $33,000.
    b. $45,000.
    c. $30,000.
    d. $12,000.
    e. none of the above

14. Entrepreneurship differs from the other factors of production in that
    a.   the return to it is always negative.
    b.   the return to it is always positive.
    c.   it cannot be measured.
    d.   the return to it is larger than the returns to the other factors of production.

15. A person buys A for $400 and sells it for $450. Which theory of profit is most consistent with this example?
    a.   Profit is the return to the entrepreneur as innovator.
    b.   Uncertainty is the source of profit.
    c.   Profit is the return to being alert to arbitrage opportunities.
    d.   a and b
    e.   none of the above

True-False
Write "T" or "F" at the end of each statement.

16. The nominal interest rate is the real interest rate minus the expected inflation rate. _____

17. Present value refers to the future worth of some current dollar amount. _____

18. No factor besides land can receive pure economic rent. _____

19. Entrepreneurship is measured in terms of entins, such that 2 entins equal 1 enton. _____

20. The word interest refers to the price paid by borrowers for loanable funds and the return on capital in the production process. _____

Fill in the Blank
Write the correct word in the blank.

21. Investors (or firms) demand loanable funds so that they can invest in productive _____ _____ of production.

22. Over time, the price for loanable funds and the return on capital tend to _____.

23. If the expected inflation rate is positive, the _____ interest rate is greater than the _____ interest rate.

24. The present value of $1,000 _____ year(s) from now is $925.92 at an 8 percent interest rate.

25. As present values _____, firms will buy more capital goods, *ceteris paribus*.

Chapter 31
Market Failure: Externalities, Public Goods and Asymmetric Information

What This Chapter Is About
Does the market sometimes fail to provide the optimal amount of a particular good? Some economists think so. This chapter is about market failure.

Key Concepts in the Chapter
- a.   market failure
- b.   externality
- c.   socially optimal output
- d.   Coase theorem
- e.   public good
- f.   free rider
- g.   asymmetric information

- **Market failure** refers to the situation in which the market does not provide the ideal or optimal amount of a particular good.
- **Externality** is a side effect of an action that affects the well-being of third parties.
- **Socially optimal output** is the output level that takes into account and adjusts for all benefits and all costs.
- The **Coase theorem** states that in the case of trivial or zero transaction costs, the property rights assignment does not matter to the resource allocative outcome.
- A **public good** is a good, which if consumed by one person, does not reduce consumption by another person.
- A **free rider** is anyone who receives the benefits of a good without paying for it.
- **Asymmetric information** exists when either the buyer or the seller in a market exchange has some information that the other does not have.

Review Questions

1.   Does the market output always differ from the socially optimal output? Explain your answer.

2.   What is market failure?

3. Do property rights assignments matter to the allocation of resources? Explain your answer.

4. What it is the objective of imposing a corrective tax? Does a corrective tax always work? Why or why not?

5. Is less pollution always preferred to the current amount of pollution? Explain your answer.

6. How does market environmentalism work?

7. What is the difference between a nonexcludable public good and an excludable public good?

8. Why doesn't the market produce nonexcludable public goods?

9. Explain how asymmetric information in a product market can lead to market failure.

10. Explain how asymmetric information in a factor market can lead to market failure.

11. How can adverse selection eliminate markets?

12. Give an example that illustrates moral hazard.

Problems

1. Using the data in the table, answer these two questions:

    a) What is the total cost of eliminating 6 units of pollution if a regulation is set mandating each firm to eliminate two units of pollution?

    b) What is the cost of eliminating 6 units of pollution if pollution permits are bought and sold for $650 each?

Cost of eliminating:	Firm A	Firm B	Firm C
1st unit of pollution	$100	$200	$1,000
2nd unit of pollution	$200	$400	$1,900
3rd unit of pollution	$300	$600	$2,300

2. Diagrammatically show how a corrective tax can go wrong (when trying to adjust for a negative externality).

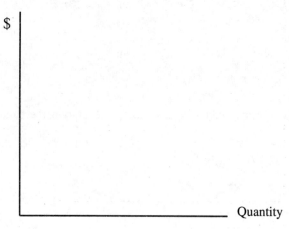

3. In the diagram that follows, the identified triangle identifies the market failure. Why?

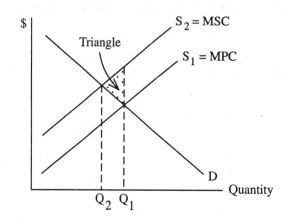

4. Under what condition will a corrective tax achieve the socially optimum output?

5. Diagrammatically explain how asymmetric information in a product market can lead to market failure?

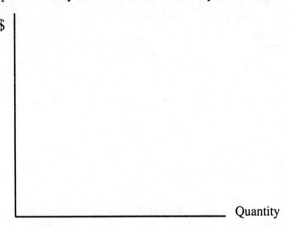

What Is the Question?
Identify the question for each of the answers that follow?

1. This exists when a person's or group's actions cause a cost to be felt by others.

2. MSC > MPC.

3. MSB > MPB.

4. In this case property rights assignments do not matter to the resource allocative outcome.

5. He stressed the reciprocal nature of externalities.

6. Consumption by one person reduces consumption by another person.

7. The person who makes it difficult, if not impossible, for the market to produce nonexcludable public goods.

8. This exists when either the buyer or the seller in a market exchange has some information that the other does not have.

9. This exists when the parties on one side of the market, who have information not known to others, self-select in a way that adversely affects the parties on the other side of the market.

What Is Wrong?
In each of the statements that follow, something is wrong. Identify what is wrong in the space provided.

1. The economist holds that less pollution is always better than the current amount of pollution because pollution is a bad.

2. A negative externality is a type of subsidy.

3. Given a positive externality, the marginal private benefit curve lies to the left of the demand curve, with the market output above the socially optimal output.

4. The side effect of an action that increases the well-being of others is called a neutral benefit.

5. If private property were established in the air, there would probably be more air pollution.

6.   If a person who generates a negative externality incorporates into his private cost-benefit calculations the effects that this externality will have on third parties, the externality has been complementarized.

7.   Generally, negative externalities result in too little of a good being produced.

8.   If there are no externalities, then the socially optimum output occurs where MPB > MPC.

9.   Exchange is a zero sum game.

10.   Marginal social costs equal marginal private costs plus internal costs.

Multiple Choice
Circle the correct answer.

1.   Market failure is a situation in which
     a.   prices are so low that producers will not produce goods.
     b.   there are too many buyers, but not enough sellers.
     c.   the market does not provide the ideal or optimal amount of a particular good.
     d.   prices are so high that buyers won't buy the quantity of goods that sellers want to sell.

2.   In which of the following situations could a negative externality potentially be involved?
     a.   Patricia is sitting at home waiting for her friend to call. He never calls.
     b.   Frank got caught in a rainstorm on his way to Miami.
     c.   Fergie went to the beauty salon and got a new hairdo. She hates it.
     d.   Xavier works late at night and tries to sleep late in the morning. Ever Tuesday and Thursday he is awakened at around 8:00 in the morning by his neighbor's television set. His neighbor is slightly deaf and turns the television up loud.
     e.   none of the above

3.   When a negative externality exists,
     a.   social costs are greater than private costs.
     b.   social costs equal private costs.
     c.   external costs are greater than private costs.
     d.   external costs are less than private costs.
     e.   none of the above

4.   When a positive externality exists,
     a.   external benefits are greater than private benefits.
     b.   external benefits are less than private benefits.
     c.   social benefits are less than private benefits.
     d.   social benefits equal private benefits.
     e.   social benefits are greater than private benefits.

5.   There are numerous ways of adjusting for externalities. One way is to persuade persons or groups that
     they ought to consider others when they act. Which of the following scenarios is consistent with this
     method of adjusting for (internalizing) externalities?
     a.   The government stipulates how much pollution (over some period of time) a factory can emit into
          the air.
     b.   Katrina is sitting at a restaurant when cigarette smoke drifts her way. She asks the manager to ask
          the person smoking if he would be considerate enough not to smoke. (The restaurant does not have
          designated smoking and nonsmoking areas.)
     c.   Mark's next-door neighbor is having a loud party at 1:00 in the morning. Mark calls his neighbor
          up on the telephone and asks him to be more considerate.
     d.   b and c
     e.   a, b, and c

6.   The Coase theorem states that
     a.   private property rights evolve when the costs of defining property rights are less than the benefits.
     b.   in the case of trivial or zero transaction costs, negative externalities are more likely to appear.
     c.   when transaction costs are high, negative externalities are more common than positive
          externalities.
     d.   in the case of trivial or zero transaction costs, the property rights assignment does not matter to the
          resource allocative outcome.

7.   Which of the following statements is true?
     a.   One way to adjust for negative externalities is for government to apply regulations to the activity
          that generates the externalities.
     b.   A subsidy is used to adjust for a positive externality, a tax is used to adjust for a negative
          externality.
     c.   Simply because taxes and subsidies are sometimes used to adjust for negative and positive
          externalities, respectively, it does not necessarily follow that the socially-optimal level of output
          will be reached.
     d.   b and c
     e.   a, b, and c

8.   When a good is nonexcludable,
     a.   it is impossible for individuals to obtain the benefits of the good without paying for it.
     b.   it is possible for individuals to obtain the benefits of the good without paying for it.
     c.   it is a government-provided good.
     d.   the benefits of producing it outweigh the costs.
     e.   none of the above

9.   Most economists contend that the market will fail to produce public goods because of the
     a.   rivalry problem.
     b.   Coase problem.
     c.   Demsetz problem.
     d.   free-rider problem.

10. Much of the air is polluted. We would expect this natural resource to be less polluted if
    a. there were stiff fines for polluting the air.
    b. private property rights were established in the air.
    c. both a and b
    d. neither a nor b

True-False
Write "T" or "F" at the end of each statement.

11. National defense is a nonexcludable public good. ____

12. A public good is the same as a government-provided good. ____

13. A good is excludable if it is possible, or not prohibitively costly, to exclude someone from obtaining the benefits of the good once it has been produced. ____

14. Economists believe that there is an optimal amount of pollution, and that this probably isn't zero. ____

15. Coase discussed the reciprocal nature of externalities. ____

Fill in the Blank
Write the correct word in the blank.

16. _____ _____ is a situation in which the market does not provide the ideal or optimal amount of a particular good.

17. An externality is _____ if the person(s) or group that generated the externality incorporate into their own private cost-benefit calculations the external benefits of costs that third parties bear.

18. A good is _____ _____ _____ if its consumption by one person does not reduce its consumption by others.

19. _____ _____ occurs when one party to a transaction changes his or her behavior in a way that is hidden from, and costly to, the other party.

20. When either negative or positive externalities exist, the market output is different from the _____ _____.

Chapter 32
Public Choice:
Economic Theory Applied to Politics

What This Chapter Is About
This chapter uses economic tools to analyze decisions made in the public sector. Specifically, it looks at the behavior of voters, politicians, special-interest groups, and bureaucrats using the tools of economics.

Key Concepts in the Chapter
    a.   median voter model
    b.   rational ignorance

- The **median voter model** suggests that candidates in a two-person political race will move toward matching the preferences of the median voter.
- **Rational ignorance** is the state of not acquiring information because the costs of acquiring the information are greater than the benefits.

Review Questions

1. A politician running for office speaks in general terms. Is this consistent with the median voter model? Explain your answer.

2. A politician running for office labels herself "middle of the road," and she labels her opponent "extremist." Is this consistent with the median voter model? Explain your answer.

3. According to the median voter model, are politicians more likely to take polls to determine their position, or to first determine their position and then take polls? Explain your answer.

4.   Why might a person who can vote choose not to vote?

5.   A person may vote even though she knows that her single vote cannot affect the outcome of the election. Why would this person vote?

6.   Give an example to illustrate why a person's vote in a presidential election may not matter to the outcome.

7.   Jim, 24 years old, doesn't know the names of his U.S. senators. What does this have to do with rational ignorance?

8.   Is everyone rationally ignorant of something? Explain your answer.

9. What are special-interest groups?

10. Why is a farmer more likely to be informed about agricultural policy than a member of the general public?

11. Even if members of the general public were well informed about special-interest legislation that would harm them, they might not lobby against it. Explain why.

12. What is rent? What is rent seeking?

13. Why is rent seeking socially wasteful?

Problems

1. A group of five persons is thinking of buying good X and splitting the cost. The group will use majority rule to decide whether good X will be purchased or not. In the table that follows, you will find the dollar value of the benefit and cost to each individual.

Person	Dollar value of the benefit to the individual	Dollar cost to the individual
A	$143	$100
B	$120	$100
C	$110	$100
D	$10	$100
E	$5	$100

    Will the group buy good X? Is the purchase of the good an efficient purchase? Explain your answer.

What Is the Question?
Identify the question for each of the answers that follow.

1. The branch of economics that deals with the application of economic principles and tolls to public-sector decision making.

2. Candidates will speak in general terms; candidates will label their opponent in extreme terms; candidates will label themselves in moderate terms; candidates will take polls and if they are not doing well in their polls they will adjust their positions.

3. The state of not acquiring information because the costs of acquiring the information are greater than the benefits.

4.   The exchange of votes to gain support for legislation.

5.   In this case rent is usually called profit.

6.   The expenditure of scarce resources to capture a pure transfer.

What Is Wrong?
In each of the statements that follow, something is wrong. Identify what is wrong in the space provided.

1.   Legislation that concentrates the benefits on many and disperses the costs over a few is likely to pass, because the beneficiaries will have an incentive to lobby for it, whereas those who pay the bill will not lobby against it because each of them pays such a small part of the bill.

2.   A public choice economist would likely state that people will not behave differently in different settings.

3.   In a two-person race, the candidate on the right of the median voter is more likely to win the race than the candidate on the left of the median voter.

4.   One of the predictions of the median voter model is that candidates will speak in specific terms instead of general terms because this is what the median voter wants.

5.   Younger people are more likely to be rationally ignorant of various subjects than older people.

6. A government bureau maximizes profit and minimizes costs.

7. Farmers, lobbying for a legislative bill, are more likely to openly state, "We need this legislation because it will be good for us," instead of "We need this legislation for America's future."

Multiple Choice
Circle the correct answer.

1. Which of the following statements would a public choice theorist have some difficulty accepting as true?
    a. The only way to genuinely reform in this country is to elect really good and moral people to government.
    b. The people who work for a large government bureaucracy are fundamentally different people than those who work for a private firm.
    c. People respond to the costs and benefits of different institutional settings.
    d. a and b
    e. a, b, and c

2. Two policians, running for the same political office, move towards the middle of the political spectrum. This is behavior consistent with the
    a. median voter model.
    b. presidential middle theory.
    c. public choice rational ignorance theory of politics.
    d. candidate theory.
    e. none of the above

3. An economist is most likely to ask which of the following questions about a theory?
    a. If the theory is right, what should I expect to see in the real world?
    b. If the theory is right, then does it follow that the assumptions of the theory are right and can be used to explain different things?
    c. If the theory is right, then how simple is it?
    d. If the theory is right, can it be tested?

4. Public choice is a branch of
    a. political science that deals with the presidential elections and how they affect the economy.
    b. sociology that deals with human behavior in group settings.
    c. economics that deals with the theory of the firm.
    d. economics that deals with the application of economic principles and tools to public-sector decision making.
    e. none of the above

5. A public choice theorist would be most likely to say that government failure is a consequence of the
    a. ineptitude of bureaucrats.
    b. rational behavior of the participants of the political process.
    c. ignorance of voters.
    d. greed of special interest groups.
    e. b, c, and d

6. The model that predicts the candidate in the two-person race that comes closer to occupying the center of the voter distribution will win, is built on the assumption that people
   a. vote for the Democratic candidate if they are Democrats and they vote for the Republican candidate if they are Republicans.
   b. don't vote in close elections.
   c. vote for the candidate who comes closer to matching their own views.
   d. vote their pocketbooks.
   e. c and d

7. Which of the following statements is false?
   a. If the costs of voting are greater than the benefits of voting, a person will decide not to vote.
   b. The simply majority decision rule can generate inefficient results.
   c. Voting does not take into account the intensity of individuals' preferences.
   d. One cannot be uninformed on government and political matters and be considered rational, too.
   e. c and d

8. Rational ignorance refers to
   a. the honeymoon period that every president experiences soon after he is elected.
   b. the fact that some voters are not smart enough to be informed on some things.
   c. the state of not acquiring information because the costs of acquiring the information are greater than the benefits.
   d. political candidates criticizing each other based on something other than the facts.
   e. none of the above

9. The "average" member of the public is likely to know less about government agricultural policies than a farmer. The reason for this is:
   a. a farmer is smarter than the "average" member of the public.
   b. government agricultural policies are more likely to directly affect a farmer than the "average" member of the public, and so a farmer has a sharper incentive to be informed about them.
   c. a farmer is a member of a special interest group, and a member of a special interest group is more informed on all issues than the "average" member of the public.
   d. a and c
   e. none of the above

10. An elected representative may vote for a piece of special-interest legislation without fear of retaliation from the general public because
    a. many voters are rationally ignorant.
    b. people forgive quickly.
    c. all politicians do it, so in relative terms one politician is no worse for doing it than another.
    d. b and c
    e. none of the above

True-False
Write "T" or "F" after each statement.

11. James Buchanan is a public choice economist. ____

12. Public choice economists contend that people exhibit different behavior in the private sector than they do in the public sector. ____

13. The simple majority decision rule does not take into account the intensity of individuals' preferences. ____

14. Logrolling is the exchange of votes to gain support for legislation. ____

15. It is irrational not to vote in a presidential election. ____

Fill in the Blank
Write the correct word in the blank.

16. _____ _____ is said to exist when government enacts policies that produce inefficient and /or inequitable results as a consequence of the rational behavior of the participants in the political process.

17. Many potential voters will not vote because the _____ of voting—in terms of time spent going to the polls and so on—outweigh the _____ of voting measured in terms of the probability of their single vote affecting the election outcome.

18. Candidates for political office will speak more in _____ terms than _____ terms.

19. Near the end of a political campaign, we would expect two candidates running for the same office to be _____ to each other in terms of their policy positions than at the beginning of the campaign.

20. _____ _____ won the Nobel Prize in Economics in 1986 for his work in public choice theory.

Chapter 33
International Trade

What This Chapter Is About

This chapter is about international trade—why people in different countries trade with each other, the effects of tariffs and quotas, and more.

Key Concepts in the Chapter

a. comparative advantage
b. consumers' surplus
c. producers' surplus

- **Comparative advantage** is the situation in which a country can produce a good at lower opportunity cost than another country.
- **Consumers' surplus** is the difference between the maximum buying price and the price paid.
- **Producers' surplus** is the difference between the price received (by the seller) and the minimum selling price.

Review Questions

1. Why do people in different countries trade with each other?

2. Why are countries better off specializing and trading (with each other) than not specializing and not trading?

3. How will a tariff affect (domestic) consumers' surplus?

4. How will a quota affect (domestic) producers' surplus?

5. Why might quotas be imposed even when the benefits of quotas (to the beneficiaries) are less than the costs of the quotas?

6. Outline the details of the infant-industry argument for trade restrictions.

7. What is the antidumping argument for trade restrictions?

8. Suppose a tariff or quota saves some domestic jobs. Would an economist say it is worth it? Explain your answer.

9. What is the role of the WTO?

10. There is a net loss from tariffs. What does this mean?

Problems

1. Fill in the blank spaces in the second table, based on the information in the first table.

Country A can produce these combinations of X and Y	Country B can produce these combinations of X and Y
120X, 0Y	60X, 0Y
80X, 60Y	40X, 20Y
40X, 120Y	20X, 40Y
0X, 180Y	0X, 60Y

Opportunity cost of one unit of X for Country A	Opportunity cost of one unit of Y for Country A	Opportunity cost of one unit of X for Country B	Opportunity cost of one unit of Y for Country B

2. Using the diagram that follows, identify the area of consumers' surplus.

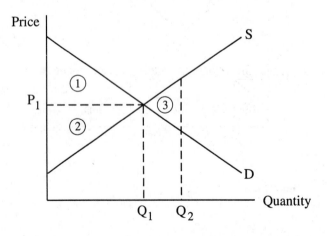

3. Using the diagram that follows, identify the area of producers' surplus.

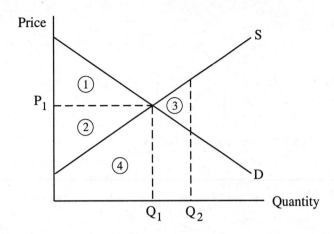

4. In the diagram (that follows), the world price is P_W. The price after a tariff has been imposed is P_T.
    Identify the change in consumers' surplus due to the tariff. Identify the change in producers' surplus
    due to the tariff.

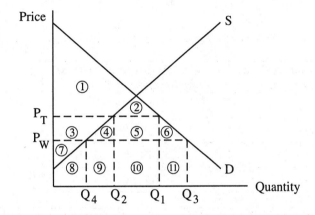

5. In the diagram (that follows), identify the gain due to the tariff. Next, identify the loss due to the tariff.

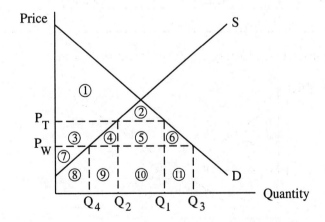

6. In the diagram (that follows), identify the net loss due to the tariff.

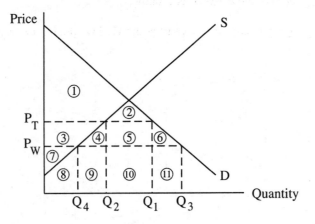

7. In the diagram (that follows), P_W is the world price and P_Q is the price after a quota has been imposed. Identify the increase in additional revenue received by importers due to the quota.

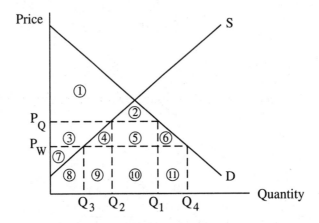

8. Using the diagram that follows, fill in the blank spaces in the table below.

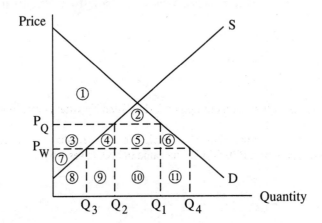

Price after quota	Loss in consumers' surplus due to the quota	Gain in producers' surplus due to the quota	Increase in revenue received by importers due to the quota	Net loss due to the quota
P_Q				

What is the Question?
Identify the questions for each of the answers that follow.

1.   This will allow the country to consume beyond its production possibilities frontier (PPF).

2.   As a result, imports decrease.

3.   The sale of goods abroad at a price below their cost and below the price charged in the domestic market.

4.   The situation in which a country can produce a good at lower opportunity cost than another country.

5.   The gains are less than the losses plus the tariff revenues.

What Is Wrong?
In each of the statements that follow, something is missing. Identify what is wrong in the space provided.

1.   A PPF for the world can be drawn when 1) countries do not specialize and trade and 2) when they do specialize and trade. The world PPF will be the same in both cases.

2. The national-defense argument states that certain goods are necessary to the national defense and therefore should be produced only by allies.

3. A quota raises more government revenue than a tariff.

4. Consumers' surplus and producers' surplus fall as a result of a tariff being imposed on imported goods.

5. What producers gain from a quota is greater than what consumers lose from a quota.

6. If the United States sells a good for less in France than it does in Brazil, then the United States is said to be dumping goods in France.

7. A voluntary export restraint is an agreement between two countries in which importing countries voluntarily agree to limit their imports of a good from another country.

8. A quota is a tax on the amount of a good that may be imported into a country.

Multiple Choice
Circle the correct answer.

EXHIBIT A

United States		Japan	
Good X	Good Y	Good X	Good Y
120	0	30	0
80	10	20	10
40	20	10	20
0	30	0	30

1. In Exhibit A, the opportunity cost of one unit of Y for the United States is _____, whereas the opportunity cost of one unit of Y for Japan is _____.
    a. 2X; 5X
    b. 10X; 2X
    c. 4X; 1X
    d. 6X; 5X
    e. none of the above

2. In Exhibit A, the United States is the lower opportunity cost producer of _____ and Japan is the lower opportunity cost producer of _____.
    a. good X; good Y
    b. both goods; neither good
    c. neither good; both goods.
    d. good Y; good X

3. Considering the data in Exhibit A, which of the following terms of trade would both countries agree to?
    a. 5.5X = 1Y
    b. 0.5X = 1Y
    c. 5X = 1Y
    d. 2X = 1Y

4. Jack paid $40 for good X and gained $10 consumers' surplus. What is the highest price Jack would have paid for the good?
    a. $50
    b. $30
    c. $60
    d. $65
    e. There is not enough information to answer the question.

5. Producers' surplus is the difference between the price _____ receive for a good and the _____ price for which they would have _____ the good.
    a. sellers; minimum; sold
    b. buyers; maximum; bought
    c. sellers; maximum; sold
    d. buyers; minimum; bought

6. The national defense argument for trade restriction contends that
    a. the president should have the authority to erect trade barriers in case of war or national emergency.
    b. free trade makes a country dependent on other countries and this weakens the national defense.
    c. a country should produce those goods necessary for national defense purposes even if it doesn't have a comparative advantage in them.
    d. if your enemy erects trade restrictions, so should you.
    e. b and c

7. Dumping refers to
   a. buying goods at low prices in foreign countries and selling them at high prices in the United States.
   b. expensive goods being sold for low prices.
   c. government actions to remedy "unfair" trade practices.
   d. the sale of goods abroad at a price below their cost and below the price charged in the domestic market.

8. A tariff is a
   a. restriction on the number of people that can work in an export business.
   b. legal limit on the amount of a good that may be imported.
   c. business fee incurred to ship goods abroad.
   d. tax on imports.
   e. none of the above

9. Under a policy of prohibiting exports,
   a. domestic consumers have greater consumers' surplus than under a policy of permitting exports.
   b. domestic consumers have less consumers' surplus than under a policy of permitting exports.
   c. domestic producers have greater producers' surplus than under a policy of permitting exports.
   d. a and c
   c. b and c

10. Under a tariff policy,
   a. domestic consumers have greater consumers' surplus than under a policy of free trade.
   b. domestic consumers have less consumers' surplus than under a policy of free trade.
   c. domestic producers have greater producers' surplus than under a policy of free trade.
   d. a and c
   c. b and c

11. Company A is a new company that produces a good that is already produced in many foreign countries and sold in the United States. Most likely, the argument it will voice in its attempt to be protected from foreign competition is the
   a. antidumping argument.
   b. low-foreign-wages argument.
   c. job creating argument.
   d. infant industry argument.
   e. national defense argument.

12. Tariffs and quotas are
   a. beneficial for producers in a protected industry, but not beneficial for the workers in the industry.
   b. beneficial for producers in a protected industry, but not beneficial for consumers.
   c. beneficial for workers in a protected industry, but not beneficial for consumers.
   d. not beneficial for the workers in a protected industry or for consumers.
   e. b and c

13. A tariff is imposed on good X. The tariff will _____ the price of good X in the domestic market, _____ the number of units of good X imported into the domestic market, and _____ consumers' surplus.
   a. lower; raise; raise
   b. raise; lower; lower
   c. raise; lower; raise
   d. lower; raise; lower
   e. none of the above

14. Tariffs and quotas are often imposed when government is responsive to _____ interests, and the benefits of tariffs and quotas are often _____.
    a. consumer; dispersed
    b. consumer; concentrated
    c. producer; dispersed
    d. producer; concentrated

15. Which of the following is not an example of a trade restriction?
    a. tariff
    b. quota
    c. dumping
    d. a and b
    e. a, b, and c

True-False
Write "T" or "F" at the end of each statement.

16. Consumers' surplus is greater at higher prices than lower prices. _____

17. There is a net loss from tariffs. _____

18. Specialization and trade allow a country's inhabitants to consume at a level beyond its production possibilities frontier. _____

19. If the price received is $40 and producers' surplus is $10, then the minimum selling price is $30. _____

20. A quota is a legal limit on the amount of a good that may be imported. _____

Fill in the Blank
Write the correct word in the blank.

21. The _____ argument states that domestic producers should not have to compete (on an unequal basis) with foreign producers that sell products below cost and below the prices they charge in their domestic markets.

22. As a result of a quota, the number of imported goods will _____.

23. As a result of a tariff, consumers' surplus _____.

24. The gains from a quota are _____ than the losses from a quota.

25. The gains from free trade are _____ than the losses from protected (non-free) trade.

Chapter 34
International Finance

What This Chapter Is About
The main subject of this chapter is exchange rates. What are exchange rates? How are exchange rates determined? What are the effects of changes in exchange rates? These questions and more are answered in this chapter.

Key Concepts in the Chapter
    a.   balance of payments
    b.   current account balance
    c.   capital account balance
    d.   merchandise trade balance
    e.   exchange rate
    f.   appreciation
    g.   depreciation
    h.   optimal currency area

- The **balance of payments** is a periodic statement of the money value of all transactions between residents of one country and residents of all other countries.
- The **current account balance** is the summary statistic for exports of goods and services, imports of goods and services, and net unilateral transfers abroad.
- The **capital account balance** is the summary statistic for the outflow of U.S. capital and the inflow of foreign capital. It is equal to the difference between the outflow of U.S. capital and the inflow of foreign capital.
- The **merchandise trade balance** is the difference between the value of merchandise exports and the value of merchandise imports.
- The **exchange rate** is the price of one currency in terms of another currency.
- **Appreciation** refers to an increase in the value of one currency relative to other currencies.
- **Depreciation** refers to a decrease in the value of one currency relative to other currencies.
- An **optimal currency area** is a geographic area in which exchange rates can be fixed or a common currency used without sacrificing domestic economic goals—such as low unemployment.

Review Questions

1. Give an example of a transaction that would be considered a debit item in the balance of payments.

2. Give an example of a transaction that would be considered a credit item in the balance of payments.

3. What is the difference between the current account balance and the merchandise trade balance?

4. What items compose the capital account?

5. What is the difference between a flexible and a fixed exchange rate system?

6. The demand for pounds is related to the supply of dollars. How so?

7. The supply of pounds is related to the demand for dollars. How so?

8. It took 106 yen to buy 1 dollar on Tuesday and 110 yen to buy 1 dollar on Wednesday. Has the dollar appreciated or depreciated from Tuesday to Wednesday? Explain your answer.

9. What factors can lead to a change in exchange rates?

10. Give an example of a currency that is overvalued.

11. What is the difference between a currency that is devalued and one that has depreciated?

Problems

Answer questions 1 through 5 based on the table that follows.

Item	Dollar amount
Merchandise exports	+ 400
Income from U.S. assets abroad	+ 36
Services (exports)	+ 80
Outflow of U.S. capital	− 33
Statistical discrepancy	− 20
Inflow of foreign capital	+ 50
Increase in U.S. official reserve assets	− 5
Decrease in foreign official assets in the U.S.	+ 4
Merchandise imports	− 410
Services (imports)	− 34
Net unilateral transfers abroad	− 18
Income from foreign assets in U.S.	− 50

1. What does the merchandise trade balance equal?

2. What does the current account balance equal?

3. What does the capital account balance equal?

4. What does the official reserve balance equal?

5. What does the balance of payments equal?

6. Suppose there are only two currencies in the world, pesos and dollars. Fill in the blank spaces in the table.

If the	Then the
demand for dollars rises in the foreign exchange market	
	supply of dollars falls on the foreign exchange market
	supply of pesos rises on the foreign exchange market

7. Fill in the blank spaces where a question mark appears in the table.

If	Then
$1 = 106 yen	1 yen = ?
$1 = 74 Kenyan shillings	1 shilling = ?
$1 = 1,500 Lebanese pounds	1 pound = ?

8. Fill in the blank spaces in the table.

The exchange rate is	And the item costs	What does the item cost in dollars?
$1 = 106 yen	18,000 yen	
$1 = £0.50	£ 34.00	
$1 = 9.44 pesos	89 pesos	

9. Fill in the blank spaces in the table.

The exchange rate changes from	Has the dollar appreciated or depreciated?
$2 = £1 to $2.50 = £1	
109 yen = $1 to 189 yen = $1	
10 pesos = $1 to 8 pesos = $1	

10. Fill in the blank spaces in the table.

If ...	The dollar will (appreciate, depreciate)
the real interest rate in the U.S. rises relative to real interest rates in other countries	
income in foreign countries (that trade with the U.S.) rises relative to income in the United States	
the inflation rate in the U.S. rises and the inflation rate in all other countries falls	

11. Fill in the blank spaces in the table.

If the equilibrium exchange rate is $1 = £ 0.50 and the official exchange rate is	Then the dollar is (overvalued, undervalued)
$1 = £ 0.60	
$1 = £ 0.30	

What is the Question?

Identify the question for each of the answers that follow.

1. Any transaction that supplies the country's currency in the foreign exchange market.

2. Any transaction that creates a demand for the country's currency in the foreign exchange market.

3. The summary statistic for the exports of goods and services, imports of goods and services, and net unilateral transfers abroad.

4. The difference between the value of merchandise exports and the value of merchandise imports.

5. One-way money payments.

6. The price of one currency in terms of another currency.

7. It predicts that the exchange rates between any two currencies will adjust to reflect changes in the relative price levels of the two countries.

8.   Raising the official price of a currency.

What Is Wrong?
In each of the statements that follow, something is wrong. Identify what is wrong in the space provided.

1.   The balance of payments is the summary statistic for the current account balance, capital account balance, net unilateral transfers abroad, and statistical discrepancy.

2.   The demand for dollars on the foreign exchange market is linked to the supply of dollars on the foreign exchange market. In short, if the demand for dollars rises, the supply of dollars rises, too.

3.   There are two countries, A and B. The income of Country B rises and the income of Country A remains constant. As a result, the currency of Country B appreciates.

4.   There are two countries, C and D. The price level in Country C rises 10 percent and the inflation rate in Country D is zero percent. As a result, the demand for Country C's goods rises, and the supply of its currency falls.

5.   A change in real interest rates across countries cannot change the exchange rate.

6.   If the equilibrium exchange rate is £1 = $1.50, and the official exchange rate is £1 = $1.60, then the dollar is overvalued and the pound is undervalued.

7.   An international monetary fund right is a special international money created by the IMF.

Multiple Choice
Circle the correct answer.

1. An international transaction that supplies the nation's currency also creates a
   a. supply of foreign currency, and is recorded as a credit in the balance of payments.
   b. demand for foreign currency, and is recorded as a credit in the balance of payments.
   c. demand for foreign currency, and is recorded as a debit in the balance of payments.
   d. supply of the nation's currency, and is recorded as a debit in the balance of payments.

2. If the French buy American computers, they
   a. demand U.S. dollars and supply French francs.
   b. demand U.S. dollars and demand French francs.
   c. supply U.S. dollars and demand French francs.
   d. supply both U.S. dollars and French francs.

Exhibit A

Components of the Balance of Payments	($ billions)
Exports of goods and services	+ 330
Merchandise exports (including military sales)	+ 150
Export services	+ 40
Income from U.S. assets abroad	+ 140
Imports of goods and services	– 390
Merchandise imports (including military sales)	– 220
Import services	– 80
Income from foreign assets abroad	– 90
Net unilateral transfers abroad	– 21
Outflow of U.S. capital	– 46
Inflow of foreign capital	+ 60
Increase in U.S. official reserve assets	– 21
Increase in foreign official assets in U.S.	+ 23
Statistical discrepancy	+ 65

3. In Exhibit A, the merchandise trade balance equals _____ billion dollars.
   a. – 80
   b. + 100
   c. – 70
   d. + 60
   e. none of the above

4. In Exhibit A, the current account balance equals _____ billion dollars.
   a. – 111
   b. – 81
   c. – 60
   d. + 63
   e. none of the above

5. In Exhibit A, the capital account balance equals _____ billion dollars.
   a. + 15
   b. – 10
   c. + 14
   d. – 14
   e. none of the above

6. In Exhibit A, the official reserve balance equals _____ billion dollars.
    a. + 2
    b. − 1
    c. + 10
    d. + 17
    e. none of the above

7. The three major components of the current account are
    a. exports of goods and services, imports of goods and services, and statistical discrepancy.
    b. outflow of U.S. foreign capital, inflow of foreign capital, and statistical discrepancy.
    c. merchandise exports, merchandise imports, and net unilateral transfers abroad
    d. exports of goods and services, imports of goods and services, and inflow of foreign capital.
    e. none of the above

8. The lower the dollar price per yen, the _____ Japanese goods are for Americans and the _____
    Japanese goods Americans will buy; thus _____ yen will be demanded.
    a. more expensive; more; fewer
    b. more expensive; fewer; fewer
    c. less expensive; more; more
    d. less expensive; more; fewer
    e. none of the above

9. An American computer is priced at $5,500. If the exchange rate between the U.S. dollar and the British
    pound is $1.70 = £1.00, approximately how many pounds will a British buyer pay for the computer?
    a. £3,235
    b. £3,052
    c. £2,543
    d. £6,599

10. If the dollar price per pound moves from $1.90 = £1.00 to $1.40 = £1.00, the pound is said to have
    _____ and the dollar to have _____.
    a. depreciated; appreciated
    b. appreciated; appreciated
    c. appreciated; depreciated
    d. depreciated; depreciated

11. The U.S. dollar has appreciated relative to the French franc if it takes
    a. fewer francs to buy a dollar.
    b. fewer dollars to buy a franc.
    c. more dollars to buy a franc.
    d. a and c
    e. none of the above

12. Suppose the current exchange rate between the dollar and pound is $1.70 = £1.00. Furthermore,
    suppose the price level in the United States rises 25 percent at a time when the British price level is
    stable. According to the purchasing power parity theory, what will be the new equilibrium exchange
    rate?
    a. $2.72 = £1.00
    b. $1.55 = £1.00
    c. $1.86 = £1.00
    d. $2.13 = £1.00

13. The purchasing power parity theory predicts less nearly accurately in the _____ run, and when there is a _____ difference in inflation rates across countries.
    a. long; small
    b. short; large
    c. long; large
    d. short; small

14. Under a fixed exchange rate system, if the British pound is overvalued then there exists
    a. a shortage of pounds.
    b. a surplus of pounds.
    c. the equilibrium level of pounds.
    d. there is not enough information to answer the question (we need to know the actual exchange rate)

15. One of the things a nation must do if it is on an international gold standard is
    a. link its money supply to its gold holdings.
    b. increase taxes.
    c. declare itself to be on a flexible exchange rate system.
    d. revalue its currency.
    e. none of the above

True-False
Write "T" or "F" after each statement.

16. From the 1870s to the 1930s, many nations tied their currencies to gold. ____

17. Under the Bretton Woods system, nations were expected to maintain fixed exchange rates (within a narrow range) by buying and selling their own currency for other currencies. ____

18. Any transaction that supplies the nation's currency is recorded as a debit in the balance of payments. ____

19. The current account balance is the summary statistic for exports of goods and services, imports of goods and services, and the statistical discrepancy. ____

20. Any transaction that supplies a foreign currency is recorded as a credit in the balance of payments. ____

Fill in the Blank
Write the correct word in the blank.

21. The _____ _____ _____ is the difference between the value of merchandise exports and the value of merchandise imports.

22. The _____ _____ _____ _____ predicts that changes in the relative price levels of two countries will affect the exchange rate in such a way that one unit of nation's currency will continue to buy the same amount of foreign goods as it did before the change in the relative price levels.

23. When nations adopt the gold standard, they automatically _____ their exchange rates.

24. A _____ occurs when the official price of currency (under the fixed exchange rate system) is lowered.

25. Central banks play a much larger role under a _____ exchange rate system than under a _____ exchange rate system.

Chapter 35
International Economic Development

What This Chapter Is About
This chapter deals with international economic development. It focuses on the differences between developed and less developed countries and on the factors that affect economic development.

Key Concepts in the Chapter
   a.   Rule of 72
   b.   Vicious circle of poverty

   •   The **rule of 72** is a simple arithmetical rule for compound calculations. It says that that the time required for any variable to double is calculated by dividing its percentage growth rate into 72.
   •   The **vicious circle of poverty** is the idea that countries are poor because they do not save and invest and they cannot save and invest because they are poor.

Review Questions

1.   What is a developed country? What is a less developed country?

2.   What is the rule of 72? Give an example of how it can be used.

3.   What is the importance of capital to economic development?

4.   What is the importance of labor productivity to economic development?

5. What is the importance of the property rights structure to economic development?

6. How can a rapid population growth rate hamper economic development?

7. What is the dependency ratio?

8. What is the vicious circle of poverty?

9. A less developed country chooses not to use an affordable technology that exists. What might explain this choice?

What is the Question?
Identify the question for each of the answers that follow.

1. It is a country with a relatively low GDP per capita.

2. The number of children who die before their first birthday out of every 1,000 live births.

3. Natural resources, capital formation, labor productivity, technological advances, property rights structure, and economic freedom.

4. Any unit is substitutable for another.

5. The combination of higher birthrates and declining death rates.

6. The number of children under a certain age plus the number of the elderly divided by the total population.

7. Low income leads to low savings, which leads to low investment, which leads to low productivity, which leads to low income, and so on.

What Is Wrong?
In each of the statements that follow, something is wrong. Identify what is wrong in the space provided.

1. If a country has an annual growth rate in GDP per capita of 4 percent, it will take 15 years for its GDP per capita to double.

2. Natural resources are a necessary but not sufficient factor for economic development.

3. One way to calculate labor productivity is to divide the number of labor hours worked by GDP.

4. The infant mortality rate tends to be lower in less developed countries than in developed countries.

5. Countries poor in natural resources do not experience economic development.

6. A high dependency ratio is something that most economists think promotes economic development.

7. The vicious circle of poverty holds that low productivity leads to low savings, which leads to low income.

Multiple Choice
Circle the correct answer.

1. Labor productivity tends to be _____ in developed countries mainly because those countries _____.
    a. low; are overpopulated
    b. low; have little capital for labor to work with
    c. high; have much capital for labor to work with
    d. high; have little capital to displace labor

2. In an economic study, economist Alvin Rabushka linked low per capita income with
    a. low marginal tax rates.
    b. high marginal tax rates.
    c. low population growth.
    d. high population growth.
    e. b and d

3. If the proponents of the vicious circle of poverty argument are right, then it would follow that
    a. no poor country could ever become a rich country.
    b. poor countries have a higher population growth rate than rich countries.
    c. the Rule of 72 would not apply to a poor country.
    d. per capita GDP would be higher in rich countries than poor countries.
    e. none of the above

4. Having more natural resources _____ economic development.
    a. assists
    b. has no effect on
    c. hinders
    d. has an uncertain effect on

5. The range of laws, rules, and regulations that define the allowed forms of the use and transfer of resources is called the _____ of the economy.
    a. monetary rights
    b. property rights
    c. microeconomics
    d. macroeconomics

6. In the early 1990s, approximately _____ people (in the world) were living in poverty.
    a. 100 million
    b. 500 million
    c. 10 million
    d. 1.25 billion
    e. 24 million

7. A less developed country is usually defined as a country with a
    a. high saving-to-investment ratio.
    b. high unemployment rate.
    c. low per capita GDP
    d. low-quality public school system.
    e. none of the above

8. Which of the following statements is true?
    a. The population growth rate is lower in the LDCs than in the developed countries.
    b. About three-quarters of the world's people live in the developed countries.
    c. The population growth rate is equal to the birthrate minus the death rate.
    d. The birthrate tends to be lower in LDCs than in developed countries.
    e. b and d

9. Which scenario best illustrates the vicious circle of poverty?
    a. Agricultural incomes are low when the weather is bad, the weather is bad in certain parts of the world, and nothing can change the weather, so agricultural incomes will continue to be low.
    b. Incomes are low, thus investment is low; because investment is low, interest rates are high; because interest rates are high, people can't buy homes; without homes people are not satisfied enough to work.
    c. Incomes are low, thus saving is low; because saving is low, investment is low; because investment is low, income is low.
    d. If you can't spend, you can't buy; if you can't buy, you can't spend.

10. Using the rule of 72, how many years will it take a country with a 6 percent growth rate per year to double in size?
    a. 10 years
    b. 12 years
    c. 18 years
    d. 24 years

True-False
Write "T" or "F" at the end of each statement.

11. Money is fungible.

12. The dependency ratio is the number of children under a certain age plus the number of the elderly divided by the total population.

13. Labor productivity refers to the amount of output a worker produces in some time period.

14. Tractors, computers, and factory machines are examples of human capital.

15. There is some evidence supporting the thesis that economic freedom is directly related to GDP per capita.

Fill in the Blank
Write the correct word in the blank.

16. Some economists have argued that rises in per capita GDP first appeared in those areas where a system of institutions and _____ _____ had evolved that encouraged individuals to direct their human capital and energy to effective economic projects.

17. _____ means that any unit is substitutable for another.

18. The _____ _____ _____ is equal to the number of children who die before their first birthday out of every 1,000 live births.

19. _____ _____ make it possible to obtain more output from the same amount of resources.

20. Natural resources are neither a _____ nor a _____ factor for economic development.

Answer Key

Chapter 1
Answers

Review Questions

1. Yes and no. This is only part of scarcity. Scarcity is the condition in which people have infinite wants *and* there are not enough resources (finite resources) to satisfy those wants.

2. A good gives a person utility or satisfaction; a bad gives a person disutility or dissatisfaction. People want goods and they don't want bads.

3. Josie likes to play music on Friday night. Music is a good on Friday night. Josie doesn't like to play music when she is studying for an exam. At that time, music is a bad.

4. The opportunity cost of your reading this study guide is whatever you would be doing if you weren't reading it. If you would be watching television, then watching television is the opportunity cost of your reading this study guide.

5. People are interested in only doing things when the benefits are greater than the costs. As the cost of smoking rises, it will be the case (for some people) that the benefits of smoking will no longer be greater than the costs, and therefore they will quit smoking.

6. marginal

7. Harriet considers what is relevant. Only the benefits of the next hour and the costs of the next hour are relevant to her. Costs and benefits in the past are not relevant. What does it matter what the costs and benefits have been? What matters is what they are expected to be. Marginal benefits and marginal costs deal with "additions," hence they deal with benefits and costs to come.

8. Answers will vary. Here is a sample answer. Someone takes a sleeping pill at night in order to get a restful sleep. Getting a restful sleep is the intended effect. The person does get a restful sleep, but also feels rather groggy for the first two hours she is up in the morning. Feeling groggy is an unintended effect.

9. Because scarcity exists—because our wants are greater than the resources available to satisfy them—we must decide (choose) which of our wants we will satisfy and which of our wants we won't satisfy. When we make choices, we necessarily incur an opportunity cost. After all, to choose to do X is to choose not to do Y. Y is the opportunity cost of doing X.

10. To think in terms of what would have been is to think in terms of opportunity cost. For example, you choose to go for a jog by the beach. What might have been had you not decided to jog by the beach? What would you have done instead? Whatever it was, it was the opportunity of your jogging by the beach.

11. A theory is an abstract representation of reality.

12. Probably so. People "build" theories (even casually) in order to answer questions that are not easily answered. In their pursuit of answers, they focus in on what they believe are key causal factors to explain what it is they want explained. Everyone does this, not only the economist, biologist, and psychologist. On some level, almost everyone builds theories or theorizes.

13. The seven steps are: (a) decide on what it is you want to explain; (b) identify the variables you think are important to explaining what you want to explain; (c) state the assumptions of a theory; (d) state the hypothesis; (e) test the theory by comparing its predictions against real-world events; (f) if the evidence supports the theory, take no further action; (g) if the evidence rejects the theory, then formulate a new theory or amend the old theory.

14. Because theories that have sounded wrong (in the past) have turned out to the right. The round-earth theory sounded wrong to many people long ago, but it predicts well. If human beings were to have complete information, and knew everything there is to know, then we might be able to judge theories by how they "sound" to us. Unfortunately, though, we do not have complete information and we make mistakes. We need to take a scientific approach to judging theories. Theories should be judged according to how well they explain and predict things.

15. An assumption is something someone believes is true but can't prove is true. Jim assumes that everyone works to be happy. He can't prove this, but he believes it is true.

16. Answers will vary. The following is an example in which association is causation: George steps on a nail and later his foot begins to hurt. George's stepping on a nail and his foot hurting are associated in time—one event comes closely before the other. Furthermore, it was stepping on the nail that caused George's foot to hurt. The following is an example in which association is not causation: It is sunny and warm today and Jennifer lost her wallet. The sunny, warm day is associated with Jennifer's losing her wallet in time, but the sunny, warm day didn't cause Jennifer to lose her wallet.

Theory on a Television Show

1. Two things might have happened: (a) when George walked up to the woman, she would have treated him the way women always treat him; or (b) when George confronted the two rowdy men in the movie theater, they would have behaved toward him the way two men would always behave toward George if he confronted them. Generally, for Jerry's theory to be incorrect, George would have to go against his every instinct, and things would have to turn out the same way as they always do.

2. It is still early in your study of economics to know the answer, but it is worth taking an educated guess. The following are some of the things that economists build theories to explain: unemployment, economic growth, business cycles (the ups and downs of the economy), why firms produce the level of output that they produce, how firms price their goods, inflation, exchange rates, and much more.

Problems

1.

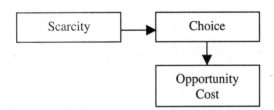

2.

Factor	Benefits of attending college	Costs of attending college	More likely to go to college? Yes or No
Jim thought he would earn $20 an hour if he didn't go to college, but learns that he will earn $35 an hour instead.		↑	No
His friends are going to college and he likes being around his friends.	↑		Yes
The salary gap between college graduates and high school graduates has widened.	↑		Yes
Jim learns something about himself: he doesn't like to study.		↑	No
The college he is thinking about attending just opened a satellite campus near Jim's home.		↓	Yes
The economy has taken a downturn and it looks like there are very few jobs for high school graduates right now.		↓	Yes

3.

Statement	The person is assuming that this does not change:
People who don't brush their teeth will get cavities.	People will not change the amount of fluoridated water they drink.
As people get older, they tend to put on weight because their metabolism slows down.	People will not change the amount they exercise.
If he studies more, he will get higher grades.	He won't change how focused he is when he studies.

4. a. microeconomics, b. macroeconomics, c. macroeconomics, d. macroeconomics, e. microeconomics, f. microeconomics, g. microeconomics

5. Answers will vary. In each case, you want to ask yourself what you would do if you chose not to do the activity specified. The following are some sample answers.

Activity	Opportunity Cost
Study one more hour each night	Watch television
Take a long trip to someplace you have always wanted to visit	Buy a new car
Sit in the back of the room in one of your classes	Sit in the middle of the room
Talk up more in class	Daydream
Get a regular medical checkup	Play tennis
Surf the Web more	Watch television

What Is Wrong?

1. People have finite wants and infinite resources.

    People have infinite wants and resources are finite. This is scarcity.

2. People prefer more bads to fewer bads.

    Since people receive disutility from bads, they want fewer bads. Alternatively, you could say that people prefer more goods to fewer goods.

3. Scarcity is an effect of competition.

    Competition is an effect of scarcity.

4. The lower the opportunity cost of playing tennis, the less likely a person will play tennis.

    The lower the opportunity cost of playing tennis, the more likely a person will play tennis. The higher the opportunity cost of playing tennis, the less likely a person will play tennis.

5. Abstract means to add more variables to the process of theorizing.

    When we abstract, we remove variables that we, as theorists, don't think explain the phenomena at hand.

6. Microeconomics is the branch of economics that deals with human behavior and choices as they relate to highly aggregate markets or the entire economy.

    Macroeconomics is the branch of economics that deals with human behavior and choices as they relate to highly aggregate markets or the entire economy.

7. Positive economics is to normative economics what opinion is to truth.

   Positive economics and truth are more closely aligned, as are normative economics and opinion.

8. Because there are rationing devices, there will always be scarcity.

   Because there is scarcity, there will always be rationing devices.

9. The four factors of production, or resources, are land, labor, capital, and profit.

   Profit is not a factor of production, it is a payment to a factor of production. The missing factor of production is entrepreneurship.

10. Karen doesn't like to study so no one likes to study. This is an example of the association is not causation issue.

    This is an example of the fallacy of composition.

Multiple Choice
   1. c
   2. b
   3. a
   4. b
   5. c
   6. c
   7. d
   8. a
   9. b
   10. a
   11. a
   12. c
   13. a
   14. c
   15. c

True-False
   16. T
   17. F
   18. T
   19. F
   20. F
   21. F

Fill in the Blank
   22. fallacy of composition
   23. association is causation
   24. ceteris paribus
   25. Macroeconomics
   26. fails to reject
   27. marginal
   28. capital
   29. entrepreneur

Chapter 2
Answers

Review Questions

1. *Ex ante* position. *Ex ante* means before the exchange.
2. $3. Consumers' surplus is the difference between maximum buying price ($10) and price paid ($7).
3. Compare your consumers' surplus (CS) before and after the change. If your CS is higher after, you have been made better off; if it is lower, you have been made worse off; if it is unchanged, then you are neither better nor worse off.
4. It means consumers prefer low to high prices for what they buy.
5. The transaction costs of buying a hamburger are lower than selling a house. There are many things involved in selling a house—finding an agent to list the house, signing contracts, etc.
6. Jake buys a cigarette from George and then smokes the cigarette while sitting next to Tabitha. Tabitha is allergic to cigarette smoke.
7. $1X = 1.5Y; 1Y = 0.66X$
8. Through specialization and trade people can consume more goods. But this doesn't answer why this happens. It happens because when people specialize, they produce those things that they can produce at a lower cost than other people. In other words, they are doing what they do best and then trading with others. If everyone does what he or she does best, you would naturally think that everyone has to be better off—at least as compared to the situation where no one does his or her best.
9. People trade to make themselves better off. The necessary condition: People have to value what they will trade for more than what they will trade with. For example, if Yvonne trades $10 for a book, she values the book (which she doesn't currently have) more than the $10 (which she currently does have).
10. We have to give up 10 units of X to produce the first 10 units of Y, but we have to give up 20 units of X to produce the second 10 units of Y.
11. It indicates constant costs.
12. It indicates increasing costs.
13. These are two points *on* its PPF, which means the two points are efficient. Efficiency implies the impossibility of gains in one area without losses in another. This is what a tradeoff is about: more of one thing, but less of something else.
14. An advance in technology; more resources.
15. Answers will vary. The example you come up with should make it possible to produce more goods with the same resources.
16. What goods will be produced? How will the goods be produced? For whom will the goods be produced?
17. According to economist Thomas Sowell, it is our sense of how the world works.

Problems

1. $140
2. $15
3. 1 hat = $30 or 1 hat = $20. Any price lower than $40 gives us the correct answer.
4. If the entrepreneur can lower Karen's transaction costs from $60 to $24 (a reduction of $36), then Karen will make the trade. Karen will think this way: I pay $370 to the seller, and $5 to the entrepreneur, for a total of $375. My maximum buying price is $400, so I will receive $25 consumers' surplus. But what about transaction costs? As long as my transaction costs are not more than, say, $24, I will receive at least $1 consumers' surplus and the exchange is worth it to me. The entrepreneur will have to lower Randy's transaction costs from $60 to $14 (a reduction of $46). Randy will think this way: I receive $370 from the buyer and I pay $5 to the entrepreneur. This leaves me with $365. My minimum selling price is $350, so I receive $15 producers' surplus. But what about transaction costs? As long as my transaction costs are not higher than, say, $14, I will receive $1 producers' surplus and the exchange is worth it to me.

5.

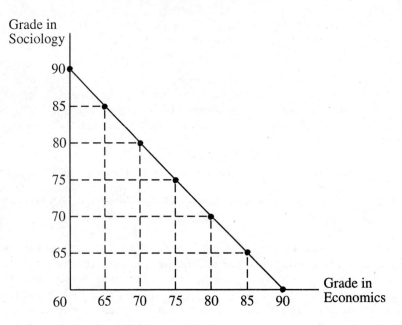

6. 5 fewer points in sociology.
7. Points A and D
8. Points B and C
9. Points E and F
10. Yes, point D could be efficient. The reason why is that there are tradeoffs moving from one efficient point to another. In other words, more of one good comes with less of another good.
11.

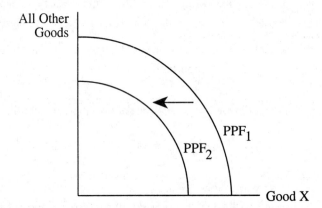

12.

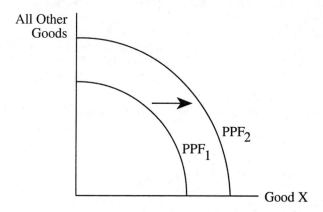

What Is Wrong?

1. If costs are increasing, the PPF is a straight (downward-sloping) line.

    If costs are increasing, the PPF is bowed outward. Alternatively you could say: If costs are constant, the PPF is a straight line.

2. Mary said that she received $40 consumers' surplus when she paid $50 for the good and only $30 consumers' surplus when she paid $45 for the good.

    Mary is wrong since the lower the price, the more consumers' surplus.

3. If Jones can produce either (a) 100 units of X and 100 units of Y or (b) 200 units of X and zero units of Y, then he has a comparative advantage in the production of Y.

    We don't know whether he has a comparative advantage in Y or not. To know this, we have to compare his costs to someone else's costs.

4. The following PPF represents a 2-for-1 opportunity cost of apples.

    It is a 1-for-1 opportunity cost of apples. For every apple produced, one orange is not produced. For every one orange produced, one apple is not produced.

5. There are probably more unemployed resources at point A than at point D.

    There are more unemployed resources at D, a point below the PPF.

6. Efficiency implies the possibility of gains in one area without losses in another area.

    Efficiency implies the impossibility of gains in one area without losses in another area. Alternatively, you could have written, Inefficiency implies the possibility of gains in one area without losses in another area.

7. If Georgina reads one more book, she will have to give up doing something else. This shows that Georgina is inefficient.

    When there is efficiency, there are tradeoffs. Georgina cannot do more of one thing without doing less of something else.

8. For a given quantity of output, a rise in price reduces producers' surplus and increases consumers' surplus.

    For a given quantity of output, a rise in price reduces consumers' surplus and increases producers' surplus. Alternatively, you could have written: For a given quantity of output, a fall in price reduces producers' surplus and increases consumers' surplus.

9. If Bobby can produce either (a) 100 units of good X and 50 units of good Y, or (b) 25 units of good X and 80 units of good Y, then the cost of 1 unit of good X is 1.5 units of good Y.

    The cost of 1 unit of good X is 0.4 units of good Y.

10. John says, "I bought this sweater yesterday and I think I got a bad deal." It follows that in the *ex ante* position John thought he would be better off with the sweater than with the money he paid for it, but in the *ex post* position he prefers the money to the sweater.

    This could be true, but it could be that John is not disheartened about the trade (of money for the sweater), but about the terms of exchange. He may simply have preferred to pay less for the sweater.

Multiple Choice
1. b
2. d
3. c
4. c
5. c
6. e
7. a
8. b
9. d
10. b
11. a
12. a
13. e
14. d
15. e

True-False
16. T
17. F
18. F
19. T
20. T

Fill in the Blank
21. What goods will be produced? How will the goods be produced? For whom will the goods be produced?
22. Inefficiency
23. Efficiency
24. 8

Chapter 3
Answers

Review Questions
1. Price and quantity demanded are inversely related, *ceteris paribus*.
2. Price and quantity demanded move in opposite directions: as price rises, quantity demanded falls, and as price falls, quantity demanded rises.
3. Amount of a good buyers are willing and able to buy at a particular price. For example, quantity demanded may be 100 units at $10 per unit.
4. Quantity demanded is a specific number—such as 100 units. Demand is a relationship between various prices and various quantities demanded.
5. income, preferences, prices of related goods (substitutes and complements), number of buyers, expectations of future price.
6. to the right
7. to the left
8. Amount of a good sellers are willing and able to produce at a particular price.
9. Quantity supplied is constant as price changes. Stated differently, quantity supplied is independent of (does not depend on) changes in price.
10. Price and quantity supplied are directly related.
11. prices of relevant resources, technology, number of sellers, expectations of future price, taxes and subsidies, government restrictions
12. to the right
13. to the left
14. Quantity is on the horizontal axis, price is on the vertical axis.
15. The absolute price of a good is the money price of a good—such as $3,000 for a computer. The relative price of a good is the price of the good in terms of some other good. For example, if the absolute price of a computer is $3,000, and the absolute price of a TV set is $1,000, then the relative price of a computer (in terms of TV sets) is 3 TV sets.
16. Equilibrium price and quantity rise.
17. Equilibrium price falls and equilibrium quantity rises.
18. Equilibrium price and quantity rise.
19. Equilibrium price rises and equilibrium quantity falls.
20. Consumers' surplus falls. Consumers' surplus equals maximum buying price minus price paid, so if price paid rises, consumers' surplus must fall.

3.

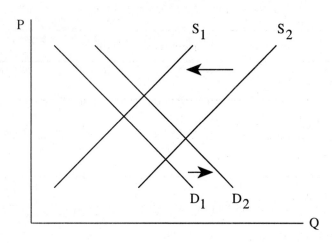

4. A + B + C
5. E + F + G + H
6. 140 – 50 = 90 units
7. 180 – 60 = 120 units
8.

Price	Quantity demanded by John	Quantity demanded by Mary	Quantity demanded (market demand)
$10	100	130	230
$12	80	120	200
$14	50	100	150

9. $6
10. Jack's first candy bar gives him more utility than the second; the second gives him more utility than the third; and so on.

What Is Wrong?

1. If the price of a good rises, the demand for the good will fall.

    If the price of a good rises, the quantity demand for the good will fall. (not demand)

2. Consumers' surplus is equal to the minimum selling price minus price paid.

    Consumers' surplus is equal to the maximum buying price minus price paid.

3. As income rises, demand for a normal good rises; as income falls, demand for an inferior good falls.

    …as income falls, demand for an inferior good rises.

4. The supply curve for Picasso paintings is upward-sloping.

    The supply curve for Picasso paintings is vertical.

5. As price rises, supply rises; as price falls, supply falls.

    As price rises, quantity supplied rises; as price falls, quantity supplied falls.

6. Quantity demanded is greater than supply when there is a shortage.

    Quantity demanded is greater than quantity supplied when there is a shortage.

7. If supply rises, and demand is constant, equilibrium price rises and equilibrium quantity rises.

    If supply rises, and demand is constant, equilibrium price falls and equilibrium quantity rises.

8. The law of diminishing marginal utility states that as a consumer consumes additional units of a good, each successive unit gives him or her more utility than the previous unit.

    …each successive unit gives him or her less utility than the previous unit.

9. According to the law of demand, as the price of a good rises, the quantity demanded of the good rises, *ceteris paribus*.

    According to the law of demand, as the price of a good rises, the quantity demanded of the good falls, ceteris paribus.

Multiple Choice
1. d
2. d
3. e
4. b
5. c
6. d
7. a
8. b
9. e
10. b
11. d
12. a
13. a
14. d
15. d

True-False
16. F
17. F
18. T
19. F
20. T

Fill in the Blank
21. falls; rises
22. market
23. inferior
24. increases
25. equals
26. tie-in

Chapter 4
Answers

Review Questions

1. It is lower for a 6-year-old than for a 20-year-old. Economists use the wage rate as the proxy for the price of friendship. A 6-year-old is probably not earning a wage, so his or her wage rate is zero. The 20-year-old is probably earning some positive wage rate.

2. This statement simply says that the higher the wage rate, the higher the price of friendship, and the fewer friends one will have. When economists make statements like this one, they are implicitly making the *ceteris paribus* assumption.

3. Look at D_1 and D_2. D_1 is closer to the origin than is D_2, but since price is so much lower, quantity demanded is greater.

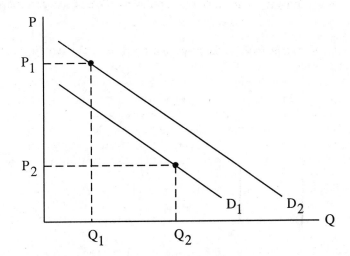

4. The price of crime = the probability of being apprehended for the crime multiplied by the punishment (jail, fine, etc.).

5. Answers will vary. Generally, you want to identify goods that have a used market. Cars were discussed in the text. Books are another good that have a used market. For example, there is a used textbook market.

6. Answers will vary. If you are nicer to nice people, your supply curve of niceness is upward sloping. If you are equally nice to everyone, no matter how nice they are to you, then your supply curve of niceness is vertical. If you are nicer to people who are less nice to you, your supply curve of niceness is downward sloping.

7. We infer from what Jack says that he believes companies can "pass off to the consumer" any percentage of the tax that they want. If this were the case, then companies would always "pass off" 100 percent of the tax. The fact is, companies don't pass off anything. They react to the tax, and then that reaction (exhibited in the supply curve) together with the demand curve determines price and, therefore, how much of the tax is paid for by the consumer.

8. Yes, there is a deadweight loss. The tax will shift the supply curve to the left, bringing about a higher price and lower quantity. Because of the lower quantity, there is a deadweight loss. See Exhibit 4 (in Chapter 4) in the textbook.

9. Raise price, raise supply, lower demand. The freeway congestion is evidence of a shortage. There are three ways to get rid of a shortage. The first is to allow price to move to its equilibrium level, where quantity demanded is equal to quantity supplied. The second is to raise supply enough so that there is no more shortage. The third is to lower demand enough so that there is no more shortage. Increasing supply, in the context of freeway congestion, means adding more freeways. Lowering demand means, perhaps, giving people an incentive to carpool to a greater degree.

10. If the university charges a below-equilibrium price for parking, there will be a shortage of parking spaces. Something will have to ration the available parking spots. It is most likely to be first-come-first-served (FCFS). What happens if you're not one of the first in line to park? You might end up being late to class.

Problems

1. Suppose there is a downward-sloping demand curve for losing one's temper. If so, the higher the price to lose one's temper, the less one will lose one's temper. Perhaps Yvonne's father charges her a higher price to lose her temper than Yvonne's mother charges her. Notice that people don't often lose their tempers with their bosses (the price you would have to pay is too high), but will lose their tempers with family members, etc.

2. Driving takes time. For example, it might take 20 minutes, going at 50 mph, to go from point X to point Y. The more valuable time is, the more a person will want to economize on time. How valuable time is may be a function of one's wage rate. The higher one's wage rate, the more valuable time is, and the more one will want to economize on time. The 68-year-old retired person may face a lower wage rate than the 32-year-old working person and so time is less valuable to the older person than to the younger person. We would expect the 68-year-old to care less about whether or not he drives slowly because time is less valuable to him or her.

3. Think back to the apple example in the text. New Yorkers bought relatively more apples than Washingtonians, because the relative price of good apples was lower in New York than in Washington. The transportation cost of apples in the apple example is similar to the transportation cost one faces when he or she goes on vacation. To illustrate, suppose there are high-quality shirts and low-quality shirts. The high-quality shirts are $60 and the low-quality shirts are $10. At home, the relative price of a high-quality shirt is 6 low-quality shirts. Now pay $400 to travel to some place on vacation. In a sense, the price of a high-quality shirt (purchased on vacation) is $400 + $60 or $460, and the price of a low-quality shirt (purchased on vacation) is $400 +10 or $410. Now what is the relative price of a high-quality shirt? Is it still 6 low-quality shirts? Not at all. Now it is 1.12 low-quality shirts. Since the relative price of high-quality shirts has fallen, we would expect people to buy relatively more high-quality shirts on vacation, *ceteris paribus*.

4. Answers will vary. Here is a sample answer. When students pay the equilibrium, professors know that the quantity demanded of students equals the quantity supplied. If they do something that students don't like, then the demand curve may fall (for education at the university) and, at the given tuition, quantity supplied will be greater than quantity demanded. In other words, there will be a surplus. Will the university get rid of some professors when this happens? Now consider the case when students pay below-equilibrium tuition. Professors know that there is a shortage of space at the university. If they do something that some of their students don't like, and the students leave the university, there are others to take their places (because of the shortage). We predict the following. *If* there is a difference between the way a professor wants to teach a class and the way students want it taught, the professor is more likely to respond to the preferences of the students in the first setting (where students pay equilibrium tuition) than in the second setting (where there is a shortage of students due to a below-equilibrium tuition being charged).

5. Broadway shows don't have slot machines in the lobby. The hotel-casino has to consider revenue from the slot machines versus revenue from the show. The owners of the Broadway show only have one business to concern themselves with—the show.

6. Answers will vary. This is a good question to think about.

7. The price of a speeding ticket is the price of the speeding ticket. The price of speeding is a function of two variables—the price of the speeding ticket and the probability of your having to pay the speeding ticket.

8. Greedy people care about money. If there is more money from conserving resources (for a future generation) than from using resources now (for the current generation), then greedy people are likely to conserve resources.

9. It appears that the steeper the slope of the demand curve, the larger the percentage of the tax paid for by the consumer.

10. Consumers lose because they lose consumers' surplus. Producers' lose because they lose producers' surplus. Government gains because it gains revenue.

What May Have Been Overlooked?

1. The higher the demand for something, the greater the quantity demanded.

    This is true at a given price. However, a lower price and lower demand can generate a greater quantity demanded than a higher price and higher demand.

2. I think how I behave is independent of the setting that I am in. I act the same way no matter what the setting.

    The person has overlooked the fact that the price of acting a certain way may be different in different settings and that people usually respond to changes in price.

3. If there were no flea markets or garage sales (where people can buy old furniture), new furniture companies would sell more (new) furniture.

    This is the used-car-market example in disguise. The person sees one factor that affects the demand for new furniture but not another. She sees the fact that if there were fewer buyers of old furniture, there would be more buyers of new furniture. What she doesn't see is that the demand for new furniture is higher if furniture (purchased) can be resold.

4. The rock band has the best interest of its fans in mind. It knows it can charge $80 a ticket, but it charges only $20 a ticket so that its fans won't have to pay so much.

    What the rock band forgets is that people pay in money or in something else. If $80 is the equilibrium price, then $20 is a below-equilibrium price, at which there will be a shortage of tickets. How will the tickets be rationed. By a combination of the $20 price and some nonprice rationing device—such as first-come-first-served (FCFS). FCFS will no doubt lead to fans standing in long lines to get tickets, some of whom will end up not getting the tickets. Fans will pay by standing in line instead of more money.

5. If my university doesn't charge for student parking, then I am definitely better off than I would be if it did charge for student parking.

    Not necessarily. If there is some positive equilibrium price for parking, then a zero price will create a shortage of parking spots and some nonprice rationing device will come into play. It will probably be first-come-first-served (FCFS), which will cause students to have to pay for parking spots in time instead of money.

6. The tuition at Harvard is very high, so Harvard must be charging the equilibrium tuition to students. Still, Harvard uses such things as GPA, SAT and ACT scores for admission purposes. It must be wrong that these nonprice rationing devices (GPA. etc.) are only used by colleges and universities that charge below-equilibrium tuition.

    The demand for Harvard may very high, such that even at the high tuition charged, there is still a shortage of spots at Harvard. In other words, Harvard can still charge a high tuition and the high tuition can still not be high enough to equal the equilibrium tuition.

7. If a good doesn't have a money price, it has no price at all.

> *Price connotes sacrifice, or giving up something to get something. Someone offers you free tickets to a concert if you will drive to his house and pick up the tickets and later that week mow his lawn. No money has changed hands, but if you accept the deal you will have to pay a nonmoney price for the tickets.*

Multiple Choice
1. b
2. e
3. b
4. d
5. a
6. a
7. b
8. e
9. e
10. d
11. e
12. b
13. b
14. d
15. b

True-False
16. T
17. T
18. T
19. T

Fill in the Blank
20. pay
21. price; quantity,
22. shortage; nonprice
23. $1
24. pays; keep

Chapter 5
Answers

Review Questions

1. Economist use a price index to measure the price level.
2. No, the CPI is not a reflection of the prices of all goods and services in the economy—only those that are in the market basket.
3. First, it means that prices in this year are higher than in the base year (whatever year that happens to be) because the CPI in the base year is always 100. By itself, the CPI of 132 doesn't mean much more. It is only when we compare the CPI of 132 to other things that we derive some meaning. For example, if the CPI is 120 in the year before, then using the CPI of 132, we can compute how much prices (on average) have risen over the year.
4. We compute real income by (1) dividing nominal income by the CPI and then (2) multiplying by 100. Two people may have the same nominal income, but if they live in different countries, and face different CPIs, then they will have different real incomes. For example, $40,000 in a country where prices are low goes much further than $40,000 in a country where prices are high.
5. $40,000 in 1987 was not the same (in terms of purchasing power) as $40,000 in 1999, unless prices were the same in 1987 as in 1999, which they weren't.
6. There are a number of steps to calculating the CPI: (1) define the market basket; (2) identify current-year prices and base-year prices; (3) use the market basket and current-year prices to determine the total expenditure on the market basket in the current year; (4) use the market basket and base-year prices to determine the total expenditure on the market basket in the base year; (5) divide the total expenditure on the market basket in the current year by the total expenditure on the market basket in the base year; and (6) multiply by 100. The process is shown in the textbook in Exhibit 2 (of the relevant chapter).
7. The civilian noninstitutional population is a larger number than the civilian labor force because the civilian labor force is a subset of the noninstitutional population. The civilian noninstitutional population is equal to the persons not in the labor force plus the persons in the civilian labor force. The civilian labor force is equal to the number of employed persons plus the number of unemployed persons. Look at it this way. Everyone in the civilian labor force is in the civilian noninstitutional population, but not everyone in the civilian noninstitutional population is in the civilian labor force. Who isn't? Obviously, the persons not in the labor force.
8. An unemployed person must satisfy any of the following: (1) he or she did not work during the survey week, has actively looked for work within the past four weeks, and is currently available for work; (2) he or she is waiting to be called back to a job from which he or she has been laid off; or (3) he or she is waiting to report to a job within 30 days.
9. No. The employment rate and the unemployment rate have different denominators, and so therefore do not have to add up to 100 percent. The denominator of the employment rate is the civilian noninstitutional population. The denominator of the unemployment rate is the civilian labor force.
10. Job leaver, job loser, reentrant, entrant.
11. A reentrant was previously employed full time, an entrant was not.
12. They do not meet any of the conditions specified in question number 8 above.
13. Mary works as an accountant. The demand for accounting services falls and Mary loses her job. No accountants are currently being hired. The only businesses that are hiring are those that are looking for computer analysts. Mary doesn't currently have the skills to be a computer analyst. Mary is structurally unemployed.
14. This is way economists believe wage offers look *on average* (or for the average person) during the job search process. An individual's wage offers may rise and fall during the process.
15. Economists are assuming that as search time moves forward (the longer one has searched), the lower wage one will accept from an employer. Is there some reason to this? Savings may decline over time, unemployment compensation may run out, and so on. A person may be more desperate for work in the 32nd week of search than in the 5th week of search.

16. If people take longer to search (that is, if optimal search time rises), then at any given point in time, more people are unemployed. This will increase the unemployment rate.

Problems
1. Multiply current-year prices by the market basket to find the total expenditure on the market basket in the current year. This is $150.95. Then multiply base-year prices by the market basket to find the total expenditure on the market basket in the base year. This is $112.55. Next divide the total expenditure on the market basket in the current year by the total expenditure on the market basket in the base year. This gives us 1.34. Finally, multiply by 100 to get the CPI of 134.
2. (160.5 – 72.6/72.6) x 100 = 121
3. Real income is $34,965.
4. Yes, Rebecca's real income did rise since her nominal income increased by a greater percentage than prices increased.
5. $10,000 in 1967 was equivalent to $49,191 in 1999. To get the answer: (a) divide the CPI in 1999 by the CPI in 1967; (b) multiply the outcome of (a) by 10,000.
6. The formula used to compute the chain-weighted price index is on page 122 in your textbook. The answer is 119.89.
7.

Category	Number of persons
Civilian noninstitutional population	200
Employed	100
Civilian labor force	120
Unemployment rate	16.67 percent
Persons unemployed	20
Persons not in the labor force	80

8. 200/280 = 71.42 percent
9. The labor force participation rate is the civilian labor force as a percentage of the civilian noninstitutional population. The employment rate is the number of employed persons as a percentage of the civilian noninstitutional population.
10. No, we would also need to know the number of entrants. Unemployed persons = job losers + job leavers + reentrants + entrants.
11. No, because to compute the cyclical unemployment rate, we also need to know the actual unemployment rate in the economy.
12.

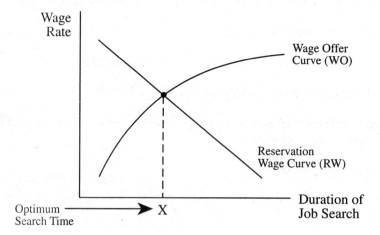

13.

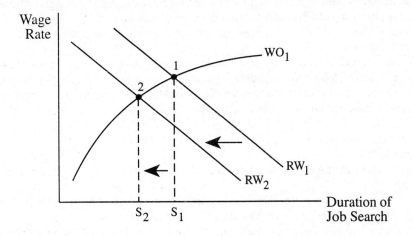

14. An increase in unemployment compensation shifts the reservation wage curve to the right and raises the optimum search time. When the optimum search time rises, so does the unemployment rate.

What is the Question?

1. The consumer price index.

    What is one price index used to measure the price level?

2. Take the nominal income and divide it by the CPI. Then take the quotient and multiply it by 100.

    How do you compute real income?

3. The number of persons employed plus the number of persons unemployed.

    What does the civilian labor force equal?

4. The natural unemployment rate minus the frictional unemployment rate.

    What does the structural unemployment rate equal?

5. This person is not considered unemployed (by the government), even though many people think this person should be considered unemployed.

    What is a discouraged worker?

6. The cyclical unemployment rate.

    What does you call the difference between the actual unemployment rate in the economy and the natural unemployment rate?

7. The lowest wage at which a person will accept a job.

    What is the reservation wage?

8. Price stability, low unemployment, and high and sustained economic growth.

    What are three macroeconomic goals or objectives?

9. The first step is to subtract the CPI in the earlier year from the CPI in the later year. The second step is to divide by the CPI in the earlier year. The third step is to multiply by 100.

    How do you compute the percentage change in prices (using the CPI)?

10. This happens if the CPI rises by more than your nominal income.

    What happens when real income falls?

11. This person did at least one hour of work as a paid employee during the survey week.

    What is an employed person?

12. This person quit his job.

    What is a job leaver?

13. This person got fired but doesn't (currently) have transferable skills.

    What is a job loser who is structurally unemployed?

14. The wage offer is equal to the reservation wage.

    What condition holds when a person has achieved the optimum search time?

Multiple Choice
   1. c
   2. c
   3. c
   4. d
   5. b
   6. e
   7. d
   8. e
   9. c
   10. b
   11. e
   12. d
   13. d
   14. d
   15. a

True-False

    16. F

    17. T

    18. T

    19. T

    20. T

Fill in the Blank

    21. unemployment rate

    22. price index

    23. real income

    24. rises

    25. base year

Chapter 6
Answers

Reveiw Questions

1. With GDP, geography matters; with GNP, citizenship matters. GDP is the total market value of all final goods and services produced annually within a country's borders. GNP is the total market value of all final goods and services produced annually by citizens in a country. If a Mexican citizen lives and works in the U.S., her production is counted in U.S. GDP. If a U.S. citizen lives and works in France, her production is not counted in U.S. GDP.
2. Total market value refers to the monetary value of something at today's prices. For example, suppose two units of good X are sold (today) for $50 per unit. Total market value of these two goods is $100.
3. A hamburger at a fast food restaurant is a final good. The lettuce on the hamburger is an intermediate good.
4. GDP only measures current production. Sales of used goods do not deal with current production. A used good is a good produced in the past that is sold today.
5. GDP measures production. A financial transaction does not deal with production. A financial transaction, such as a purchase of 100 shares of stock, deals with a change in ownership rights. When John buys 100 shares of stock from Taylor, there is no production involved. John simply owns what Taylor used to own.
6. Durable goods, nondurable goods, and services.
7. Fixed investment is the sum of the purchases of new capital goods and the purchases of new residential housing.
8. GDP measures production. Transfer payments have nothing to do with production. A transfer payment is a payment to a person that is not made in return for goods and services currently supplied (produced).
9. National income is equal to compensation of employees plus proprietors' income plus corporate profits plus rental income plus net interest.
10. GDP minus the capital consumption allowance.
11. Personal income is the income that people actually receive. There is some component of national income that is earned but not received (such as corporate profits taxes) and some part of national income that is received but not earned (such as transfer payments). You may want to think of national income as income earned, and personal income as income received.
12. Disposable income is personal income minus personal taxes.
13. No, it is possible for GDP to rise and Real GDP to remain unchanged. GDP is equal to prices multiplied by output. Real GDP is simply output (in base year prices). It is possible for prices to rise, the level of output to stay the same, and therefore GDP will rise. Real GDP will not change, though.
14. Economic growth is the percentage change in Real GDP. The formula to find the percentage change in Real GDP is on page 153 (in the relevant chapter) of the textbook.

Problems

1. Only the $23 price goes into the computation of GDP. GDP measures the total market value of *final goods and services...*
2. GDP equals $100. Everything except Carl's production is not included in GDP.
3. Yes, since the purchases of new residential housing is a component of fixed investment.
4. C + I + G + (EX – IM)
5. A fall in output or a fall in prices. Think of GDP as being equal to current-year prices multiplied by current-year quantity. If either prices or quantities fall, so does GDP.
6. Some of the items in the table are not relevant to computing GDP. GDP = C + I + G + (EX – IM). Consumption is the sum of durable goods, nondurable goods, and services. Investment is given. Government purchases is the sum of purchases by all levels of government—federal, state, and local. Exports is given, as is imports. GDP is equal to $1,125 million.

7. Some of the items in the table are not relevant to computing national income. National income is the sum of compensation of employees, proprietors' income, corporate profits, rental income, and net interest. National income is equal to $1,060 million.

8. Some of the items in the table are not relevant to computing personal income. Personal income is equal to national income minus undistributed corporate profits minus social insurance taxes minus corporate profits taxes plus transfer payments. Personal income is equal to $900 million.

9. GDP is equal to the sum of current-year quantities multiplied by current-year prices. GDP = $2,600. Real GDP is equal to the sum of current-year quantities multiplied by base-year prices. Real GDP = $1,200.

10. To find per capita GDP, simply divide GDP by population.

GDP	Population	Per capita GDP
$1,200 billion	100 million	$12,000
$500 billion	67 million	$7,462
$3,000 billion	50 million	$60,000

11. GNP is equal to GDP minus income earned by the rest of the world plus income earned from the rest of the world. Here's the explanation of how we get this equation. U.S. GDP, we know, includes the income a noncitizen (who lives in the U.S.) earns. This income a noncitizen earns is called "income earned by the rest of the world." First, subtract this amount from GDP. Then to turn what we have left into GNP, we have to add the income a U.S. citizen earns in another country. This we call "income earned from the rest of the world." So, GNP is equal to GDP minus income earned by the rest of the world plus income earned from the rest of the world.

12. GDP is equal to GNP minus income earned from the rest of the world plus income earned by the rest of the world. Here's the explanation of how we get this equation. We know that GNP contains the income a U.S. citizens earns in another country. This income is called "income earned from the rest of the world." First, subtract this amount GNP. Then take what we are left with and add income earned by the rest of the world to get GDP. In other words, GDP is equal to GNP minus income earned from the rest of the world plus income earned by the rest of the world.

13. Yes, since we know that NDP is equal to GDP minus capital consumption allowance, it follows that GDP is equal to NDP plus capital consumption allowance.

14. No, there is a contraction, recovery, and expansion between one peak and the next. Knowing that peak to peak is March to July doesn't give us any information on how long the contraction is, or how long the recovery is, or how long the expansion is. If we knew the length of peak to peak, and knew the length of the contraction, and the length of the recovery, we could then figure out the length of the expansion.

15. 12 + 13 + 12 = 37 months.

What Is Wrong?

1. The expansion phase of a business cycle is generally longer than the recovery stage.

    There is no telling how long each stage will be.

2. A stock variable makes little sense without some time period specified.

    A flow variable makes little sense without some time period specified. Alternatively, you could write, A stock variable makes sense without some time period specified.

3. Fixed investment includes business purchases of new capital goods, inventory investment, and purchases of new residential housing.

    Fixed investment includes only business purchases of new capital goods and purchases of new residential housing.

4.   GDP = C + I + G + EX + IM

$$GDP = C + I + G + EX - IM$$

5.   Net domestic product is equal to GDP minus capital consumption allowance. Another name for capital consumption allowance is capital good.

Another name for the capital consumption allowance is depreciation.

6.   A business cycle is measured from trough to peak.

A business cycle is measured from peak to peak.

7.   The largest expenditure component of GDP is government purchases.

The largest expenditure component of GDP is consumption.

What Is the Question?

1.   GDP divided by population.

What is per capita GDP equal to?

2.   Five phases: peak, contraction, trough, recovery, and expansion.

How many phases are there in a business cycle and what are the phases?

3.   First, subtract Real GDP in the earlier year from Real GDP in the current year. Second, divide by Real GDP. Third, multiply by 100.

How do you compute the economic growth rate?

4.   National income minus undistributed corporate profits minus social insurance taxes minus corporate profits taxes plus transfer payments.

What is personal income equal to?

5.   Personal income minus personal taxes.

What is disposable income equal to?

Multiple Choice

1. a
2. b
3. e
4. e
5. e
6. c
7. c
8. e
9. e
10. e
11. e
12. a
13. e
14. b
15. a

True False

16. F
17. F
18. F
19. T
20. F

Fill in the Blank

21. two
22. five
23. trough
24. flow
25. Investment

Chapter 7
Answers

Review Questions

1. According to economists, aggregate demand curves slope downward because of the (1) real-balance effect, (2) interest-rate effect, and (3) international-trade effect. The real-balance effect can be described as follows: As the price level rises, purchasing power falls, monetary wealth falls, and people end up buying fewer goods. As the price level falls, purchasing power rises, monetary wealth rises, and people end up buying more goods. See Exhibit 2 in the relevant chapter of the text.

2. A change in the quantity demanded of Real GDP is a movement from one point to another point on a given AD curve. It is caused by a change in the price level. A change in aggregate demand refers to a rightward shift or leftward shift in the entire AD curve. It can be brought about by a change in consumption, government purchases, investment, and so on. A change in AD is representative of a change in the quantity demanded of Real GDP at a given price level.

3. Consumption, investment, government purchases, exports, and imports.

4. No, a lower price level will change the quantity demanded of Real GDP, it will not change AD.

5. wealth, expected future prices and income, interest rate, income taxes

6. interest rate, expected future sales, business taxes

7. real national income, exchange rate

8. (1) Firms agree to a certain nominal wage for a specified period of time, (2) the price level falls, (3) as a result of a fall in the price level, the real wage rises, (4) firms hire fewer workers at higher real wages, (5) because fewer people are working, firms produce less output. Notice that a lower price level has led to less output. This gives us an upward-sloping SRAS curve.

9. (1) The demand for goods and services fall, (2) some prices fall, (3) some prices are sticky because of menu costs, (4) since some prices fall and others do not, the average price, or price level, falls, (5) firms who have not lowered prices do not sell as much at lower demand, (6) because they do not sell as much, they cut back on production. In the end, the price level has fallen and less output is being produced. This gives us an upward-sloping SRAS curve.

10. (1) Both the price level and the price a seller charges for his goods rise by the same percentage, (2) the seller believes his price has risen by more than the price level, (3) because of (2), the seller believes the relative price of producing his good has risen, (4) he produces more output, (5) if all sellers act this way, output in the economy rises. Notice that a higher price level has led to more output. This gives us an upward-sloping SRAS curve.

11. (1) Both the price level and nominal wage fall by the same percentage, (2) the real wage does not change, (3) workers believe that the nominal wage has fallen by more than the price level and that their real wage has fallen, (4) in reaction to the "perceived" lower real wage, the quantity supplied of labor falls, (5) with less labor, firms produce less output. Notice that a lower price level has led to less output. This gives us an upward-sloping SRAS curve.

12. wage rates, prices of nonlabor inputs, productivity, supply shocks (adverse and beneficial)

13. Real GDP and the unemployment rate are inversely related, *ceteris paribus*.

Problems

1.

If...	AD curve shifts to the (right or left?)
consumption rises	right
investment rises	right
exports rise	right
imports rise	left
government purchases rise	right
consumption falls	left
net exports rise	right

2.

If...	SRAS curve shifts to the (right or left?)
wage rates rise	left
prices of nonlabor inputs fall	right
productivity increases	right
adverse supply shock	left
beneficial supply shock	right
wage rates fall	right

3.

Factor	How does the factor change affect C, I, G, EX, and/or IM?
wealth rises	C rises
individuals expect higher (future) prices	C rises
individuals expect higher (future) income	C rises
interest rate rises	C falls, I falls
income taxes fall	C rises
businesses expect higher (future) sales	I rises
business taxes rise	I falls
foreign real national income falls	EX rises
dollar appreciates	EX falls, IM rises
dollar depreciates	EX rises, IM falls

4.

Factor	Does the AD curve shift? (right, left, no change)	Does the SRAS curve shift? (right, left, no change)	Is there a change in the price level? (up, down, no change)	Is there a change in Real GDP? (up, down, no change)	Is there a change in the unemployment rate? (up, down, no change)
interest rate falls	right	no change	up	up	down
wage rates rise	no change	left	up	down	up
productivity rises	no change	right	down	up	down
adverse supply shock	no change	left	up	down	up
wealth falls	left	no change	down	down	up
businesses expect lower (future) sales	left	no change	down	down	up
dollar appreciates	left	no change	down	down	up
prices of nonlabor inputs rise	no change	left	up	down	up
beneficial supply shock	no change	right	down	up	down
wealth rises	right	no change	up	up	down
dollar depreciates	right	no change	up	up	down
wage rates fall	no change	right	down	up	down

5.

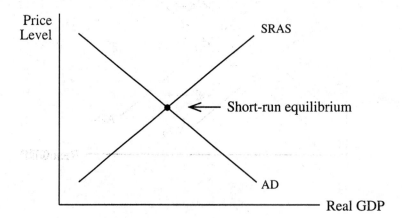

6.

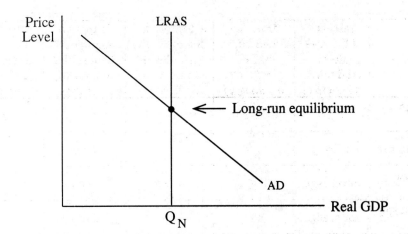

7.

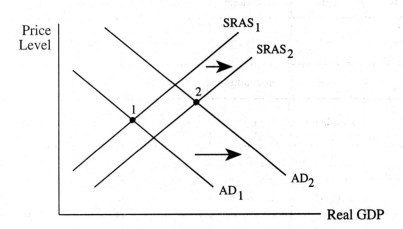

8.

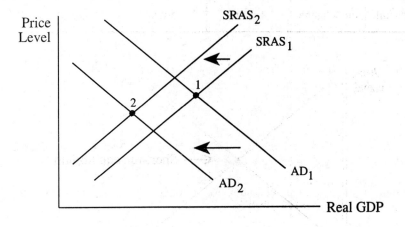

9.

Suppose...	Does the price level rise, fall, or remain constant?	Does Real GDP rise, fall, or remain constant?	Does the unemployment rate rise, fall, or remain constant?
AD rises	rise	rise	fall
AD rises by more than SRAS falls	rise	rise	fall
SRAS falls	rise	fall	rise
SRAS rises by the same amount as AD rises	remain constant	rise	fall
SRAS rises	fall	rise	fall
AD falls	fall	fall	rise

10. $225
11. $200

What Is Wrong?

1. Real GDP increased and the price level fell. This was because the AD curve shifted to the right.

    If the AD curve shifted to the right, the price level wouldn't fall. If the SRAS curve shifted to the right, Real GDP would rise and the price level would fall.

2. Real GDP and the price level increased. This was because the SRAS curve shifted to the right.

    If the SRAS curve shifted to the right, the price level would not increase. If the AD curve shifted to the right, Real GDP and the price level would increase.

3. If SRAS increases, the SRAS curve shifts upward and to the left.

    If SRAS increases, the SRAS curve shifts downward and to the right. Alternatively, you could write: If SRAS decreases, the SRAS curve shifts upward and to the left.

4. The price level increased and Real GDP decreased. This is because the AD curve shifted to the left.

    If the AD curve shifted to the left, the price level would not increase. If the SRAS curve shifts to the left, the price level would increase and Real GDP would decrease.

5. A change in interest rates will affect both consumption and government purchases.

    A change in interest rates will affect both consumption and investment.

6. If the dollar appreciates, this means it takes more dollars to buy a unit of foreign currency.

    If the dollar appreciates, this means it takes fewer dollars to buy a unit of foreign currency. Alternatively, you could write: If the dollar depreciates, this means it takes more dollars to buy a unit of foreign currency.

7. An increase in wealth will raise consumption, aggregate demand, and the price level. It will lower Real GDP.

An increase in wealth will not lead to lower Real GDP, it will lead to higher Real GDP.

8. A decline in interest rates will raise consumption and investment, lower aggregate demand, shift the AD curve left, and raise the price level.

A decline in interest rates will not lead to lower aggregate demand and to a leftward shift in the AD curve. It will lead to higher aggregate demand and a rightward shift in the AD curve.

9. The LRAS curve is vertical at the current level of Real GDP.

The LRAS curve is vertical at the Natural Real GDP level.

10. Long-run equilibrium is at the intersection of the AD curve and the upward-sloping LRAS curve, while short-run equilibrium is at the intersection of the AD curve and the vertical SRAS curve.

The LRAS curve is not upward sloping, it is vertical. The SRAS curve is not vertical, it is upward-sloping.

Multiple Choice
1. b
2. a
3. c
4. d
5. c
6. b
7. d
8. b
9. c
10. c
11. c
12. d
13. b
14. a
15. e

True-False
16. T
17. F
18. T
19. T
20. F

Fill in the Blank
21. falls
22. rises
23. Productivity
24. AD
25. right

Chapter 8
Answers

Review Questions
1. Yes, according to classical economists, Say's law still holds. The savings simply lowers the interest rate and leads to a rise in investment. The rise in investment will be equal to the difference between income and consumption, or $100.
2. More saving leads to lower interest rates. Lower interest rates lead to more investment.
3. Classical economists believed that wages and prices were flexible. There are economists who believe this today.
4. The economy can remove itself from both inflationary and recessionary gaps.
5. The Real GDP that the economy is producing is less than Natural Real GDP.
6. The Real GDP that the economy is producing is greater than Natural Real GDP.
7. greater than
8. less than
9. surplus
10. shortage
11. The wage rate falls, the SRAS curve shifts to the right, and eventually intersects both the AD curve and LRAS curve at Natural Real GDP.
12. The wage rate rises, the SRAS curve shifts to the left, and eventually intersects both the AD curve and the LRAS curve at Natural Real GDP.

Problems
1.

State of the economy	The labor market is in (shortage, surplus, equilibrium)	The wage rate will (rise, fall, remain unchanged)	The SRAS curve will shift (right, left)
Recessionary gap	surplus	fall	right
Inflationary gap	shortage	rise	left
Long-run equilibrium	equilibrium	remain unchanged	remain unchanged

2. (b) the economy is removing itself from an inflationary gap. When the price level is falling, the SRAS curve is shifting to the right, which is what it does when the economy is removing itself from a recessionary gap. When it is removing itself from an inflationary gap, the SRAS curve is shifting to the left, and the price level is rising.
3. (b) the economy is removing itself from an inflationary gap. When Real GDP is rising, the SRAS curve is shifting to the right, which is what it does when the economy is removing itself from a recessionary gap. When it is removing itself from an inflationary gap, the SRAS curve is shifting to the left, and Real GDP is falling.
4. (a) the economy is removing itself from a recessionary gap. When Real GDP is rising, the SRAS curve is shifting to the right, which is what it does when the economy is removing itself from a recessionary gap.
5. (a) the economy is removing itself from a recessionary gap. When the price level is falling, the SRAS curve is shifting to the right, which is what it does when the economy is removing itself from a recessionary gap.
6. The price level is higher in Year 2 than in Year 1. The process is illustrated in Exhibit 7a in the relevant chapter of the text. Initially, the AD curve shifts to the right and the economy is in an inflationary gap. To remove itself from an inflationary gap, wage rates rise, and the SRAS curve shifts left (back into long-run equilibrium). Since the economy is back in long-run equilibrium, it is producing Natural Real GDP again. But it is doing this at a higher price level. When the SRAS curve shifts to the left, the price level necessarily rises.

374

7. The price level is lower in Year 2 than in Year 1. The process is illustrated in Exhibit 7b in the relevant chapter of the text. Initially, the AD curve shifts to the left and the economy is in a recessionary gap. To remove itself from a recessionary gap, wage rates fall, and the SRAS curve shifts right (back into long-run equilibrium). Since the economy is back in long-run equilibrium, it is producing Natural Real GDP again. But it is doing this at a lower price level. When the SRAS curve shifts to the right, the price level necessarily falls.

8. The price level is the same in Year 2 as in Year 1. Initially, the SRAS curve shifts to the left and the price level rises. But then the economy is in a recessionary gap. To remove itself, wage rates fall, and the SRAS curve shifts right (back to its original position). Since the SRAS curve is in its original position, and neither the LRAS curve nor the AD curve have shifted, the price level must be what it was originally (in Year 1).

What Is the Question?

1. These economists believe that Say's law holds in a money economy.

   Who are classical economists?

2. (Current) Real GDP is less than Natural Real GDP.

   What is the condition that specifies a recessionary gap?

3. The economy is operating at Natural Real GDP.

   What is the condition that specifies long-run equilibrium?

4. (Current) Real GDP is greater than Natural Real GDP.

   What is the condition that specifies an inflationary gap?

5. The economy is operating beyond its institutional production possibilities frontier (PPF).

   Where is the economy operating (with respect to its institutional PPF) when it is in an inflationary gap?

6. The economy is operating below its institutional production possibilities frontier (PPF).

   Where is the economy operating (with respect to its institutional PPF) when it is in a recessionary gap.

7. In the long run, the price level is higher, but Real GDP and the unemployment rate are unchanged.

   If the economy is initially in long-run equilibrium, and the economy is self regulating, what will happen to the price level and Real GDP (in the long run) if aggregate demand rises?

8. In the long run, the price level is lower, but Real GDP and the unemployment rate are unchanged.

   If the economy is initially in long-run equilibrium, and the economy is self regulating, what will happen to the price level and Real GDP (in the long run) if aggregate demand falls?

What Is Wrong?

1. The economy is initially in long-run equilibrium. Then, aggregate demand rises. In the short run, the price level and Real GDP rise. If the economy is not self regulating, in the long run the price level has risen and Real GDP has been unchanged (from its initial long-run position).

    The economy is initially in long-run equilibrium. Then, aggregate demand rises. In the short run, the price level and Real GDP rise. If the economy is self regulating, in the long run the price level has risen and Real GDP has been unchanged (from its initial long-run position).

2. The economy is initially in long-run equilibrium. Then, short-run aggregate supply falls. In the short run, the price level and Real GDP rise. If the economy is self regulating, in the long run the price level has fallen back to its original level and Real GDP has been unchanged (from its initial long-run position).

    The economy is initially in long-run equilibrium. Then, short-run aggregate supply falls. In the short run, the price level rises and Real GDP falls. If the economy is self regulating, in the long run the price level has fallen back to its original level and Real GDP has been unchanged (from its initial long-run position).

3. The economy is in a recessionary gap if it is operating at the natural unemployment rate.

    The economy is in long-run equilibrium if it is operating at the natural unemployment rate.

4. The economy is in an inflationary gap if the unemployment rate is greater than the natural unemployment rate.

    The economy is in an inflationary gap if the unemployment rate is less than the natural unemployment rate.

5. The diagram (that follows) shows an economy in a recessionary gap.

    The diagram shows an economy in an inflationary gap.

6. If wage rates fall, the SRAS curve shifts to the left.

    If wage rates fall, the SRAS curve shifts to the right. Alternatively, you could write: If wage rates rise, the SRAS curve shifts to the left.

Multiple Choice
   1. c
   2. b
   3. b
   4. c
   5. c
   6. d
   7. a
   8. e
   9. e
  10. d

True-False

11. F
12. F
13. T
14. F
15. T

Fill in the Blank

16. recessionary
17. rise; leftward
18. fall; rightward
19. physical; institutional
20. Laissez-faire

Chapter 9
Answers

Review Questions

1. Keynes believed that it is possible for consumption to fall, savings to rise, but investment not to rise by the amount that savings has increased. In other words, he did not believe that Say's law necessarily holds in a money economy.

2. Because wage rates are inflexible downward. In other words, wages aren't adjusting in the recessionary gap. If wages don't adjust downward, then the SRAS curve doesn't shift to the right and remove the economy from the recessionary gap.

3. Wages and prices may be inflexible.

4. The price level is constant, there is no foreign sector, and the monetary side of the economy is excluded.

5. $C = Co + MPC (Yd)$, where Co = autonomous consumption, MPC = marginal propensity to consume, and Yd = disposable income.

6. A rise in autonomous consumption, a rise in disposable income, and a rise in the marginal propensity to consume.

7. It is equal to the change in consumption divided by the change in disposable income.
$MPC = \Delta C / \Delta Yd$.

8. The APC is the ratio of consumption to disposable income; the marginal propensity to consume is the ratio of the change in consumption to the change in disposable income. $APC = C/Yd$; $MPC = \Delta C / \Delta Yd$.

9. Vertically sum consumption, investment, and government purchases at all Real GDP levels. For example, suppose that at Real GDP = Q_1, consumption is $200, investment is $100, and government purchases are $100. It follows that the sum, or $400, is total expenditures. One point on a TE curve represents $400 at Q_1.

10. If inventories rise above the optimum inventory level, firms cut back on production and Real GDP falls. If inventories fall below the optimum inventory level, firms increase production and Real GDP rises. In the process, the economy achieves equilibrium where TP = TE and inventories are at their optimum levels.

11. Inventories fall below their optimum levels, firms increase output, and Real GDP rises. The economy ends up moving from disequilibrium (TE > TP) to equilibrium (TP = TE).

12. Yes, equilibrium is where TE = TP, but there is nothing in the Keynesian framework of analysis that says that where TE = TP, Natural Real GDP has to exist. In other words we can have this condition: TE > TP and Real GDP is either above or below Natural Real GDP.

13. The multiplier = $1 \div (1 - MPC)$. For example, if MPC = 0.80, then the multiplier equals 5.

14. The private sector cannot always remove the economy out of a recessionary gap.

Problems

1.

Change in income	Change in consumption	MPC (marginal propensity to consume)
$2,000	$1,000	0.50
$1,000	$800	0.80
$10,000	$9,500	0.95
$3,456	$2,376	0.6875

2.

If consumption is	And disposable income is	And the marginal propensity to consume is	Then autonomous consumption is
$400	$1,000	0.20	$200
$1,600	$1,900	0.80	$80
$1,700	$2,000	0.75	$200

3.

Consumption	Investment	Net Exports	Total expenditure curve shifts (up, down)
rises	falls by less than consumption rises	rises	up
falls	rises by more than consumption falls	falls by more than investment rises	down
rises	rises	falls by more than investment rises, but falls by less than consumption rises	up

4.

MPC	Multiplier
0.75	4
0.80	5
0.60	2.5

5.

Disposable income	Change in disposable income	Consumption	Change in consumption	Saving
$10,000	$0	$8,200	$0	$1,800
$12,000	$2,000	$9,800	$1,600	$2,200
$14,000	$2,000	$11,400	$1,600	$2,600

6.

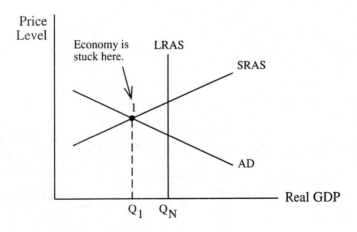

7.

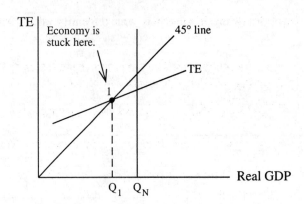

8.   At Q_1, TE > TP; at Q_2, TE = TP; at Q_3, TP > TE.

9.   Inventories will fall below optimum levels and firms will increase production. Real GDP will begin to rise.

10. Inventories will rise above optimum levels and firms will decrease production. Real GDP will begin to fall.

What Is the Question?

1.   Wages and prices may be inflexible.

     What is the Keynesian position on wages and prices?

2.   Autonomous consumption.

     What is consumption that is independent of income called?

3. $1 \div (1\text{-MPC})$

     How do you calculate the multiplier?

4.   Consumption divided by disposable income.

     What is the average propensity to consume equal to?

5.   Inventories rise above optimum levels.

     What initially happens when TP > TE?

6.   It must be horizontal so that changes in aggregate demand change only Real GDP and not the price level, too.

     What must the aggregate supply curve look like if changes in aggregate demand lead to only changes in Real GDP and not the price level, too?

What Is Wrong?
In each of the statements that follow, there is something wrong. Identify what is wrong in the space provided.

1. If the AS curve is horizontal, then an increase in aggregate demand will raise Real GDP, but a decrease in aggregate demand will lower Real GDP and the price level, too.

    A decrease in aggregate demand will not lower the price level if the AS curve is horizontal.

2. According to Keynes, saving is more responsive to changes in interest rates than to changes in income.

    According to Keynes, saving is not more responsive to changes in interest rates than to changes in income.

3. Keynes's major work was titled, *The General Theory of Employment, Income and Prices,* and it was published in 1937.

    The major work was titled The General Theory of Employment, Income and Money, *and it was published in 1936.*

4. When TE is greater than TP, inventories rise above the optimum inventory level.

    When TE is greater than TP, inventories fall below the optimum inventory level. Alternatively, you could write: When TP is greater than TE, inventories rise above the optimum inventory level.

5. When the economy is in disequilibrium, inventories are at their optimum levels.

    When the economy is in equilibrium, inventories are at their optimum levels. Alternatively, you could write: When the economy is in disequilibrium, inventories are not at their optimum levels.

Multiple Choice
1. e
2. b
3. c
4. c
5. d
6. b
7. b
8. b
9. b
10. a
11. d
12. b
13. b
14. c
15. b

True-False

16. T
17. T
18. F
19. T
20. T

Fill in the Blank

21. Efficiency wage
22. inflexible
23. AS curve
24. 0.60
25. fall

Chapter 10
Answers

Review Questions

1. Automatic fiscal policy kicks in automatically when the economy changes. Discretionary fiscal policy is deliberately brought about by Congress. For example, suppose the economy turns down. As a result, unemployment compensation spending rises. Congress doesn't have to meet to direct increases in unemployment compensation spending; it is simply the result of more people (during economic bad times) losing their jobs and collecting unemployment compensation. This is an example of automatic fiscal policy. If the Congress meets, proposes legislation to cut income tax rates, and then passes the legislation (all in order to jump start the economy), then this is an example of discretionary fiscal policy.

2. Expansionary fiscal policy (lower taxes, increases in government expenditures). Expansionary fiscal policy will raise aggregate demand (if there is either zero or incomplete crowding out) and thus reduce or eliminate the recessionary gap.

3. For every $1 increase in government spending, private spending falls by $0.60.

4. No, more government spending on libraries does not necessarily lead to less private spending on books. If it does, though, there is some degree of crowding out. Our point is that there doesn't have to be crowding out.

5. If the budget is initially balanced, and then spending rises, a budget deficit occurs. Government will need to borrow to finance the deficit. As a result, the demand for credit (or loanable funds) rises, and the interest rate rises. If the U.S. interest rate is now higher than foreign interest rates, foreigners will want to buy U.S. interest-paying Treasury securities. To do this, they need to supply their home currency and demand U.S. dollars. The increased demand for U.S. dollars will lead to an appreciation in the value of the dollar.

6. No, it is not necessarily the case that interest rates rise. Because of the deficit, the demand for credit (or loanable funds) will rise. But the supply of loanable funds may rise, too. This will happen if individuals translate a higher budget today into higher taxes in the future. They will end up saving more today in order to pay the higher taxes in the future. The increased saving will put downward pressure on interest rates. Will interest rates rise, fall, or remain constant on net? It depends on the increase in the demand for loanable funds relative to the increase in the supply of loanable funds.

7. It is the time after policymakers decide on what type of fiscal policy measure is required and the actual passage of the fiscal policy measure.

8. Suppose the economy's SRAS curve is shifting to the right, but this is unknown to policymakers. They institute expansionary fiscal policy and push the AD curve rightward more than they would have had they known the SRAS curve is shifting right. In the end, the economy goes from a recessionary gap to an inflationary gap. This process is described in Exhibit 5 in the relevant chapter of the text.

9. Suppose someone earns and income of $40,000 and pays $10,000 in income taxes. His average tax rate is equal to his income taxes divided by his income, or 25 percent. Now suppose the person earns an additional $1,000, and must pay $333 additional income taxes as a result. His marginal tax rate is the change in his taxes ($333) divided by the change in his income ($1,000), or 33 percent.

10. Not necessarily. Higher income tax rates will raise tax revenue if the economy is on the upward-sloping portion of the Laffer curve; higher income tax rates will lower tax revenue if the economy is on the downward-sloping portion of the Laffer curve.

Problems

1.

If the objective is to raise Real GDP by...	And the MPC is...	Then autonomous government spending should be increased by...
$400 billion	0.80	$80 billion
$500 billion	0.75	$125 billion
$100 billion	0.60	$40 billion

2.

If the objective is to raise Real GDP by...	And the MPC is...	Then taxes should be cut by...
$400 billion	0.80	$100 billion
$500 billion	0.75	$166.67 billion
$100 billion	0.60	$66.67 billion

3.   Yes, if expansionary fiscal policy can shift the AD curve to the right by enough to intersect the LRAS curve at point 2. See Exhibit 1a in the relevant chapter in the text.

4.   The economy is initially at point 1 in a recessionary gap. Unbeknownst to policymakers, the SRAS curve is shifting to the right. Policymakers enact expansionary fiscal policy and shift the aggregate demand curve from AD_1 to AD_2. They hope to move the economy to point 1A. Instead, since the SRAS curve has shifted to the right from $SRAS_1$ to $SRAS_2$, the economy moves from point 1 to 2, from a recessionary gap into an inflationary gap.

5.

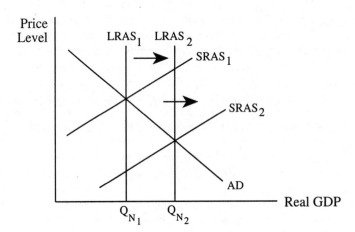

6.

Income	Taxes Paid	Marginal tax rate	Average tax rate
$10,000	$2,200	22 percent	22 percent
$11,000	$2,900	70 percent	26.36 percent
$12,000	$3,700	80 percent	30.83 percent

7.

Taxable income	Tax rate	Tax revenue
$100 million	12.3 percent	$12.4 million
$190 million	10.0 percent	$19 million
$200 million	9.0 percent	$18 million

What Is the Question?

1. Changes in government expenditures and/or taxes that occur automatically without (additional) congressional action.

   What is automatic fiscal policy?

2. Saving increases as a result of the higher future taxes implied by the deficit.

   What do new classical economists think will happen to saving if the budget deficit rises?

3. Deficits do not necessarily bring higher interest rates.

   What is the new classical economic position with respect to budget deficits and interest rates?

4. The time if takes before policymakers know of a change in the economy.

   What is the data lag?

5. The change in the tax payment divided by the change in taxable income.

   What is the marginal tax rate?

6. The downward-sloping part of the Laffer curve.

   Higher tax rates bring about lower tax revenues in what part of the Laffer curve? Alternatively, you could write, Lower tax rates bring about higher tax revenues in what part of the Laffer curve?

Multiple Choice
1. e
2. b
3. b
4. c
5. e
6. c
7. d
8. b
9. b
10. e
11. c
12. a
13. b
14. c
15. b

True-False

16. T
17. T
18. T
19. F
20. T

Fill in the Blank

21. 132
22. marginal
23. downward-sloping
24. tax rate
25. Crowding out

Chapter 11
Answers

Review Questions

1. If a person earns $40,000 a year, she pays a tax rate of 20 percent. If she earns $45,000 a year, she pays $8,000 plus a tax rate of 25 percent on everything over $40,000 (that is, on the additional $5,000 income).

2. Two people, Smith and Jones, each earn $400 for a job. The $400 is enough to move Smith up into a higher tax (rate) bracket, but not enough to move Jones into a higher tax bracket. At the higher tax bracket (that Smith is now in), the marginal tax rate is 13 percent, but at the lower tax bracket (that Jones is in), the marginal tax rate is 10 percent. It follows, then, that Jones pays a tax rate of 10 percent on the $400 income, but Smith pays a tax rate of 13 percent on the $400 income. Smith's after-tax pay is less than Jones's after-tax pay, although their pay ($400) is exactly the same.

3. $4,998.

4. A person would be taxed on the difference between his income and what he saved. For example, if a person's income is $40,000 and he saves $2,000, then he is taxed on $38,000 of consumption.

5. The structural deficit is that part of the total budget deficit that would exist even if the economy were operating at full employment. The cyclical deficit is that part of the total budget deficit that is a result of a downturn in the economy.

6. The nominal budget deficit has not been adjusted for the decline in the real value of the public debt (when inflation exists). The real budget deficit has been adjusted accordingly.

7. The net public debt is that part of the public debt that is held exclusively by the public. The public debt is composed of the debt held by the public (net public debt) and the debt held by government agencies.

8. Government increases its spending on some project. To finance the spending, it borrows the funds. Because more resources are used to finance the project, fewer resources are left to produce other goods (television sets, houses, etc.). So, in the end, the current generation pays for the project (and the debt that is incurred because of it) in terms of consuming fewer television sets, houses, etc.

9. Government increases its spending on some project. To finance the spending, it borrows the funds. When the debt (incurred by the project) comes due, in the future, taxpayers have to pay off the debt.

What Are the Facts?

1. 13.8 percent
2. 30.2 percent
3. 48.8 percent
4. 4.6 percent
5. 48.11 percent
6. 33.71 percent
7. 4.4 percent
8. $91,964
9. 15.5 percent
10. 23 percent
11. 14 percent
12. $5.72 trillion
13. 1835
14. 15.3 percent
15. 5
16. 74 percent
17. 1998

Problems
1. $1,500
2. $2,372
3. $3,558.32
4. 12 percent
5. 14 percent ; 10.756 percent

6.

Total budget deficit	Structural deficit	Cyclical deficit
$250 billion	$100 billion	$150 billion
$100 billion	$25 billion	$75 billion
$150 billion	$100 billion	$50 billion

7.

Nominal budget deficit	Public debt	Inflation rate	Real budget deficit
$200 billion	$4,000 billion	2 percent	$120 billion
$200 billion	$2,000 billion	8 percent	$40 billion
$250 billion	$4,000 billion	5 percent	$50 billion

What Is the Question?

1. Half of the tax is imposed on the employer and half is imposed on the employee.

   How is the Social Security tax imposed?

2. The same tax rate is used for all income levels.

   What is a proportional income tax?

3. A multistage tax that is collected from firms at each stage in the production and distribution process.

   What is a value-added tax (VAT)?

4. One of the arguments in its favor is that it would encourage saving, thus permitting more investment.

   What is one of the arguments in favor of a national consumption tax?

5. It is equal to the total budget deficit minus the cyclical deficit.

   What is the structural budget deficit equal to?

Multiple Choice
1. a
2. d
3. d
4. a
5. e
6. a
7. c
8. b
9. b
10. b

True-False
11. T
12. F
13. T
14. T
15. T
16. T

Fill in the Blank
17. Social Security
18. flat
19. cyclical deficit
20. lower future taxes

Chapter 12
Answers

Review Questions

1. Here is an example in a barter economy: Bob has a Swiss army knife and wants a telephone. Jack has a telephone and wants a Swiss army knife. Here is an example in a money economy: Harry has $40 and wants a shirt. Mike has a shirt and wants $40.
2. It means money serves as a common measurement in which relative values are expressed. Stated differently, it means money serves as the "common language" in which relative values are expressed.
3. It is out of self interest that people (in a barter economy) try to reduce the costs of making exchanges. They simply want to make their lives easier. In pursuit of this goal, they begin to accept the good that is the most marketable of all goods. In time, this good emerges into money. The people didn't intend for there to be money; they intended only to make their lives easier.
4. With money, people do not have to take as much time finding the person with whom they have a double coincidence of wants. Everyone will take money. With less time spent making exchanges, people have more time to work and/or play.
5. Money is valuable because it is generally accepted by everyone.
6. The two monies have the same face value, different intrinsic values, and are fixed at an exchange rate of one-for-one.
7. Currency plus checkable deposits plus traveler's checks
8. M_1 plus small-denomination time deposits plus savings deposits plus money market accounts plus overnight repurchase agreements plus overnight Eurodollar deposits
9. A money is not only widely accepted for purposes of exchange, but also in the repayment of debt. A credit card debt cannot be paid off with your credit card. A credit card is not money, it is a loan.
10. A bank's reserves consist of vault cash and bank deposits at the Fed.
11. Certainly if checkable deposits rise, required reserves will rise, too. Required reserves = r x Checkable deposits. Whether or not the bank will have to hold more reserves depends on what reserves it is currently holding. For example, suppose checkable deposits = $400 million and the required-reserve ratio is 10 percent. It follows that required reserves are $40 million. Now, suppose the bank is holding $50 million in reserves. It is holding more reserves than it has to. What happens if checkable deposits now rise to $500 million. Required reserves are now $50 million. Will the bank have to hold more reserves than it is presently holding? Not at all. It is holding the amount of reserves ($50 million) that it is supposed to be holding. Of course, if was only holding $40 million in reserves before, it would have to hold $10 million more in reserves.
12. George sells a television set and receives a $400 check for it. He takes the check to his bank, asks for $100 cash, and deposits the remainder, $300, into his checking account. The $100 is a cash leakage.
13. The simple deposit multiplier is 1 divided by the required-reserve ratio (1/r). The required-reserve ratio is the percentage of each dollar that is deposited in a bank that must be held in reserve form.

Problems
1.

Required-reserve ratio	Simple deposit multiplier
0.10	10
0.12	8.33
0.09	11.11

2.

Currency	Checkable deposits	Traveler's checks	M_1 money supply
$200 billion	$500 billion	$8 billion	$708 billion
$100 billion	$591 billion	$9 billion	$700 billion
$190 billion	$300 billion	$10 billion	$500 billion

3.

Checkable deposits	Required-reserve ratio	Required reserves
$400 million	0.10	$40 million
$300 million	0.12	$36 million
$1,000 million	0.15	$150 million

4.

Checkable deposits	Required-reserve ratio	Required reserves	Reserves	Excess reserves
$400 million	0.10	$40 million	$60 million	$20 million
$500 million	0.15	$75 million	$80 million	$5 million
$872 million	0.12	$104.64 million	$200 million	$95.36 million

5.

Checkable deposits	Required-reserve ratio	Required reserves	Vault cash	Bank deposits at the Fed	Excess reserves
$230 million	0.13	$29.9 million	$10 million	$30 million	$10.1 million
$367 million	0.10	$36.7 million	$1 million	$43 million	$7.3 million
$657 million	0.12	$78.84 million	$23 million	$60 million	$4.16 million

6.

Change in reserves	Required-reserve ratio	Maximum change in the money supply
+ $4 million	0.10	$40 million
+ $50 million	0.12	$416.67 million
− $41 million	0.10	− $410 million

7.

Checkable deposits	Required-reserve ratio	Required reserves	Vault cash	Bank deposits at the Fed	Excess reserves
$1,000 million	0.10	$100 million	$50 million	$50 million	$0
$230 million	0.12	$27.6 million	$20 million	$7.6 million	$0
$498 million	0.10	$49.8 million	$10 million	$39.8 million	$0

What Is the Question?

1. Medium of exchange, unit of account, and store of value.

    What are the three functions of money?

2. Exchanging goods and services for other goods and services.

    What is barter?

3. The least exclusive function of money.

    What is the store-of-value function of money?

4. General acceptability.

    What makes money valuable?

5. Deposits on which checks can be written.

    What are demand deposits?

6. An asset that can easily and quickly be turned into cash.

    What is a liquid asset?

7. The central bank of the United States.

    What is the Fed (or the Federal Reserve System)?

8. Bank deposits at the Fed plus vault cash.

    What are reserves equal to?

9. The difference between reserves and required reserves.

    What are excess reserves equal to?

10. 1 divided by the required-reserve ratio.

    What is the simple deposit multiplier equal to?

What Is Wrong?

1. How much money did you earn last week?

    How much income did you earn last week?

2. A double coincidence of wants is not a necessary condition for trade to take place.

    A double coincidence of wants is a necessary condition for trade to take place.

3. Gresham's law states that bad money drives good money out of circulation if the bad money and the good money have different face values, the same intrinsic values, and are fixed at a ratio of 1-for-1.

   Gresham's law states that bad money drives good money out of circulation if the bad money and the good money have the same face value, different intrinsic values, and are fixed at a ratio of 1-for-1.

4. The largest component of M_1 is currency.

   The largest component of M_1 is checkable deposits.

5. M_1 is the broad definition of the money supply.

   M_1 is the narrow definition of the money supply. Alternatively, you could write: M_2 is the broad definition of the money supply.

6. Excess reserves equal reserves plus required reserves.

   Excess reserves equal reserves minus required reserves.

7. The maximum change in checkable deposits = $r \times \Delta R$.

   The maximum change in checkable deposits = $1/r \times \Delta R$

8. The greater the cash leakages, the larger the increase in the money supply for a given positive change in reserves.

   The greater the cash leakages, the smaller the increase in the money supply for a given positive change in reserves. Alternatively, you could write: The smaller the cash leakages, the larger the increase in the money supply for a given positive change in reserves.

9. Our money today has value because it is backed by gold.

   Our money today has value because of its general acceptability. Alternatively, you could write, Our money today is not backed by gold.

Multiple Choice
1. e
2. c
3. c
4. b
5. b
6. d
7. a
8. d
9. b
10. a
11. a
12. c
13. a
14. c
15. d

True-False
16. T
17. F
18. T
19. T
20. F

Fill in the Blank
21. double coincidence of wants
22. Federal Reserve notes
23. fractional reserve
24. 10
25. general acceptability

Chapter 13
Answers

Review Questions

1. Seven
2. Twelve
3. Boston, New York, Philadelphia, Cleveland, Richmond, Atlanta, Dallas, Chicago, St. Louis, Minneapolis, Kansas City, San Francisco
4. control the money supply
5. There are 12 members of the FOMC. Seven of the 12 are the Board of Governors of the Federal Reserve System, one is the president of the New York Fed, and the remaining four are (on a rotating basis) presidents of the remaining 11 Fed banks.
6. A person endorses a check and turns it over to her bank. The bank sends it to its Federal Reserve District bank. If the check was written on a bank in another Fed district, then the Fed bank sends the check to the Fed bank in that district. The Fed bank in that district sends the check to the bank on which the check was written. What about funds? Funds are moved from the reserve account of the bank on which the check is written into the reserve account of the bank in which the recipient of the check has an account.
7. The Treasury is a budgetary agency; its job is to collect taxes and borrow funds to manage the affairs of the financial government. The Fed is a monetary agency. Its major responsibility is to control the money supply.
8. Reserves plus currency held outside banks. Alternatively, it is equal to bank deposits at the Fed plus vault cash plus currency held outside banks.
9. Suppose the Fed buys the services of an economic consultant. It pays the consultant (writes a check for) $50,000. The consultant will take the check and deposit it in her bank and either (1) ask for $50,000 currency, or (2) not ask for $50,00 currency. If (1), the currency held outside banks has risen by $50,000, and so the monetary base (which is composed of bank deposits at the Fed, vault cash, and currency held outside banks) changes. Alternatively, if (2), the $50,000 can either end up in the reserve account of the bank (which changes the monetary base), or as vault cash (which also changes the monetary base) if the bank asks the Fed for $50,000 currency instead of $50,000 in its reserve account.
10. The Fed buys $10 million of government securities from, say, Bank A. It pays for the purchase by increasing the balance of Bank A's reserve account by $10 million. Thus, Bank A has $10 million more in reserves. As a result of increased reserves, Bank A ends up with more excess reserves, which it uses to create loans. As it extends loans to customers, it creates checkable deposits which are part of the money supply. The money supply rises.
11. The Fed lowers the discount rate and banks begin to borrow from the Fed. The Fed extends loans to these banks by increasing the balance in their reserve accounts. The banks end up with more excess reserves which they use to create loans. As the banks extend loans, they create checkable deposits which are part of the money supply. The money supply rises.
12. Suppose checkable deposits = $400 million, the required-reserve ratio is 10 percent, required reserves are $40 million, reserves are $40 million, and excess reserves are $0. Now suppose the required-reserve ratio is lowered to 5 percent. Required reserves now fall from $40 million to $20 million. This means reserves minus required reserves (or excess reserves) are now $20 million instead of $0. Banks use the excess reserves to create new loans and checkable deposits and so the money supply rises.
13. The discount rate is set by the Fed (specifically, the Board of Governors of the Fed). There are no market forces that determine the discount rate. The federal funds rate is set by the supply of, and demand for, reserves. The federal funds rate is set in a market, the discount rate is not.

Problems

1.

Change in the monetary base	Money multiplier	Change in the money supply
$300 million	2.5	$750 million
$146.34 million	4.1	$600 million
$530 million	3.3	$1,749 million

2.

Vault cash	Bank deposits at the Fed	Currency (held outside banks)	Monetary base
$30 billion	$70 billion	$200 billion	$300 billion
$180 billion	$420 billion	$400 billion	$1,000 billion
$37 billion	$100 billion	$210 billion	$347 billion

3.   Checkable deposits = $400 million
        Required-reserve ratio = 5 percent
        Required reserves = $20 million
        Reserves = $40 million
        Excess reserves = $20 million

4.   Checkable deposits = $500 million
        Required-reserve ratio = 12 percent
        Required reserves = $60 million
        Reserves = $70 million
        Excess reserves = $10 million

5.   Checkable deposits = $610 million
        Required-reserve ratio = 10 percent
        Required reserves = $61 million
        Reserves = $70 million
        Excess reserves = $9 million

6.   Checkable deposits = $600 million
        Required-reserve ratio = 10 percent
        Required reserves = $60 million
        Reserves = $70 million
        Excess reserves = $10 million

7.

Fed action...	Money supply (rises, falls, remains unchanged)
Conducts an open market purchase	rises
Lowers required-reserve ratio	rises
Raises the discount rate to a level higher than the federal funds rate	falls
Conducts an open market sale	falls
Lowers the discount rate to a level substantially lower than the federal funds rate	rises
Raises the required-reserve ratio	falls

8.

Fed action...	Maximum change in the money supply
Buys $100 million worth of government securities from Bank A	$1,000 million
Gives a $10 million discount loan to Bank B	$100 million
Sells $20 million worth of government securities to Bank C	– $200 million

What Is the Question?

1. Any of these changes in Fed policy tools will cause the money supply to rise.

   What will a decrease in the required-reserve ratio, an open market purchase, and a decrease in the discount rate (relative to the funds rate) do to the money supply?

2. This group conducts open market operations.

   What is the Federal Open Market Committee (FOMC)?

3. These are sold to raise funds to pay the government's bills.

   What are U.S. Treasury securities?

4. Bank deposits at the Fed plus vault cash plus currency held outside banks.

   What does the monetary base equal?

5. The money supply divided by the monetary base.

   What does the money multiplier equal?

6. The Fed buys and sells government securities.

   What is an open market operation?

7. Either to the federal funds market or to the Fed for a discount loan.

   Where can a bank go to obtain a loan?

What Is Wrong?

1. The president of the St. Louis Fed holds a permanent seat on the FOMC.

   The president of the New York Fed holds a permanent seat on the FOMC.

2. The Fed is a budgetary and monetary agency and the Treasury is a budgetary agency only.

   The Fed is a monetary agency and the Treasury is a budgetary agency.

3. If the monetary base rises by $400 million and the money supply rises by $1,200 million dollars, the multiplier is 4.

   ...the multiplier is 3.

4. An open market purchase refers to a commercial bank buying government securities from the Fed.

   An open market purchase refers to the Fed buying government securities from a commercial bank. Alternatively, you could write: An open market sale refers to a commercial bank buying government securities from the Fed. (The Fed sells.)

5. An increase in the discount rate is likely to raise the money supply.

   A decrease in the discount rate is likely to raise the money supply. Alternatively, you could write: An increase in the discount rate is likely to lower the money supply.

6. Open market operations are flexible, can easily be reversed, but can only be implemented over a substantial period of time.

   Open market operations are flexible, can easily be reversed, and can be implemented quickly.

7. Every time the Fed buys or sells something, reserves change.

   Every time the Fed buys or sells something, the monetary base changes.

8. The simple deposit multiplier is likely to be smaller than the money multiplier.

   The simple deposit multiplier is likely to be larger than the money multiplier.

9. The major responsibility of the Fed is to clear checks.

   The major responsibility of the Fed is to control the money supply.

Multiple Choice
1. a
2. b
3. e
4. b
5. a
6. a
7. d
8. e
9. e
10. b
11. a
12. c
13. d
14. d
15. b

True-False

    16. F

    17. T

    18. F

    19. T

    20. T

Fill in the Blank

    21. money multiplier

    22. federal funds rate

    23. increase; decrease

    24. monetary base

    25. high-powered or base

Chapter 14
Answers

Review Questions

1. If $1 changes hands 3 times (in a year) to buy goods and services, then velocity is 3.
2. The equation of exchange is simply an identify. It simply says that the money supply multiplied by velocity equals the price level multiplied by Real GDP. Stated differently, it says that total spending must equal total receipts. The simply quantity theory of money is a theory that offers a particular prediction. The simple quantity theory of money is built on the equation of exchange. It assumes that two of the variables in the equation (velocity and Real GDP) are constant; then it predicts that changes in the money supply lead to strictly proportional changes in the price level.
3. The simple quantity theory of money predicts that changes in the money supply lead to strictly proportional changes in the price level.
4. In the simple quantity theory of money, Real GDP is constant. It follows, then, that the AS curve is vertical.
5. The equation of exchange is MV = PQ. What will cause an increase in P (inflation)? The answer is an increase in M and V and a decrease in Q. What will cause a decrease in P (deflation)? The answer is a decrease in M and V and an increase in Q.
6. a. The SRAS curve is upward sloping
    b. the money supply and velocity
    c. velocity changes in a predictable way
    d. the economy is self regulating, prices and wages are flexible.
7. Yes, we agree. Either a rightward shift in the AD curve, or a leftward shift in the SRAS curve, can cause the price level to rise.
8. It is a demand-side phenomenon. It is caused by continued increases in aggregate demand.
9. The liquidity effect refers to the change in the interest rate that is brought about by a change in the supply of loanable funds.
10. The expectations effect refers to the change in the interest rate that is brought about by a change in the expected inflation rate.
11. A change in the money supply can affect the interest rate via the liquidity, income, price-level, and expectations effects.
12. The nominal interest rate is equal to the real interest rate plus the expected inflation rate. The (*ex ante*) real interest rate is the nominal interest rate minus the expected inflation rate.
13. The *ex ante* real interest rate is the nominal interest rate minus the expected inflation rate. The *ex post* real interest rate is the nominal interest rate minus the actual inflation rate.

Problems

1.

Percentage change in the money supply	Percentage change in the price level
+25	+25
− 10	− 10
+ 9	+9

2.

Money supply	Velocity	Real GDP	Will there be inflation or deflation?
rises	rises	stays constant	inflation
falls	stays constant	rises	deflation
falls	falls	rises	deflation

3.

Expected inflation rate	Actual inflation rate	Nominal interest rate	*Ex ante* real interest rate	*Ex post* real interest rate
3 percent	2 percent	6 percent	3 percent	4 percent
1 percent	1 percent	5 percent	4 percent	4 percent
2 percent	4 percent	7 percent	5 percent	3 percent

4. In the short run the price level and Real GDP will rise. In the long run, only the price level will rise.
5. In the short run the price level and Real GDP will fall. In the long run, only the price level will fall.
6.

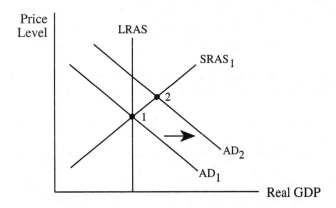

7.

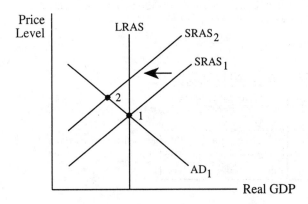

8. The SRAS curve would continually shift to the left, and while the price level would continually rise, Real GDP (Q) would get increasingly smaller.

9.

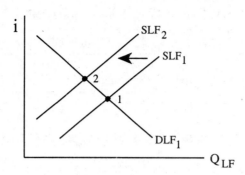

10.

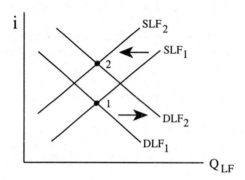

11. short run goes from A to B; long run goes from A to F (via B)
12. short run goes from A to D; long run goes from A to E (via D)

What Is the Question?

1. In the theory, velocity is assumed constant.

    What is the simple quantity theory of money?

2. In the theory, the AS curve is vertical.

    What is the simple quantity theory of money?

3. This can happen if the money supply rises, velocity rises, or if Real GDP falls.

    Using the variables in the equation of exchange, what causes the price level to rise?

4. According to these economists, changes in velocity can change aggregate demand.

    Who are the monetarists?

5. The change in the interest rate due to a change in the expected inflation rate.

    What is the expectations effect?

6. The change in the interest rate due to a change in the price level.

   What is the price-level effect?

7. The real interest rate plus the expected inflation rate.

   What does the nominal interest rate equal?

What Is Wrong?

1. An increase in velocity and a decrease in Real GDP will lead to a decline in the price level.

   An increase in the velocity and a decrease in Real GDP will lead to an increase *in the price level.*

2. In both the simple quantity theory of money and the monetarist theory, the aggregate demand curve will shift right or left if either the money supply or interest rates change.

   In the simple quantity theory of money, the AD curve will shift right or left if the money supply changes. In monetarist theory, the AD curve will shift right or left if either the money supply or velocity change.

3. According to monetarists, prices are flexible but wages are inflexible.

   According to monetarists, both prices and wages are flexible.

4. The CPI rises from 100 to 120, to 130, to 135, to 145, and so on. This is indicative of one-shot inflation.

   This is indicative of continued inflation.

5. Continued decreases in short-run aggregate supply can lead to continued deflation.

   Continued decreases in short-run aggregate supply can lead to continued inflation.

Multiple Choice
1. e
2. b
3. d
4. e
5. e
6. c
7. e
8. c
9. b
10. b
11. b
12. d
13. d
14. b
15. e

True-False

    16. F

    17. F

    18. F

    19. F

    20. T

Fill in the blank

    21. demand-induced

    22. supply-induced

    23. money supply

    24. demand for; supply of

    25. real interest rate

Chapter 15
Answers

Review Questions

1. People will hold more money the lower the opportunity cost of holding money. The opportunity cost of holding money is the interest rate. As the interest rate falls (the opportunity cost of holding money falls) and people will hold more money, *ceteris paribus*.

2. If investment is not interest insensitive, and there is no liquidity trap, then the Keynesian transmission mechanism will work for an increase in the money supply as follows: An increase in the money supply lowers the interest rate; as the interest rate falls, investment rises; greater investment leads to higher aggregate demand. Higher aggregate demand leads to greater Real GDP.

3. If there is a surplus of money, the interest rate falls; if there is a shortage of money, the interest rate rises.

4. If investment is interest insensitive it means that changes in the interest rate do not lead to changes in investment. If investment is interest insensitive, then the Keynesian transmission mechanism is short-circuited; the link to the money market and goods and services market is broken. It follows that changes in the money market will not affect the goods and services market. Monetary policy is ineffective at changing Real GDP.

5. If Bond A pays 10 percent interest each year, and a new bond (Bond B) is offered that pays 12 percent interest each year, then no one will buy Bond A at the same price they would pay for Bond B. The price of Bond A will have to fall to make it competitive with Bond B. In short, the prices of existing bonds (like Bond A) move down as current interest rates rise.

6. The monetarist transmission mechanism is direct: changes in the money market directly impact the goods and services market. For example, a rise in the money supply will create a surplus of money at the given interest rate. This surplus of money will go to buy goods and services.

7. Expansionary monetary policy refers to an increase in the money supply. Contractionary monetary policy refers to a decrease in the money supply.

8. Expansionary monetary policy (increase in the money supply) is supposed to increase aggregate demand. As the AD curve shifts to the right, the economy begins to produce more Real GDP and thus the recessionary gap is eliminated.

9. Contractionary monetary policy (decrease in the money supply) is supposed to decrease aggregate demand. As the AD curve shifts to the left, the economy begins to produce less Real GDP at a lower price level and thus the inflationary gap is eliminated.

10. a) the economy does not always equilibrate quickly enough at Natural Real GDP; b) activist monetary policy is effective at smoothing out the business cycle; c) activist monetary policy is flexible.

11. Expansionary monetary policy is supposed to remove the economy from Point 1 to Point 2. However, if the SRAS curve is shifting to the right, and monetary authorities do not take this into account, then the economy will move from Point 1 (recessionary gap) to an inflationary gap (Point 3).

12. If the market price of gold is greater than the official price of gold, the public will buy gold from the government. It pays for the gold with money, and the government takes the money out of circulation. Consequently, the money supply (in the economy) falls. With a reduced money supply, the price level drops. Now if the market price of gold is less than the official price of gold, things work in reverse. The public will sell gold to the government and get money in return. The money supply rises. With an increased money supply, the price level rises.

Problems

1.

If the money supply...	And the demand for money curve is...	And investment is...	Then Real GDP will (rise, fall, remain unchanged)
rises	downward sloping	interest sensitive	rise
falls	horizontal	interest sensitive	remain unchanged
rises	downward sloping	interest insensitive	remain unchanged
falls	downward sloping	interest sensitive	fall
rises	horizontal	interest sensitive	remain unchanged

2.

If the money supply...	And the demand for money curve is...	And investment is...	Then Real GDP will (rise, fall, remain unchanged)
rises	downward sloping	interest sensitive	rises
falls	downward sloping	interest sensitive	falls
rises	downward sloping	interest insensitive	rises
falls	downward sloping	interest sensitive	falls

3.

If the money supply...	And the demand for money curve is...	And investment is...	Then the price level will (rise, fall, remain unchanged)
rises	downward sloping	interest sensitive	remain unchanged
falls	horizontal	interest sensitive	remain unchanged
rises	downward sloping	interest insensitive	remain unchanged
falls	downward sloping	interest sensitive	remain unchanged
rises	horizontal	interest sensitive	remain unchanged

4.   A surplus of money will cause the AD curve to shift to the right.

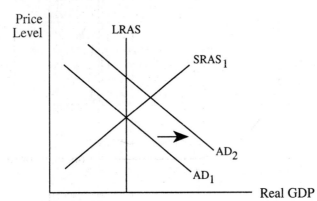

5. A surplus of money will cause the interest rate to fall, which will cause investment to rise, which will cause the AD curve to shift to the right.

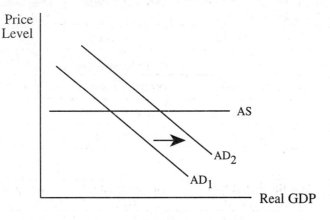

6. It will end up higher because the AD curve has shifted to the right.
7. It will end up lower because the AD curve has shifted to the left.
8.

Percentage change in velocity	Percentage change in Real GDP	Percentage change in the money supply
+ 2 percent	+ 3 percent	+ 1 percent
− 1 percent	+ 2 percent	+ 3 percent
+ 2 percent	− 3 percent	− 5 percent

9.

Market price of gold (per ounce)	Official price of gold	Will the public buy gold from the government or sell gold to the government? (buy, sell)	The supply of gold in the market will (rise, fall)	The money supply will (rise, fall)	The price level will (rise, fall)
$300	$280	buy gold	rise	fall	fall
$259	$280	sell gold	fall	rise	rise

10.

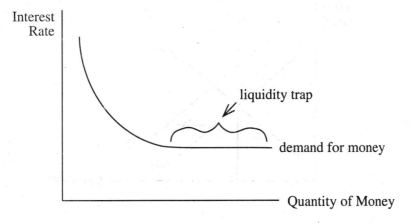

11.

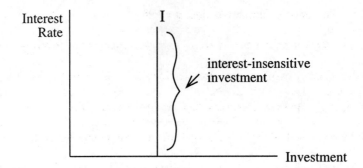

12.

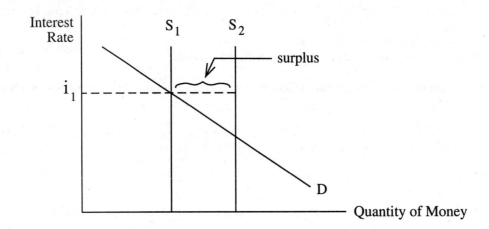

13.

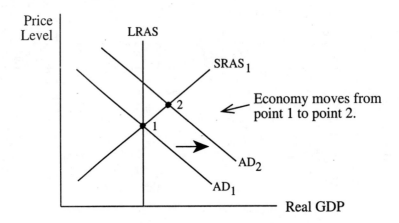

What Is the Question?

1. The money supply rises but the interest rate does not fall.

    What happens when the money supply rises but the economy is in a liquidity trap?

2. The interest rate falls, but investment does not increase.

    What happens if investment is insensitive and the interest rate falls?

3. A change in the money supply directly leads to a change in aggregate demand.

    How does the monetarist transmission mechanism work if there is a change in the money supply?

4. Activist monetary policy may not work, activist monetary policy may be destabilizing, and wages and prices are sufficiently flexible to allow the economy to equilibrate at reasonable speed at Natural Real GDP.

    What are the arguments against activist monetary policy?

5. If velocity rises by 2 percent, and Real GDP rises by 3 percent, then increase the money supply by 1 percent.

    By how much should the money supply be changed if the objective is price stability and velocity rises by 2 percent and Real GDP rises by 3 percent?

Multiple Choice
   1. d
   2. a
   3. c
   4. b
   5. d
   6. b
   7. c
   8. d
   9. a
   10. d
   11. a
   12. b
   13. c
   14. d

True-False
   16. T
   17. F
   18. F
   19. F
   20. F

Fill in the Blank
   21. insensitive; liquidity trap
   22. directly
   23. contractionary; expansionary
   24. Real GDP; velocity
   25. nonactivist

Chapter 16
Answers

Review Questions
1. A. W. Phillips identified the relationship between wage inflation and unemployment. Samuelson and Solow identified the relationship between price inflation and unemployment.
2. If the Phillips curve is downward sloping, then there is a tradeoff between inflation and unemployment. High inflation goes with low unemployment and low inflation goes with high unemployment. Stagflation—which is both high inflation and high unemployment—cannot occur.
3. According to Friedman, when there is a difference between the expected and actual inflation rates, there is a tradeoff between inflation and unemployment. In short, workers can be "fooled" into believing their real wages are higher than in fact they are. In time, workers learn, and the expected inflation rate equals the actual inflation rate. When this occurs, there is no tradeoff between inflation and unemployment.
4. Consider the issue of inflation. What will the inflation rate be over the next year? With adaptive expectations, a person only considers what the inflation rate has been in forming his expected inflation rate. With rational expectations, a person considers what the inflation rate has been, what is happening now in the economy, and what he thinks will happen in the future in the economy when forming his expected inflation rate.
5. Because workers are sometimes "fooled" into thinking their real wages are higher than they are.
6. No. If policy is unanticipated, we get the same results whether individuals hold adaptive or rational expectations. Compare Exhibit 5 (adaptive expectations) with Exhibit 6a (rational expectations).
7. Yes. With adaptive expectations, there is a change in Real GDP in the short run; with rational expectations, there is no change in Real GDP. Compare Exhibit 5 (adaptive expectations) with Exhibit 6b (rational expectations).
8. Changes in Real GDP can originate on the supply-side of the economy. In other words, changes in LRAS can bring about changes in Real GDP (ups and downs in Real GDP). Moreover, most business cycle theorists not only believe that changes in Real GDP can originate on the supply-side of the economy, but do originate on the supply-side of the economy.
9. The PIP says that under certain conditions (such as flexible wages and prices, rational expectations, and correctly anticipated policy) expansionary fiscal and monetary policy is ineffective at meeting macroeconomic objectives (such as increasing Real GDP or lowering the unemployment rate).
10. Expectations are formed rationally and some prices and wages are inflexible.
11. Yes. Changes in AD or LRAS can change Real GDP.

Problems
1.

Starting point	People hold	Change in the economy	Change is	Prices and wages are	Short run change in Real GDP (rise, fall, remain unchanged)	Long run change in the price level (rise, fall, remain unchanged)
Long-run equilibrium	adaptive expectations	AD rises	unanticipated	flexible	rise	rise
Long-run equilibrium	rational expectations	AD rises	correctly anticipated	flexible	remain unchanged	rise
Long-run equilibrium	rational expectations	AD rises	unanticipated	flexible	rise	rise

2. The economy will move from Point 1 to Point 2.

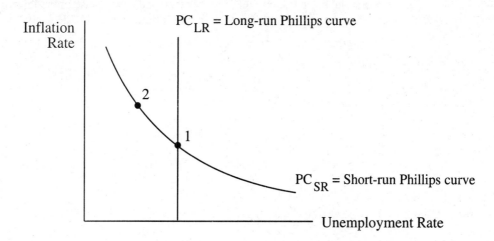

3. The economy will move from Point 1 to Point 2 on the long-run Phillips curve.

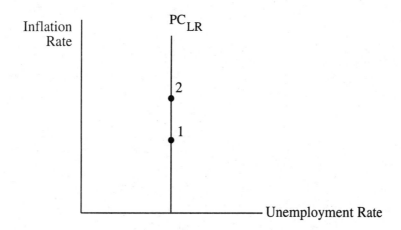

4. The economy will move from Point 1 to Point 2 if some wages and prices are inflexible. It will move from Point 1 to Point 3 if wages and prices are flexible.

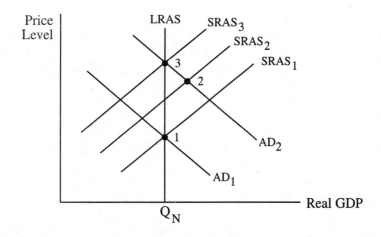

5. Real GDP might be lower because the money supply has fallen and therefore the AD curve has shifted to the left. But it need not be. It could be lower because the LRAS curve first shifted to the left, lowering Real GDP, and later the money supply fell. In other words, the real cause of the lower Real GDP was a decline in LRAS, not a decline in the money supply (originating on the demand-side of the economy).

6. The economy moves from Point 1 to Point 2.

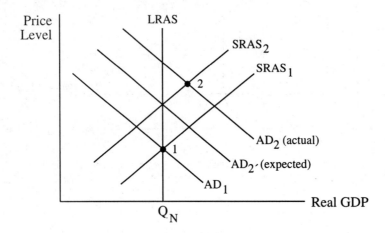

7. The economy moves from Point 1 to Point 2.

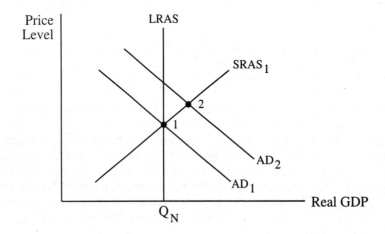

8. The economy moves from Point 1 to Point 2.

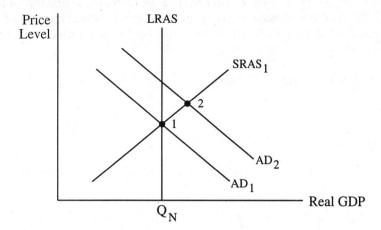

9.

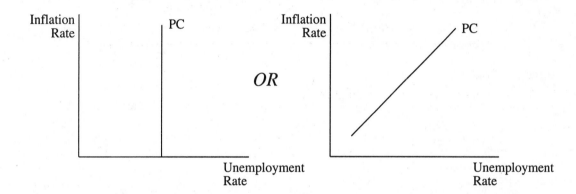

10. It says the PIP holds. PIP holds that policy cannot bring about certain macroeconomic outcomes. If there is only one Phillips curve, and it is always vertical, then the unemployment rate is not changing. This is likely to be at the natural unemployment rate. Increases in AD, then, cannot change the unemployment rate. But this can only occur if wages and prices are flexible, expectations are rational, and policy is correctly anticipated. These are the conditions necessary for the PIP to hold.

11. If there is only one Phillips curve, and it is always vertical, then the unemployment rate is not changing. This is likely to be at the natural unemployment rate. Increases in AD, then, cannot change the unemployment rate. But this can only occur if wages and prices are flexible, expectations are rational, and policy is correctly anticipated.

What Is the Question?

1. It posited an inverse relationship between wage inflation and unemployment.

    What type of relationship did the original Phillips curve (by A.W. Phillips) posit between wage inflation and unemployment?

2. In the short run, the economy moves away from its natural unemployment rate, but in the long run, the economy operates at its natural unemployment rate.

    What happens in the short run and long run in the Friedman natural rate theory as a result of an increase in aggregate demand?

3. The expected inflation rate changes faster in this theory.

    What is rational expectations theory (as opposed to adaptive expectations theory)?

4. Expectations are rational and some prices and wages are inflexible.

    What are two assumptions of New Keynesian theory?

5. Stagflation is precluded.

    What does a downward-sloping Phillips curve preclude?

6. According to this theory, there is a tradeoff between inflation and unemployment—but only in the short run.

    What does the Friedman natural rate theory say about the tradeoff between inflation and unemployment in the short run and in the long run?

7. Initially, both Real GDP and the price level fall. Later, the money supply may decline.

    What does business cycle theory say about the sequencing of changes in Real GDP, the price level, and the money supply?

What Is Wrong?

1. Stagflation over time is consistent with a short-run Phillips curve that continually shifts to the left.

    Stagflation over time is consistent with a short-run Phillips curve that continually shifts to the right. Alternatively, you could write: Stagflation over time is not consistent with a short-run Phillips curve that continually shifts to the left.

2. If the economy is in long-run equilibrium, then it is not on the long-run vertical Phillips curve.

    If the economy is in long-run equilibrium, then it is on the long-run Phillips curve.

3. Rational expectations theory assumes that people are smarter today than they were yesterday, but not as smart as they will be tomorrow.

    Rational expectations theory assumes that people base their expected inflation rate on past inflation rates, and on the policy effects of what is currently occurring (in the present) and what may happen (in the future).

4. In real business cycle theory, the LRAS curve shifts to the left after the money supply has fallen.

    In real business cycle theory, the LRAS curve shifts to the left before the money supply falls.

5. New Keynesian theory holds that wages are not completely flexible because of things such as rational expectations.

    New Keynesians hold that wages are not completely flexible because of things such as long-term contracts.

6. The policy ineffectiveness proposition holds under the conditions that (1) policy changes are anticipated correctly, (2) wages and prices are flexible, and (3) expectations are adaptive.

The policy ineffectiveness proposition holds under the conditions that (1) policy changes are anticipated correctly, (2) wages and prices are flexible, and (3) expectations are rational.

Multiple Choice
1. d
2. b
3. b
4. a
5. b
6. b
7. c
8. e
9. d
10. a
11. d
12. a
13. c
14. a
15. d

True-False
16. F
17. F
18. T
19. F
20. T

Fill in the Blank
21. long-run equilibrium
22. Stagflation
23. New classical
24. supply-side
25. new classical theory

Chapter 17
Answers

Review Questions

1. Absolute real economic growth is an increase in Real GDP from one period to the next. Per capita real economic growth is an increase in per capita Real GDP (Real GDP divided by population) from one period to the next.
2. It means it occurs from a point below the production possibilities frontier (PPF). If the economy is at a point below its PPF, there are some unemployed resources.
3. It means it occurs from a point on the PPF. With economic growth from an efficient level of production, the PPF shifts rightward.
4. It means a country does not need natural resources to experience economic growth, and if a country does have natural resources it is not guaranteed that it will experience economic growth.
5. Human capital is education, training, and experience.
6. Combining people (labor) with certain capital goods makes people more productive. A person with a tractor is more productive at farming than a person with a stick. Capital investment refers to purchases of capital goods. As capital investment rises, the people that work with the capital become more productive.
7. Property rights refer to the range of laws, rules, and regulations that define rights for the use and transfer of resources.
8. Industrial policy is a government policy of those industries that are most likely to be successful in the global marketplace.
9. The critics argue that it is difficult, if not impossible, for government officials to figure out which industries are most likely to be successful in the global marketplace. They also argue that government is likely to respond and turn industrial policy into some form of political policy, where certain industries are assisted, not based on their merit, but on their political power.
10. labor and capital
11. It means that technology is part of the economic system as opposed to being outside the economic system. Since technology is endogenous, it follows that people can do certain things to promote it.
12. Ideas, specifically ideas on how to rearrange resources in valuable ways, are what cause economic growth.
13. It means that when we take what is given—the resources that exist—and rearrange them in different ways, we sometimes come up with a more valuable arrangement than existed before. This new, more valuable arrangement is critical to the process of economic growth.
14. Yes. Suppose economic growth occurs as a result of the LRAS curve shifting to the right. If AD does not change, then the price level will fall.

Problems

1.

If the annual growth rate in Real GDP is	then it will take _____ years for the economy to double in size.
3 percent	24
4 percent	18
5 percent	14.4

2. A movement from Point 1 to Point 2.

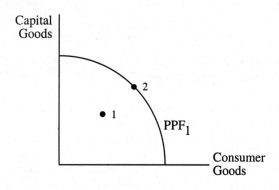

3. A movement from Point 1 on PPF₁ to Point 2 on PPF₂.

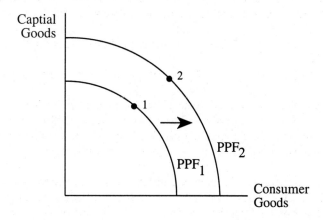

4. A movement from Point 1 to Point 2.

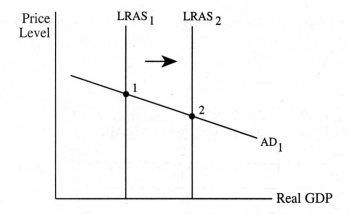

5. A movement from Point 1 to Point 2.

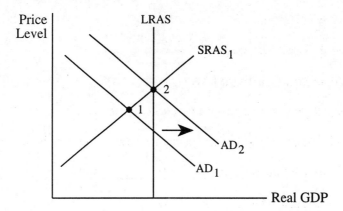

6. A movement from Point 1 to Point 2.

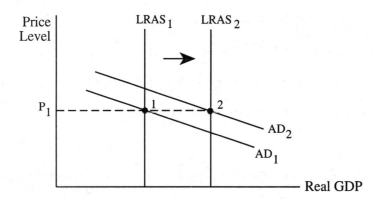

7. A movement from Point 1 to Point 2.

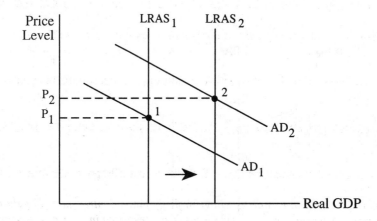

What is the Question?

1. Real GDP divided by population.

   How is per capita Real GDP computed?

2. This type of economic growth shifts the LRAS curve rightward.

   What is economic growth from an efficient level of production?

3. It makes it possible to obtain more output from the same amount of resources.

   What is an advancement in technology?

4. It emphasized both capital and labor.

   What resources did neoclassical growth theory emphasize?

5. According to this theory, technology is endogenous.

   What is new growth theory?

6. He asks us to think about technology the way we think about prospecting for gold.

   How does Paul Romer ask us to think about technology?

What Is Wrong?

1. Absolute real economic growth refers to an increase in per capita GDP from one period to the next.

   Absolute real economic growth refers to an increase in Real GDP from one period to the next.

2. Economic growth can occur from below, on, or beyond the production possibilities frontier.

   Economic growth can occur from below or on the production possibilities frontier—but not from beyond it.

3. Economic growth that occurs from an inefficient level of production shifts the LRAS curve to the right.

   Economic growth that occurs from an efficient level of production shifts the LRAS curve to the right.

4. Countries rich in natural resources will grow faster than countries poor in natural resources.

   Countries rich in natural resources will grow faster than countries poor in natural resources, ceteris paribus. *Alternatively, you could write: Countries rich in natural resources will not necessarily grow faster than countries poor in natural resources.*

5. According to neoclassical growth theory, technology is endogenous; according to new growth theory, technology is exogenous.

   According to neoclassical growth theory, technology is exogenous; according to new growth theory, technology is endogenous.

Multiple Choice

1. d
2. a
3. c
4. a
5. b
6. e
7. a
8. a
9. c
10. b
11. c
12. e
13. b
14. c
15. e

True-False

16. T
17. F
18. T
19. F
20. T

Fill in the Blank

21. rise
22. rise
23. Rule of 72
24. population
25. inefficient

Chapter 18
Answers

Review Questions

1. Price elasticity of demand is equal to the percentage change in quantity demanded divided by the percentage change in price. It is a measure of the responsiveness in quantity demanded to a change in price.
2. The more substitutes for a good, the higher the price elasticity of demand. The fewer substitutes for a good, the lower the price elasticity of demand.
3. No. The more substitutes for a good, the higher the price elasticity of demand, but still the elasticity coefficient can be less than 1 (which makes demand for the good inelastic).
4. The more time that has passed (since a change in price), the higher price elasticity of demand.
5. The larger one's budget that goes for the purchase of a good, the higher price elasticity of demand.
6. Cross elasticity of demand measures the responsiveness in quantity demanded of one good given a change in the price of another good.
7. It means that the percentage change in quantity demanded of a good is less than the percentage change in income. For example, if income rises by 10 percent and quantity demanded for good A rises by 5 percent, then good A is income inelastic.
8. It is a measure of the responsiveness in quantity supplied to a change in price.

Problems

1.

Price and quantity demanded at point A		Price and quantity demanded at point B		Price elasticity of demand is equal to	Is demand (elastic, unit elastic, or inelastic)?
$10	100	$8	140	1.5	elastic
$8	200	$15	120	0.82	inelastic
$7	40	$10	33	0.54	inelastic

2.

Price elasticity of demand is	Change	Price elasticity of demand (rises, falls, remains unchanged)
0.34	more substitutes for the good	rises
1.99	more time passes since change in price	rises
2.20	smaller percentage of one's budget spent on the good	falls

3.

Demand is	Price (rises, falls)	Total revenue (rises, falls, remains unchanged)
elastic	falls	rises
inelastic	rises	rises
unit elastic	rises	remains unchanged
inelastic	falls	falls
elastic	rises	falls

4.

Price of good X (rises, falls)	Quantity demanded of good Y (rises, falls)	Cross elasticity of demand is	The two goods, X and Y, are (substitutes, complements)
rises by 10 percent	falls by 5 percent	0.5	complements
falls by 20 percent	rises by 4 percent	5	substitutes
rises by 8 percent	rises by 5 percent	0.625	complements

5.

Income (rises, falls)	Quantity demanded (rises, falls)	Income elasticity of demand is
rises by 20 percent	rises by 10 percent	0.5
falls by 10 percent	falls by 15 percent	1.5
rises by 5 percent	rises by 20 percent	4.0

6.

Price (rises, falls)	Quantity supplied (rises, falls)	Is supply (elastic, inelastic, unit elastic)?
rises 3 percent	rises 4 percent	elastic
rises 1 percent	rises 6 percent	elastic
falls 20 percent	falls 10 percent	inelastic

7.

Initial equilibrium price and quantity		New equilibrium price and quantity (after $1 tax has been placed on supplier)		Percentage of the tax paid by the seller in terms of a higher price	Percentage of the tax paid by the seller in terms of a lower price kept
$40	100	$40.44	90	44 percent	56 percent
$9	87	$9.57	80	57 percent	43 percent
$10	200	$10.76	150	76 percent	24 percent

8. $1 tax (per unit of production) is placed on the seller. With D_1, price rises more than with D_2.

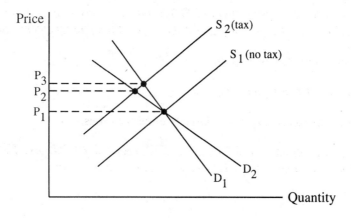

What Is the Question?

1. Measures the responsiveness of quantity demanded given a change in price.

   What is price elasticity of demand?

2. Price and total revenue are directly related.

   What is the relationship between price and total revenue if demand is inelastic?

3. Quantity demanded changes by 20 percent if price changes by 10 percent.

   What does price elasticity of demand equal to 2 mean?

4. There is no change in quantity demanded as price changes.

   What is the relationship between price and quantity demanded if demand is perfectly inelastic?

5. The number of substitutes, the percentage of one's budget spent on the good, and time (since the change in price).

   What are the three determinants of price elasticity of demand?

6. Price of one good rises and quantity demanded for another good rises.

   What does it mean if cross elasticity of demand is greater than zero and two goods are substitutes?

7. In either of these cases, the tax placed on the seller is fully paid by the buyer.

   What happens if demand is perfectly inelastic or supply is perfectly elastic?

What Is Wrong?

1. If price rises, and total revenue falls, then demand is inelastic.

   If price rises, and total revenue falls, then demand is elastic.

2. The elasticity coefficient is greater than 1 for a good that is income inelastic.

   The elasticity coefficient is greater than 1 for a good that is income elastic. Alternatively, you could write: The elasticity coefficient is less than 1 for a good that is income inelastic.

3. Cars have more substitutes than Ford cars.

   Cars have fewer substitutes than Ford cars.

4. As we move down a demand curve, price elasticity of demand rises.

   As we move down a demand curve, price elasticity of demand falls. Alternatively, you could write: As we move up a demand curve, price elasticity of demand rises.

5. For inelastic demand, quantity demanded changes proportionately more than price changes.

    For inelastic demand, quantity demanded changes proportionately less than price changes. Alternatively, you could write: For elastic demand, quantity demanded changes proportionately more than price changes.

6. A perfectly inelastic demand curve can be downward-sloping.

    A perfectly inelastic demand curve is vertical. Alternatively, you could write: An inelastic demand curve is downward-sloping.

7. The elasticity coefficient is greater than zero for goods that are complements.

    The elasticity coefficient is less than zero for goods that are complements. Alternatively, you could write: The elasticity coefficient is greater than zero for goods that are substitutes.

8. If demand is inelastic, buyers pay the full tax that is placed on sellers.

    If demand is perfectly inelastic, buyers pay the full tax that is placed on sellers.

9. If income elasticity of demand is 1.24, it means that for every 1 percent change in income there is a 1.24 percent change in price.

    If income elasticity of demand is 1.24, it means that for every 1 percent change in income there is a 1.24 percent change in quantity demanded.

10. Price elasticity of supply measures the responsiveness of quantity supplied to changes in income.

    Price elasticity of supply measures the responsiveness of quantity supplied to changes in price.

Multiple Choice
1. a
2. c
3. b
4. a
5. c
6. d
7. a
8. a
9. b
10. d
11. c
12. a
13. d
14. a
15. b

True-False
16. T
17. T
18. F
19. F
20. F

Fill in the Blank
21. elasticity coefficient, elastic
22. inelastic
23. increases
24. lower
25. elastic

Chapter 19
Answers

Review Questions

1. John eats the first apple and receives 10 utils of utility. He eats the second apple and receives 8 utils of utility. The total utility he receives from eating two apples is 18 utils. The marginal utility of the first apple is 10 utils; the marginal utility of the second apple is 8 utils.

2. Yvonne gets more utility from walking the first mile than the second mile and more utility from the second mile than the third mile.

3. If a person makes an interpersonal utility comparison, he states that one person receives more utility from doing X than another person receives from doing X. For example, John watches April and Rebecca, two young children, playing in the sandbox. John says that April gets more utility from playing in the sandbox than Rebecca. John is making an interpersonal utility comparison. How does John know how much utility each of the two children receive? The answer is, he doesn't.

4. Diamonds, which are not necessary for life, sell for a higher price than water, which is necessary for life. Water, which has more use value than diamonds, sells for less than diamonds.

5. Goods that have high total utility (a reflection of high use value) may have lower marginal utility than goods that have relatively low total utility. Price is a reflection of marginal utility, not total utility.

6. It says that a person receives more utility per unit of money (say, $1) buying A than B. When the consumer has not equated MU-P ratios, he will rearrange his purchases until he has equated MU-P ratios and is in consumer equilibrium.

7. They buy more of some goods and less of other goods until the MU-P ratio of all the goods they purchase is the same.

8. Price falls from $10 to $8 and, as a result, quantity demanded rises from 100 to 150. Because of the price fall, real income rises. Because of the higher real income, the person buys 20 more units of the good. It follows that 30 of the additional units of the good were purchased because relative price fell. This change in quantity demanded due to a change in relative price (and nothing else) is referred to as the substitution effect.

9. Price falls from $10 to $8 and, as a result, quantity demanded rises from 100 to 150. Because of the price fall, real income rises. Because of the higher real income, the person buys 20 more units of the good. It follows that 20 of the additional units of the good were purchased because price fell causing real income to rise. This change in quantity demanded due to a change in income (brought about by a change in price) is referred to as the income effect.

10. It is the additional cost of producing and selling an additional unit of a good.

11. The efficient amount of time to exercise is that amount of time at which the marginal benefits of exercise equal the marginal costs.

Problems

1.

Unit	Total utility (utils)	Marginal utility (utils)
1st	100	100
2nd	146	46
3rd	174	28

2. 3 units of X and 2 units of Y.

3.

Price falls by	Change in quantity demanded	Additional units consumer would buy due to higher real income	Additional units purchased due to the substitution effect
$2	133	60	73
$4	187	85	102
$3	222	125	97

4.

Units of good X	Total cost	Marginal cost
1	$40	$40
2	$89	$49
3	$149	$60

5.

Number of hours playing baseball	Total benefits (in utils)	Marginal benefits (in utils)
1	100	100
2	178	78
3	210	32

6.   Efficiency occurs when MB = MC. Here we have shown the MB and MC of exercising. The efficient amount of time to exercise is 50 minutes. Under 50 minutes, MB > MC; over 50 minutes, MC > MB.

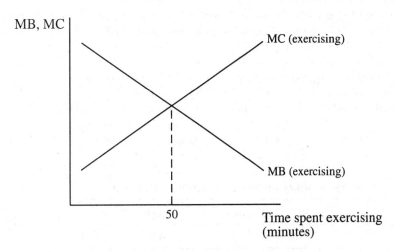

What Is the Question?

1.   The additional utility gained from consuming an additional unit of good X.

   What is marginal utility?

2.   Marginal utility turns negative.

   What happens to marginal utility when total utility declines.

3.   The consumer will buy more of good X and less of good Y.

     If $MU_X/P_X > MU_Y/P_Y$ what will the consumer do?

4.   That portion of the change in the quantity demanded of a good that is attributable to a change in its relative price.

     What is the substitution effect?

5.   The change in total cost divided by the change in quantity of output.

     What is marginal cost equal to?

6.   It slopes downward (left to right) because of the law of diminishing marginal utility.

     What is the shape of the marginal utility or marginal benefit curve?

7.   The point at which marginal benefits equal marginal costs.

     What is the efficient point?

What Is Wrong?

1.   If total utility is falling, then marginal utility is greater than zero.

     If total utility is falling, then marginal utility is negative.

2.   A millionaire gets less utility from an additional $100 than a poor person receives from an additional $100.

     We don't know if this is true or not. A millionaire may get less utility, more utility, or the same amount of utility from an additional $100 as a poor person receives.

3.   The income effect refers to that portion of the change in the quantity demanded of a good that is attributable to a change in its relative price.

     The substitution effect refers to that portion of the change in the quantity demanded of a good that is attributable to a change in its relative price. Alternatively, you could write, The income effect refers to that portion of the change in the quantity demanded of a good that is attributable to a change in real income (brought about by a change in price).

4.   If total cost rises, marginal cost must rise, too.

     Marginal cost doesn't have to rise as total cost rises. For example, if total cost is $100 for one unit of a good and $180 for two units of the good, marginal cost goes from $100 to $80. In other words, marginal cost is falling as total cost is rising.

5.   If total benefits rise, then marginal benefits must rise, too.

     Marginal benefits don't have to rise as total benefits rise. For example, if total benefit is 100 utils for one unit of a good and 180 utilis for two units of the good, marginal benefit goes from 100 to 80. In other words, marginal benefit is falling as total benefit is rising.

6. If the marginal utility-price ratio for good A is greater than the marginal utility-price ratio for good B, then a consumer will buy more of both good A and B.

> *If the marginal utility-price ratio for good A is greater than the marginal utility-price ratio for good B, then a consumer will buy more of good A. The person may reallocate dollars from the purchase of B to A.*

Multiple Choice
1. c
2. b
3. d
4. b
5. e
6. b
7. c
8. c
9. b
10. b
11. d
12. d
13. a
14. a
15. a

True-False
16. T
17. T
18. T
19. T
20. F

Fill in the Blank
21. diamond-water paradox
22. (consumer) equilibrium
23. income effect
24. marginal utility
25. higher (or greater)

Chapter 20
Answers

Review Questions

1. Firm X produces desks. Due to an increased demand for desks, the price of desks rises. Firm X responds to the higher price of desks by producing more desks.
2. The manager of a firm (that produces doors) tells the employees to paint the doors a different color than they have been painting the doors.
3. The sum of what individuals can produce as a team is greater than the sum of what the individuals can produce working alone.
4. The benefits and costs of shirking. This chapter focused on the costs of shirking and stated that the lower the costs of shirking (to the individual), the more likely the individual will shirk.
5. A person who takes the profits or incurs the losses of the firm.
6. Potential shirkers may be less likely to shirk if they are currently earning above-market wages. That's because there would be a cost to their shirking. Namely, if they are caught shirking, and lose their jobs, they then will be faced with earning market wages instead of above-market wages.
7. Outside the firm, supply and demand are determining prices, to which the firm responds. For example, as the price of the good the firm produces rises, the firm may decide to produce more units of the good. Inside the firm, employees are trading some of their independence for a monitor who will make sure they don't shirk. Why do the employees want to make sure they don't shirk? Because shirking reduces the benefits they expect to receive by joining the firm.
8. Satisficing behavior is directed at meeting some profit target. Maximizing profit is directed at obtaining the most profit possible.
9. Unlimited liability is a legal term that signifies that the personal assets of the owners of a firm may be used to settle the debts of the firm.
10. There are three disadvantages: (1) partners face unlimited liability; (2) decision making can be complex and frustrating; (3) withdrawal or death of a partner can end the partnership or cause its restructuring.
11. There are two disadvantages: (1) profit is taxed twice; (2) problems may arise due to separation of ownership from control.
12. A person who has unlimited liability can be sued by creditors for the debts incurred by the firm; a person who has limited liability cannot be.
13. Net worth is equal to assets minus liabilities.
14. The person who buys the bond is making a loan to the firm; the person who buys shares of stock is buying an ownership right in the firm. In short, the bond buyer is a lender, the stock buyer is an owner.
15. There are no residual claimants in a nonprofit firm. There are residual claimants in a business firm.

Problems

1.

Type of firm	Example
Proprietorship	hair salon
Partnership	advertising agency
Corporation	Dell Computer Corporation

2.

Advantages of proprietorships	Disadvantages of proprietorships
1. Easy to form and to dissolve.	1. Proprietor faces unlimited liability.
2. All decision-making power resides with the sole proprietor.	2. Limited ability to raise funds for business expansion.
3. Profit is taxed only once.	3. Usually ends with death of proprietor.

3.

Assets ($ millions)	Liabilities ($ millions)	Net worth ($ millions)
10	7	3
100	65	35
198	77	121

4.

Face value of bond	Coupon rate	Annual coupon payments
$10,000	5.0 percent	$500
$20,000	7.5 percent	$1,500
$10,000	6.5 percent	$650

What Is the Question?
Identify the question for each of the answers that follow.

1. These economists suggest that firms are formed when benefits can be obtained from individuals working as a team.

    Who are Alchian and Demsetz?

2. The process in which managers direct employees to perform certain tasks.

    What is managerial coordination?

3. This rises as the cost of shirking falls.

    What happens to the amount of shirking as the cost of shirking falls?

4. This is the person in a business firm who coordinates team production and reduces shirking.

    Who is the monitor?

5. Persons who share in the profits of a business firm.

    Who are residual claimants?

6. Richard Cyert, James March, and Herbert Simon.

    Who are the economists that argue that firms seek only to achieve some satisfactory target profit level?

7. This type of business firm generated the largest percentage of total business receipts.

    What is a corporation?

8. One advantage is that they are easy to form and to dissolve.

    What is one advantage of a sole proprietorship?

9. One disadvantage is that profits are taxed twice.

    What is one disadvantage of a corporation?

10. It is also known as equity.

    What is net worth also known as?

11. Assets minus liabilities.

    What is net worth equal to?

What Is Wrong?

1. Alchian and Demsetz argue that firms are formed when there are benefits to forming firms.

    Not exactly. There may be benefits to forming a firm, but that is not enough. Alchian and Demsetz argue that firms are formed (by individuals) when the sum of what individuals can produce in a firm is greater than the sum of what individuals can produce working alone.

2. Five people form a firm and decide to equally split the proceeds of what they produce and sell. The individual costs of shirking are lower in this setting than in a setting where ten people form a firm and decide to equally split the proceeds of what they produce and sell.

    For a given level of profit, the individual costs of shirking are higher in this setting than in a setting where ten people form a firm and decide to equally split the proceeds of what they produce and sell.

3. Economists who advance the efficiency wage theory argue that paying employees above-market wage rates will cause them to shirk more than if they were simply paid market wage rates.

    Economists who advance the efficiency wage theory argue that paying employees above-market wage rates will cause them to shirk less than if they were simply paid market wage rates.

4. Partnerships are the most common form of business organization in the United States.

    Proprietorships are the most common form of business organization in the United States.

5. Assets plus liabilities equal net worth.

    Assets minus liabilities equal net worth.

6. Total liabilities plus net worth equal accounts payable.

    Total liabilities plus net worth equal assets.

7. When a person buys a share of stock issued by a firm, the person effectively grants a loan to the firm.

   When a person buys a share of stock issued by a firm, the person becomes an owner of the firm. Alternatively, you could write: When a person buys a bond issued by a firm, the person effectively grants a loan to the firm.

8. There are fewer residual claimants in a business firm than in a nonprofit firm.

   There are no residual claimants in a nonprofit firm.

9. In private and public nonprofit firms, taxpayers pay the costs of the firm.

   In public nonprofit firms, taxpayers pay the costs of the firm. In private nonprofit firms, private citizens pay the costs.

Multiple Choice
1. c
2. d
3. b
4. c
5. b
6. b
7. c
8. c
9. c
10. e
11. e
12. a
13. a
14. d
15. a

True-False
16. T
17. T
18. T
19. T
20. T

Fill in the Blank
21. Unlimited liability
22. corporation
23. residual claimants
24. limited partnership
25. Limited liability

Chapter 21
Answers

Review Questions

1. A producer of a good pays $100 to buy some inputs necessary to produce the good.
2. An accountant who works for a firm, and earns $70,000 a year, quits her job to start her own accounting business. The forfeited $70,000 salary is an implicit cost of her new accounting business.
3. Economic profit is smaller than accounting profit because when calculating economic profit both explicit and implicit costs are subtracted from total revenue. When calculating accounting profit only explicit costs are subtracted from total revenue.
4. It is covering all its opportunity costs; stated differently, it is covering both its explicit costs and implicit costs.
5. Examples will vary here. Your example should be consistent with the definition of sunk cost. A sunk cost is a cost incurred in the past, that cannot be undone, and cannot be recovered.
6. James buys a pair of shoes that cannot be resold or returned to the store from which he purchased the shoes. The shoes are a sunk cost. The shoes hurt his feet but he decides to wear them anyway because he wants to get his money's worth out of the shoes. Really, he wants to recover the cost of the shoes somehow. He is trying to undo a sunk cost. He is worse off doing this than simply ignoring the sunk cost and choosing not to wear the shoes. When he wears the shoes, he increases the probability that he will have problems with his feet and have to visit a podiatrist. If he doesn't wear the shoes, he doesn't have this problem. He has lost the money he spent to buy the shoes in either case, so why not lose the money and have comfortable feet than lose the money and have uncomfortable feet.
7. The factory a producer rents.
8. The labor a producer hires.
9. Average total cost is total cost divided by output. Marginal cost is the change in total cost divided by the change in output. Marginal cost considers all "changes," average total cost does not.
10. With the addition of the sixth unit of a variable input, output rises from 100 to 120 units. With the addition of the seventh unit of a variable input, output rises from 120 to 135. The marginal physical product falls from 20 to 15. To see a more extensive example, see Exhibit 4 in the text chapter.
11. As diminishing marginal returns set in (and marginal physical product is declining), marginal cost begins to rise.
12. Marginal productivity is the change in output divided by the change in the variable input. Average productivity is output divided by the number of units of the variable input used to produce the output.
13. As diminishing marginal returns set in, marginal cost rises. At some point as marginal cost rises, it will rise above average total cost. When this happens, average total cost will rise.
14. The temperature in San Diego has been 70 degrees each day for the seven days. The average temperature for the week is 70 degrees. Then, the temperature falls to 60 degrees one day. Since the temperature on the additional day (the marginal day) is less than the average temperature, the average temperature will fall. The new average for the last seven days is 68 degrees.
15. It is a curve that shows the lowest unit cost at which the firm can produce any given level of output.
16. It means that its output increases by a greater percentage than the increase in its inputs, causing unit costs to fall.
17. A tax may affect fixed costs but not variable costs. Also, a tax may affect variable costs but not fixed costs. To illustrate, suppose a firm has to pay a lump-sum tax, no matter how much it produces. This tax will raise the firm's fixed costs. If a firm has to pay a tax per unit of output it produces, then this tax affects its variable costs.
18. The AFC curve continually declines (over output) because AFC = TFC/Q. TFC is constant, so that as Q rises, AFC must decline. The more Q rises, the smaller AFC becomes.

Problems
1. Fill in the blanks in the table.

Explicit costs	Implicit costs	Total revenue	Economic profit	Accounting profit
$40,000	$40,000	$100,000	$20,000	$60,000
$150,000	$30,000	$230,000	$50,000	$80,000
$30,000	$40,000	$300,000	$230,000	$270,000

2. Fill in the blank spaces in the table.

Variable cost	Fixed cost	Units of output produced	Average variable cost	Average fixed cost
$500	$1,000	100	$5.00	$10.00
$400	$500	200	$2.00	$2.50
$1,000	$200	400	$2.50	$0.50

3. Fill in the blank spaces in the table.

Variable cost	Fixed cost	Units of output produced	Average total cost
$500	$200	100	$7.00
$300	$400	50	$14.00
$400	$1,000	75	$18.67

4. Fill in the blank spaces in the table.

Average total cost is	Marginal cost is	Average total cost is (rising, fall, remaining unchanged)
$40	$45	rising
$30	$20	falling
$20	$37	rising

5. Fill in the blank spaces in the table.

Variable input (units)	Fixed input (units)	Quantity of output	Marginal physical product of variable input
0	1	0	0
1	1	20	20
2	1	45	25

6. Fill in the blank spaces in the table.

Marginal physical product (units)	Variable cost	Marginal cost
20	$400	$20
18	$360	$20
33	$660	$20

7. TFC does not change as output changes (rises or falls).

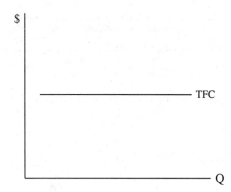

8. AFC is TFC/Q. TFC does not change as Q rises, so AFC must continually decline.

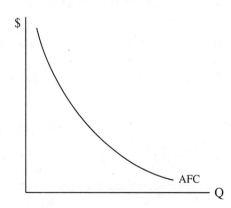

9. The MC curve must cut the ATC curve at its low point.

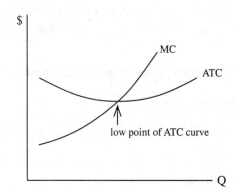

10. When the firm experiences increasing marginal returns, MC is falling; when it experiences constant marginal returns, MC is stable and neither rising nor falling; and when it experiences diminishing marginal returns, MC is rising.

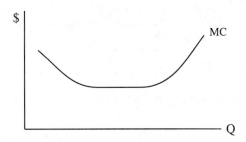

What Is the Question?

1. A cost that is incurred when an actual monetary payment is made.

    What is an explicit cost?

2. It is a cost that cannot be recovered.

    What is a sunk cost?

3. When marginal physical product is rising, this cost is declining.

    What is marginal cost?

4. These costs do not vary with output.

    What are fixed costs?

5. Total cost divided by output.

    What is average total cost or unit cost?

6. When this cost is above average total cost, average total cost is rising.

    What is marginal cost?

7. As output increases, the difference between average variable cost and this cost becomes smaller.

    What is average total cost?

8. The lowest output level at which average total costs are minimized.

    What is the minimum efficient scale?

9. This exists when inputs are increased by some percentage and output increases by a smaller percentage, causing unit costs to rise.

    What are diseconomies of scale?

What Is Wrong?

1. Economic profit is the difference between total revenue and explicit costs.

    Economic profit is the difference between total revenue and the sum of explicit and implicit costs. Alternatively, you could write: Accounting profit is the difference between total revenue and explicit costs.

2. When a firm earns zero economic profit it has not covered its total opportunity costs.

    When a firm earns zero economic profit it has covered its total opportunity costs. Alternatively, you could write: When a firm earns less than zero economic profit it has not covered its total opportunity costs.

3. The difference between the ATC curve and the AVC curve gets larger as output rises.

    The difference between the ATC and the AVC curves gets smaller as output rises.

4. Marginal physical product is equal to output divided by units of the variable input.

    Marginal physical product is equal to the change in output divided by a change in the units of the variable input. Alternatively, you could write: Average physical product is equal to output divided by units of the variable input.

5. When marginal physical product falls, marginal cost falls, too.

    When marginal physical product falls, marginal cost rises. Alternatively, you could write: When marginal physical product rises, marginal cost falls.

6.

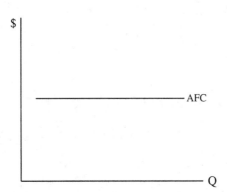

AFC curve is not supposed to be horizontal. It declines as output rises.

7.

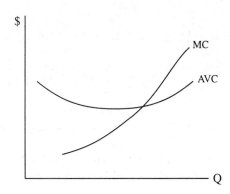

MC cuts AVC at wrong point. MC is supposed to cut AVC at the low point of AVC.

8.

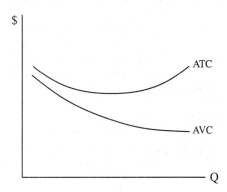

AVC is supposed to be closer to ATC as output rises.

9.

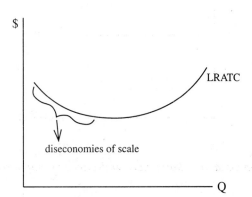

Diseconomies of scale is misrepresented. The area shown represents what happens to LRATC if economies of scale exist, not diseconomies of scale.

Multiple Choice

1. c
2. d
3. b
4. c
5. c
6. d
7. d
8. a
9. a
10. a
11. b
12. c
13. a
14. a
15. c

True-False

16. F
17. T
18. T
19. F
20. F

Fill in the Blank

21. long-run average total cost (LRATC)
22. minimum efficient scale
23. rise; diseconomies of scale
24. falls
25. marginal physical product

Chapter 22
Answers

Review Questions

1. There are many sellers and many buyers, none of which are large in relation to total sales or purchases. Each firm produces and sells a homogeneous product. Buyers and sellers have all relevant information about prices, product quality, sources of supply, and so forth. Firms have easy entry and exit.
2. It means that the seller does not have the ability to control the price of the product it sells; it takes (or sells its good at) the price determined in the market.
3. Plotting price against quantity derives a demand curve. Plotting marginal revenue against quantity derives a marginal revenue curve. Since, for a perfectly competitive firm, price equals marginal revenue, the two curves are the same.
4. To be resource-allocative efficient, price equals marginal cost at the quantity of output the firm produces. A firm will try to maximize profits by producing the quantity of output at which MR = MC. Since, for a perfectly competitive firm, MR = P, it follows that when a firm maximizes profit, it also meets the resource-allocative condition, P = MC.
5. Suppose MR declines and MC rises. Also suppose that the quantity at which MR = MC is 120 units. It follows then that for any quantity less than 120, MR > MC. Why then stop producing where the biggest difference between MR and MC appears? To do this would be to ignore the net benefit derived anytime MR is greater than MC. Take a look at Exhibit 3 in your text chapter. If the firm stops producing at 50 units, where the largest difference between MR and MC appears, it forfeits all net benefits derived by producing the next 75 units of the good.
6. It considers how much it loses if it shuts down and compares this to how much it loses (or earns) if it doesn't shut down. Essentially, this means it compares the price at which it sells the good to its average variable cost. If price is greater than average variable cost, it continues to produce in the short run. If price is less than average variable cost, it shuts down in the short run.
7. No. The firm earns profit only if, at the quantity of output at which MR = MC, price is greater than average total cost.
8. The firm will not produce if price is below AVC, so that portion of the MC curve that is below the AVC curve is not relevant to production.
9. The market supply curve is the horizontal summation of the individual firms' supply curves. For example, if there are two firms in the industry, A and B, and Firm A supplies 10 units at a $10 price, and Firm B supplies 20 units at a $10 price, then one point on the market supply curve represents $10 and 30 units.
10. The market supply curve is upward sloping. This is because the individual firms' supply curve is upward sloping. The firm's supply curve is upward sloping because its supply curve is that portion of its MC curve above its AVC curve, and this portion of its MC curve is upward sloping. But why do MC curves slope up at all? In the last chapter we learned that MC rises when marginal physical product declines (or, in other words, when diminishing marginal returns set in).
11. Here are the three conditions: P = MC, P = SRATC, and LRATC = SRATC.
12. If price is above short-run average total cost, the firm is earning positive economic profits and there is an inconsistency with one of the long-run equilibrium conditions (specifically, P = SRATC).
13. If SRATC is greater than LRATC, then the firm is not producing its output at the lowest possible cost, which is one of the conditions of long-run equilibrium (specifically SRATC = LRATC).
14. A constant-cost industry is one in which average total costs do not change as industry output increases or decreases, and when firms enter or exit the industry, respectively.
15. The firms in the market will increase output and new firms will enter the market. In time, price will fall and the profits will be no longer. In the long run, there will be only normal profits (zero economic profit) in the market.

16. No, because it sells a homogeneous good and to advertise its product is to advertise its competitors' products, too. While a firm may not advertise, the industry may advertise. The industry advertises in the hopes of increasing the market demand for the goods that the sellers produce and sell.

17. It means that the firm is not producing its output at the lowest per unit costs possible.

Problems

1.

Price	Quantity	Total revenue	Marginal revenue
$10	1	$10	$10
$10	2	$20	$10
$10	3	$30	$10

2.

Price	Quantity	Total revenue
$40	100	$4,000
$40	50	$2,000
$40	80	$3,200

3.

Price	Quantity	Marginal revenue
$15	1	$15
$15	2	$15
$15	3	$15

4.

Price	Quantity	Average variable cost	Average total cost	Total variable cost	Will the firm (continue to produce, shut down)
$10	100	$7	$9	$700	continue to produce
$15	50	$13	$16	$650	continue to produce
$23	1,000	$24	$26	$2,400	shut down

5.

Price	Quantity	Average variable cost	Average total cost	Average fixed cost	Total cost
$10	100	$4	$6	$2	$600
$40	2,000	$45	$46	$1	$92,000
$25	198	$21	$23	$2	$4,554

6.

Price	Marginal cost	ATC	Is the perfectly competitive firm earning profits? (yes, no)	Is the perfectly competitive firm in long-run equilibrium? (yes, no)
$40	$40	$30	yes	no
$30	$30	$35	no	no
$25	$25	$23	yes	no

7.

Price	Quantity	ATC	AVC	Profit (+) or Loss (−)
$33	1,234	$31	$30	+ $2,468
$55	2,436	$25	$20	+ $73,080
$100	1,000	$110	$99	− $10,000

What Is the Question?

1. A seller that does not have the ability to control the price of the product it sells.

    What is a price taker?

2. The firm sells its good at market equilibrium price.

    At what (per unit) price does the perfectly competitive firm sell its good?

3. When price is below average variable cost.

    When does the firm shut down in the short run?

4. That portion of its MC curve above its AVC curve.

    What portion of the firm's MC curve is its supply curve?

5. The horizontal summation of the individual firms' supply curves.

    What is the market supply curve equal to?

6. There is no incentive for firms to enter or exit the industry, there is no incentive for firms to produce more or less output, and there is no incentive for firms to change plant size.

    What are the conditions that specify long-run competitive equilibrium?

7. P = SRATC, P = MC, and SRATC = LRATC.

    What are the conditions that specify long-run competitive equilibrium?

8. The long-run supply curve is upward sloping.

    What does the long-run supply curve look like for an increasing-cost industry?

9. The long-run supply curve is downward-sloping.

    What does the long-run supply curve look like for a decreasing-cost industry?

10. P = MC.

   What condition specifies resource allocative efficiency?

11. The firm produces its output at the lowest possible per unit cost.

   If a firm is productive efficient, what condition holds?

What Is Wrong?

1. Firms in a perfectly competitive market have easy entry into the market and costly exit from the market.

   Firms in a perfectly competitive market have easy entry into the market and easy exit from the market.

2. In long-run competitive equilibrium, the average or representative firm may earn positive economic profit.

   In long-run competitive equilibrium, the average or representative firm earns zero economic profit (or normal profit).

3. Price is greater than marginal revenue for a perfectly competitive firm.

   Price is equal to marginal revenue for a perfectly competitive firm.

4. A perfectly competitive firm will shut down in the short run if its price is below average total cost.

   A perfectly competitive firm will shut down in the short run if its price is below average total cost. Alternatively, you could write: A perfectly competitive firm will not necessarily shut down if its price is below average total cost.

5. If a firm produces the quantity of output at which MR = MC, it is guaranteed to earn profits.

   If a firm produces the quantity of output at which MR = MC, it is not guaranteed to earn profits. It only earns profits if price is greater than average total cost.

6. The market supply curve is the vertical summation of the individual firms' supply curves.

   The market supply curve is the horizontal summation of the individual firms' supply curves.

7. If SRATC = LRATC for a firm, there is no incentive for the firm to enter or exit the industry.

   If SRATC = LRATC for a firm, there is no incentive for a firm to change plant size. Alternatively, you could write: If P = SRATC, there is no incentive for the firm to enter or exit the industry.

8. The long-run supply curve is downward-sloping for an increasing-cost industry.

   The long-run supply curve is downward-sloping for a decreasing-cost industry. Alternatively, you could write: The long-run supply curve is upward-sloping for an increasing-cost industry.

9. When average fixed cost is positive, average total cost is usually, but not always, greater than average variable cost.

   When average fixed cost is positive, average total cost is always greater than average variable cost.

10. A firm that produces its output at the lowest possible per-unit cost is said to exhibit resource-allocative efficiency.

> *A firm that produces its output at the lowest possible per-unit cost is said to exhibit productive efficiency.*

Multiple Choice
1. d
2. a
3. a
4. e
5. e
6. d
7. a
8. d
9. c
10. d
11. d
12. a
13. b
14. c
15. a

True-False
16. F
17. F
18. F
19. T
20. T

Fill in the Blank
21. resource allocative efficiency
22. zero
23. MR = MC
24. short-run supply
25. more

Chapter 23
Answers

Review Questions

1. There is one seller; the single seller sells a product for which there are no close substitutes; there are extremely high barriers to entry.
2. A natural monopoly is a firm for which economies of scale are so pronounced that it will end up being the only firm that will survive in the industry.
3. A price searcher is a seller that can, to some degree, control the price of the product it sells. A monopolist fits this description. A monopoly can sell different quantities at different prices. It can raise price and still sell some of its output; it can lower price and sell more of its output. Contrast this with a perfectly competitive firm (which is a price taker). If the perfectly competitive firm raises price above market equilibrium, it sells nothing.
4. It produces the quantity of output at which MR = MC.
5. Look at Exhibit 6 in your text chapter. The perfectly competitive seller produces and sells the quantity at which the demand curve intersects the marginal cost curve, or Q_{PC}. The monopoly seller produces and sells the quantity at which the marginal revenue curve intersects the marginal cost curve, or Q_M. The perfectly competitive seller charges P_{PC} and the monopoly seller charges P_M.
6. It is rational for the individual to seek monopoly rents if the expected benefits of the rents are greater than the costs of obtaining the rents. However, from society's perspective, resources are wasted because resources that could be used to produce goods and services are instead used to bring about transfers.
7. Perfect price discrimination occurs when the seller charges the highest price each consumer would be willing to pay for the product rather than go without. Second-degree price discrimination occurs when the seller charges a uniform price per unit for one specific quantity, a lower price for an additional quantity, and so on. Third-degree price discrimination occurs when the seller charges different prices in different markets or charges a different price to different segments of the buying population.
8. The seller must exercise some control over price (it must be a price searcher); the seller must be able to distinguish among buyers who would be willing to pay different prices; it must be impossible or too costly for one buyer to resell the good to other buyers.
9. Yes. A perfectly price-discriminating monopolist charges the highest price for each unit of the good it sells. This means its price is always equal to marginal revenue. In short, its demand curve and marginal revenue curve are the same (as is the case for the perfectly competitive firm, which is resource-allocative efficient). The perfectly price-discriminating monopolist will produce the quantity of output at which MR = MC, and since P = MR, then P = MC. P = MC is the condition that must be satisfied before a seller is resource-allocative efficient.

Problems

1.

Price	Quantity	Total revenue	Marginal revenue
$10	1	$10	$10
$9	2	$18	$8
$8	3	$24	$6

2. Consumers' surplus under perfect competition = P_1AB
   Consumers' surplus under monopoly = P_2AC

3. The triangle is CBD.

4. It produces the quantity at which MR = MC (which is Q_1 in the exhibit) and charges the highest (per unit) price consistent with this quantity (which is P_1 in the exhibit).

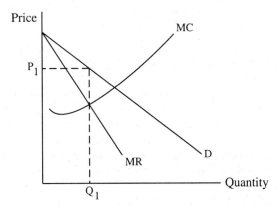

5.

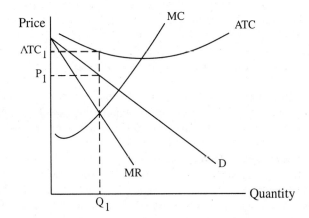

What Is the Question?

1. A right granted to a firm by government that permits the firm to provide a particular good or service and excludes all others from doing the same.

    What is a public franchise?

2. An exclusive right to sell something.

    What was the original meaning of the word monopoly?

3. Price is greater than marginal revenue.

    What is the relationship between price and marginal revenue for the monopolist?

4. Actions of individuals and groups who spend resources to influence public policy in the hope of redistributing (transferring) income to themselves from others.

    What is rent seeking?

5.   This occurs when the seller charges a uniform price per unit for one specific quantity, a lower price for an additional quantity, and so on.

   What is second-degree price discrimination?

6.   The increase in costs and organizational slack in a monopoly resulting from the lack of competitive pressure to push costs down to their lowest possible level.

   What is X-inefficiency?

7.   Total revenue is greater if the monopolist can do this.

   What happens to total revenue for the monopolist if it can go from being a single-price monopolist to a price-discriminating monopolist?

8.   If it does this, the monopolist will be resource-allocative efficient.

   What will happen if a single-price monopolist becomes a perfectly price-discriminating monopolist?

What Is Wrong?

1.   The single-price monopolist exhibits resource-allocative efficiency.

   The single-price monopolist does not exhibit resource-allocative efficiency. Alternatively, you could write: The perfectly price-discriminating monopolist exhibits resource-allocative efficiency. Or, from the last chapter: The perfectly competitive firm exhibits resource-allocative efficiency.

2.   One of the assumptions in theory of monopoly is that the single seller sells a product for which there are no perfect substitutes.

   One of the assumptions in theory of monopoly is that the single seller sells a product for which there are no close substitutes.

3.   For the monopolist, price is equal to marginal revenue.

   For the monopolist, price is greater than marginal revenue.

4.   If fixed costs exist, then a firm that maximizes revenue automatically maximizes profit, too.

   If fixed costs exist, then a firm that maximizes revenue does not automatically maximize profit.

5.   The monopoly seller produces the quantity of output at which MR = P and charges the highest price per unit for this quantity.

   The monopoly seller produces the quantity of output at which MC = MR and charges the highest price per unit for this quantity.

6.   A monopoly seller cannot incur losses, since it is the single seller of a good.

   A monopoly seller can incur losses; it will incur losses if the highest price at which it can sell its output is less than its ATC.

7. Perfect price discrimination occurs when the seller charges a uniform price per unit for one specific quantity, a lower price for an additional quantity, and so on.

    Second-degree price discrimination occurs when the seller charges a uniform price per unit for one specific quantity, a lower price for an additional quantity, and so on. Alternatively, you could write: Perfect price discrimination occurs when the seller charges the highest price each consumer would be willing to pay for the product rather than go without it.

8. A monopoly seller can charge any price it wants for the good it produces and sells.

    A monopoly seller cannot charge any price it wants for the good it produces and sells; it is limited by the height of the demand curve it faces.

Multiple Choice
1. c
2. b
3. c
4. d
5. d
6. e
7. c
8. d
9. a
10. a
11. e
12. a
13. c
14. d
15. d

True-False
16. F
17. T
18. F
19. T
20. F

Fill in the Blank
21. Natural monopoly
22. Price searcher
23. arbitrage
24. X-inefficiency
25. Gordon Tullock

Chapter 24
Answers

Review Questions
1. There are many buyers and sellers, each firm produces and sells a slightly differentiated product, there is easy entry and exit.
2. A perfectly competitive firm and a monopolistic competitive firm face many rivals.
3. A monopolistic competitive firm and a monopoly firm face a downward-sloping demand curve and each is a price searcher.
4. The quantity at which MR = MC.
5. No. To be resource-allocative efficient, a firm must produce the quantity of output at which P = MC. For the quantity of output the monopolistic competitive firm faces, P > MC.
6. Essentially because it faces a downward-sloping demand curve.
7. There are few sellers and many buyers, firms produce and sell either homogeneous or differentiated products, there are significant barriers to entry.
8. The percentage of industry sales accounted for by the four largest firms.
9. The essence is that individually rational behavior leads to an outcome that is less-than-best for all parties concerned.
10. To act as if there is only one seller so that monopoly profits can be captured.
11. If a firm cheats, and other firms do not cheat, it earns higher profits.
12. There is easy entry into the market and costless exit from the market, new firms entering the market can produce the product at the same cost as current firms, firms exiting the market can easily dispose of their fixed assets by selling them elsewhere.

Problems
1.

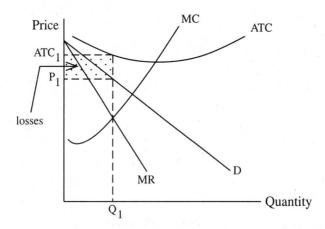

2.

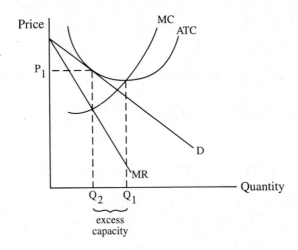

3. P_1CDB; P_1EFA
4. The top four firms in the industry have 12 percent, 10 percent, 8 percent, and 3 percent of industry sales, respectively. The four-firm concentration ratio is 33 percent.
5. The problem of forming the cartel, the problem of formulating policy, the problem of entry into the industry, and the problem of cheating.

What Is the Question?

1. States that a monopolistic competitor in equilibrium produces an output smaller than the one that would minimize its costs of production.

    What does the excess capacity theorem state?

2. It does not produce at the lowest point on its ATC curve because the demand curve it faces is downward-sloping.

    Why doesn't a monopolistic competitive firm produce at the lowest point on its ATC curve?

3. There are significant barriers to entry in this market structure.

    What is oligopoly?

4. Individually rational behavior leads to a jointly inefficient outcome.

    What is a prisoner's dilemma (game)?

5. The key behavioral assumption is that oligopolists in an industry act as if there is only one firm in the industry.

    What is the key behavioral assumption of cartel theory?

6. This is a way out of the prisoner's dilemma for two firms trying to form a cartel.

    What role does the enforcer play in a prisoner's dilemma (game)?

7. If a single firm lowers price, other firms will do likewise, but if a single firm raises price, other firms will not follow suit.

   What is the key behavioral assumption of the kinked demand curve theory?

8. The theory fails to explain how the original price comes about.

   What is a criticism of the kinked demand curve theory?

9. One firm determines price and the all other firms take this price as given.

   What is the key behavioral assumption of the price leadership theory?

10. There is easy entry into the market and costless exit from the market, new firms entering the market can produce the product at the same cost as current firms, and firms exiting the market can easily dispose of their fixed assets by selling them elsewhere.

   What are the conditions that characterize a contestable market?

What Is Wrong?

1. The monopolistic competitor is a price taker and the oligopolist is a price taker.

   Both the monopolistic competitor and the oligopolist are price searchers.

2. For the monopolistic competitor, price lies below marginal revenue.

   For the monopolistic competitor, price lies above marginal revenue.

3. When profits are normal, the monopolistic competitor exhibits resource-allocative efficiency.

   It doesn't matter whether profits are normal are not, the monopolistic competitor does not exhibit resource-allocative efficiency.

4. The cartel theory assumes that firms in an oligopolistic industry act in a manner consistent with there being only a few firms in the industry.

   The cartel theory assumes that firms in an oligopolistic industry act in a manner consistent with there being only one firm in the industry.

5. The kinked demand curve theory assumes that if a single firm raises price, other firms will do likewise, but if a single firm lowers price, other firms will not follow.

   The kinked demand curve theory assumes that if a single firm raises price, other firms will not follow, but if a single firm lowers price, other firms will do likewise.

6. The price leadership theory assumes that the dominant firm in the industry determines price and all other firms sell below this price.

   The price leadership theory assumes that the dominant firm in the industry determines price and all other firms will sell at this price.

7. Both monopolistic competitive firms and oligopolistic firms produce the quantity of output at which price equals marginal revenue.

   Both monopolistic competitive firms and oligopolistic firms produce the quantity of output at which marginal cost equals marginal revenue.

8. A contestable market is one in which there is easy entry into the market and costless exit from the market, new firms entering the market can produce the product at the same costs as current firms, and firms exiting the market only have to suffer the loses of their fixed assets.

   A contestable market is one in which there is easy entry into the market and costless exit from the market, new firms entering the market can produce the product at the same costs as current firms, and firms exiting the market can easily dispose of their fixed assets (less depreciation).

Multiple Choice
1. d
2. a
3. d
4. a
5. c
6. b
7. b
8. c
9. c
10. d
11. b
12. b
13. b
14. a
15. b

True-False
16. F
17. T
18. T
19. T
20. F

Fill in the Blank
21. George Stigler
22. cartel
23. cheat
24. excess capacity theorem
25. hit-and-run

Chapter 25
Answers

Review Questions
1. Selling to a retailer on the condition that the retailer will not carry any rival products.
2. The more broadly the market is defined, the more substitutes that exist for the good that a firm produces, and the less likely the antitrust authorities will identify the firm as a monopolist.
3. Suppose there are four firms in an industry and each firm has 25 percent of the market. The Herfindahl index is the sum of each firm's market share squared, or $25^2 + 25^2 + 25^2 + 25^2$.
4. A vertical merger is between two firms in the same industry, but at different stages of production. For example, a car manufacturer could merge with a tire manufacturer. A horizontal merger is between two firms in the same industry that sell the same good. For example, two companies that sell office-supply products could merge.
5. price discrimination
6. The higher switching costs are, the greater the permanency of the network monopoly.
7. The complaint charged that Microsoft possessed monopoly power in the market for personal computing operating systems and was using that monopoly power to gain dominance in the Internet browser market.
8. An agency initially regulates an industry but, in time, the industry ends up controlling the agency.
9. If a firm is guaranteed a profit rate, then it has no incentive to keep its costs down.
10. Economists believe that there are both costs and benefits to regulation and that regulation, should only be undertaken if the benefits are greater than the costs.

Problems

1.

Provision of the antitrust act	Name of the Act
Every person who shall monopolize, or attempt to monopolize, or combine or conspire with any other person or persons to monopolize any part of the trade or commerce...shall be guilty of a misdemeanor.	Sherman Act
Prohibits suppliers from offering special discounts to large chain stores unless they also offer the discounts to everyone else.	Robinson-Patman Act
Empowers the Federal Trade Commission to deal with false and deceptive acts or practices.	Wheeler-Lea Act
Declares illegal unfair methods of competition in commerce.	Federal Trade Commission Act
Declares illegal exclusive dealing and tying contracts.	Clayton Act

2.

Number of firms in the industry	Market shares of the firms, in order from top to bottom	Herfindahl index
6	20, 20, 20, 20, 10, 10	1,800
10	20, 10, 10, 10, 10, 10, 10, 10, 5, 5	1,150
10	10, 10, 10, 10, 10, 10, 10, 10, 10, 10	1,000

3.

Proposed merger	What type of merger? (horizontal, vertical, conglomerate)
Between two firms, each of which produces and sells tires.	horizontal
Between two firms, one of which produces and sells houses and the other which produces and sells wood.	vertical
Between two firms, one of which produces and sells books and one of which produces and sells bottled water.	conglomerate

4. P_1
5. P_2
6. If the firm charges P_1 it will incur losses. Losses are identified.

What Is the Question?

1. This antitrust act made interlocking directorates illegal.

    What is the Clayton Act?

2. One advantage is that it provides information about the dispersion of firm size in an industry.

    What is one advantage of the Herfindahl index over the four- or eight-firm concentration ratio?

3. This is descriptive of the situation where a particular product or technology becomes settled upon as the standard and is difficult or impossible to dislodge as the standard.

    What is the lock-in effect?

4. This is the time period between when a natural monopoly's costs change and when the regulatory agency adjusts prices of the natural monopoly.

    What is regulatory lag?

5. Holds that regulators are seeking to do, and will do through regulation, what is in their best interest.

    What is the essence of the public choice theory of regulation?

6. One criticism is that it does not explain which specific acts constitute "restraint of trade."

    What is one criticism of the Sherman Act?

7. This theory holds that regulators are seeking to do, and will do through regulation, what is in the best interest of the public or society at larger.

    What is the public interest theory of regulation?

What Is Wrong?

1. The size of the market is irrelevant to whether a firm is a monopolist or not.

    No, the size of the market matters. The more broadly the market is defined (and therefore the larger the market is), the less likely a firm will be considered a monopolist.

2. A conglomerate merger is a merger between companies in the same market.

A horizontal merger is a merger between companies in the same market. Alternatively, you could write: A conglomerate merger is a merger between companies in different markets (or industries).

3.   For a network good, its value increases as the expected number of units bought decreases.

For a network good, its value increases as the expected number of units sold increases.

4.   The lock-in effect reduces switching costs.

The lock-in effect increases switching costs.

5.   The more broadly a market is defined, the more likely a firm will be considered a monopolist.

The more broadly a market is defined, the less likely a firm will be considered a monopolist.

6.   George Stigler and Claire Friedland studied both unregulated and regulated electric utilities and found a small difference in the rates charged by them.

George Stigler and Claire Friedland studied both unregulated and regulated electric utilities and found no difference in the rates charged by them.

7.   The federal government looks more closely at proposed vertical mergers than horizontal mergers.

The federal government looks more closely at proposed horizontal mergers than vertical mergers.

8.   A profit-maximizing natural monopoly will produce the quantity of output at which MR = MC and charge the price that equals its ATC.

A profit-maximizing natural monopoly will produce the quantity of output at which MR = MC and charge the highest (per unit) price possible.

9.   The capture theory of regulation holds that no matter what the motive for the initial regulation and the establishment of the regulatory agency, eventually the bureaucrats that run the agency will control the industry.

The capture theory of regulation holds that no matter what the motive for the initial regulation and the establishment of the regulatory agency, eventually the regulated industry will control the regulators.

Multiple Choice
1.   a
2.   b
3.   b
4.   d
5.   a
6.   c
7.   b
8.   d
9.   d
10. d
11. b
12. a
13. b
14. a
15. d

True-False

16. T
17. F
18. F
19. T
20. T

Fill in the Blank

21. public interest theory of regulation
22. Federal Trade Commission Act
23. natural monopoly
24. market
25. size; market power

Chapter 26
Answers

Review Questions

1. Demand is inelastic. If price falls and total revenue falls, too, then demand must be inelastic.
2. Major changes in the weather affect the supply curve and price. If demand is inelastic, then quantity demanded will not change much as price changes a lot. Since price and quantity demanded change in opposite directions, a large fall in price combined with a small change in quantity demanded will dramatically lower total revenue. Alternatively, a large rise in price combined with a small change in quantity demanded will dramatically raise total revenue.
3. To avoid the risk of lower prices in the future.
4. Bad weather for all farmers but Farmer Jones means price is high (for Jones) and so is his output. High price and high output mean high total revenue, at least higher total revenue than would be the case if there is good weather for all and price is low.
5. A surplus, fewer exchanges, higher prices paid by consumers, and government purchase and storage of the surplus.
6. If the target price is $6, farmers will want to supply Q_1. At this quantity, the market price is $2. The deficiency payment is $4 per unit; the total deficiency payment is $4 multiplied by Q_1.

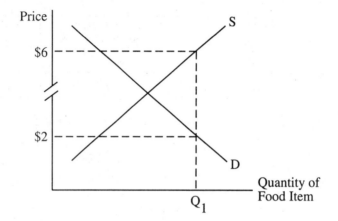

7. A price support program could make farming more profitable and therefore farmers will bid up land prices.
8. Direct payments to farmers who produce certain crops.
9. Instead of trying to change the prices of certain food items, the government (after the FAIR Act) simply subsidizes farmers' incomes.
10. In the past, farmers' might produce the same crop on a piece of land because the crop's price was supported, etc. Continuing to produce the same crop on a piece of led to certain environmental problems. Now farmers plant the crop that is best for them to plant in order to generate income. This usually ends up with their planting a variety of crops, which turns out to be better for the environment.
11. With FAIR there are set amounts that the government will spend, so farm spending is (largely) predetermined. Before FAIR, government may have to spend more than it anticipated depending on market conditions. For example, it may not know what its deficiency payments would total from year to year because this depended on the market price of crops. Market prices of crops are determined by market forces, which might be hard to predict in advance.
12. A farmer pledges so many bushels of his or her crop —say 1,000 bushels. In return, the farmer receives a loan which equals the loan rate times the 1,000 bushels. The farmer can either repay the loan with interest and get back his 1,000 bushels, or simply forfeit the 1,000 bushels and keep the loan. If the market price of the crop is greater than the loan rate, the farmer will repay the loan and sell the crop at the market price. If the market price of the crop is less than the loan rate, the farmer will not repay the loan.

458

Problems

1.

If demand for the food item is	And supply of the food item	Then farmers' income (rises, falls, remains unchanged)
elastic	rises	rises
inelastic	rises	falls
inelastic	falls	rises

2.

Target price	Market price	Quantity supplied at target price	Deficiency payment
$4	$1	4,000 units	$12,000
$5	$5	3,000 units	$0
$6	$3	10,000 units	$30,000

3.

Contract acreage (acres)	Yield per acre (bushels)	Crop payment rate (per bushel)	Production flexibility contract payment
1,000	110	$0.33	$30,855
2,000	210	$0.54	$192,780

4. The policy shifts the supply curve from S_1 to S_2 and raises the price of the food item (or crop).

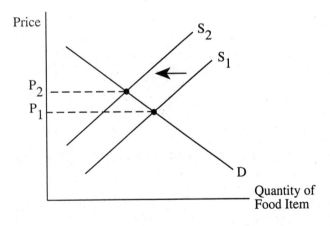

What Is the Question?

1. An obligation to make or take delivery of a specified quantity of a good at a particular time in the future at a price agreed on when the contract is signed.

   What is a futures contract?

2. A government-mandated minimum price for agricultural products.

   What is a price support?

3. It restricts output by limiting the number of farm acres that can be used to produce a particular crop.

    How does the acreage allotment program work?

4. It repealed target prices and deficiency payments.

    What did the FAIR Act do?

5. Contract acreage multiplied by 0.85 multiplied by yield per acre multiplied by crop payment rate.

    What does the production flexibility contract payment equal?

6. April 4, 1996.

    When did President Clinton sign the FAIR Act?

What Is Wrong?

1. When agricultural productivity increases, the supply of food items shifts right, price falls, and total revenue (received by farmers) rises if demand is inelastic.

    When agricultural productivity increases, the supply of food items shifts right, price falls, and total revenue (received by farmers) falls if demand is inelastic. Alternatively, you could write: When agricultural productivity increases, the supply of food items shifts right, price falls, and total revenue (received by farmers) rises if demand is elastic.

2. The demand for many farm products is income inelastic, which means that quantity demanded changes by a larger percentage than income changes.

    The demand for many farm products is income inelastic, which means that quantity demanded changes by a smaller percentage than income changes.

3. In the past, the three major agricultural policies to assist farmers were price supports, which attempted to set the prices of agricultural products indirectly; supply-restricting policies, which attempted to decrease supply and bring about a higher price for agricultural products indirectly; and target prices, which neither tried to set prices directly nor decrease supply, but instead paid farmers a production flexibility contract payment if the market price for their goods did not equal the target price.

    In the past, the three major agricultural policies to assist farmers were price supports, which attempted to set the prices of agricultural products directly; supply-restricting policies, which attempted to decrease supply and bring about a higher price for agricultural products indirectly; and target prices, which neither tried to set prices directly nor decrease supply, but instead paid farmers a deficiency payment if the market price for their goods did not equal the target price.

4. Under the FAIR Act, farmers have less flexibility to grow crops than they had under the old farm policies.

    Under the FAIR Act, farmers have more flexibility to grow crops than they had under the old farm policies.

5. Today, one farmer in the United States produces enough food to feed 100 people.

    Today, one farmer in the United States produces enough food to feed 35 people.

Multiple Choice
1. a
2. c
3. e
4. d
5. c
6. a
7. c
8. b
9. a
10. a

True-False
11. T
12. F
13. F
14. T
15. T

Fill in the Blank
16. inelastic; falls
17. market quota system (program)
18. Income elasticity of demand
19. price floor
20. higher prices

Chapter 27
Answers

Review Questions

1. There is a demand for restaurant meals. If the demand for restaurant meals increases, the demand for restaurant workers will increase. The demand for restaurant workers is a derived demand—it depends on changes in the demand for restaurant meals.

2. The factor demand curve is the MRP curve. MRP is equal to MR x MPP. At some point, MPP will decline, which will make MRP decline, which will cause the factor demand curve to be downward sloping.

3. When P = MR.

4. It should buy the quantity at which MRP = MFC. As long as MRP > MFC, the benefits of purchasing another factor unit are greater than the costs, that is, there is a net benefit of purchasing another factor unit.

5. The least-cost rule states that the MPP-to-factor price ratio is the same for all factors. If the ratio is higher for factor X than Y, then it is cheaper to buy less of Y and more of X. Why? Because there is a greater change in output for a $1 expenditure on X than Y. That is essentially what a higher MPP-to-factor price ratio says.

6. Elasticity of demand for the product that labor produces, ratio of labor costs to total costs, and number of substitute factors.

7. No, the income effect may arise, but simply be outweighed by the substitution effect.

8. Product demand and supply (and therefore product price and marginal revenue), and the MPP of labor. See Exhibit 11 in the text chapter.

9. Wage rates in other markets, nonpecuniary aspects of the job, number of persons who can do the job, training costs, and moving costs. See Exhibit 11 in the text chapter.

10. It may be too costly for an employer to generate full information on a potential employee, and therefore the employer may make a decision to hire (not to hire) based on less than full information. Had the employer known more, the decision might have been different.

Problems

1.

Quantity of factor Z	Quantity of output	Product price	Total revenue	Marginal revenue product
1	30	$40	$1,200	$1,200
2	50	$40	$2,000	$800
3	60	$40	$2,400	$400

2.

Quantity of factor Z	Price of factor Z	Total cost	Marginal factor cost
1	$10	$10	$10
2	$10	$20	$10
3	$10	$30	$10

3.

MPP of factor X (units)	Price of factor X	MPP of factor Y (units)	Price of factor Y	Should the firm buy more of factor X or factor Y?
30	$2	40	$1.25	Y
50	$4	100	$5.00	Y
100	$30	100	$40.00	X

4.

Change	Does this affect the demand for labor (yes, no)?	Does this affect the supply of labor (yes, no)?	Effect on wage (up, down, no change)
product supply falls	yes	no	down
product demand rises	yes	no	yes
training costs rise	no	yes	up
positive change in the nonpecuniary aspects of the job	no	yes	down

5.

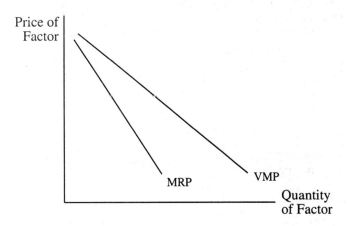

6.

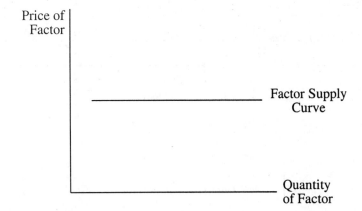

What Is the Question?

1. The additional revenue generated by employing an additional factor unit.

    What is marginal revenue product?

2. It is also the factor demand curve.

    What is the MRP curve?

3. It slopes downward because the MPP of the factor eventually declines.

    Why does the factor demand curve (or MRP curve) slope downward?

4. It will buy the number of factor units for which MRP = MFC.

    What quantity of factor units will the firm purchase?

5. The firm will buy more of factor X and less of factor Y.

    What will the firm do if the MPP-to-price ratio for factor X is greater than the MPP-to-price ratio for factor Y?

6. It is equal to the MPP of the factor divided by the cost of the factor.

    What does output produced per $1 of cost equal?

7. The percentage change in the quantity demanded of labor divided by the percentage change in the wage rate.

    What does elasticity of demand for labor equal?

8. It is upward sloping because the substitution effect outweighs the income effect.

    Why is the supply of labor curve upward sloping?

9. One of the reasons is that jobs have different nonpecuniary qualities.

    Why are supply conditions in different labor markets different?

10. States that firms in competitive or perfect product and factor markets pay factors their marginal revenue products.

    What does the marginal productivity theory state?

What Is Wrong?

1. If price equals marginal revenue, then VMP is greater than MRP.

    If price equals marginal revenue, then VMP equals MRP.

2. The factor demand curve usually lies above the MRP curve.

    The factor demand curve is the MRP curve.

3. The firm will purchase the quantity of a factor at which the difference between the MRP and MFC of the factor are maximized.

    The firm will purchase the quantity of a factor at which MRP = MFC.

4. An increase in MPP will shift the factor demand curve to the left.

    An increase in MPP will shift the factor demand curve to the right. Alternatively, you could write, A decrease in MPP will shift the factor demand curve to the left.

5. If the demand for the product that labor produces is highly elastic, a small percentage increase in price will decrease quantity demanded of the product by a relatively small percentage.

    If the demand for the product that labor produces is highly elastic, a small percentage increase in price will decrease quantity demanded of the product by a relatively large percentage.

6. The more substitutes for labor, the lower the elasticity of demand for labor; the fewer substitutes for labor, the higher the elasticity of demand for labor.

    The more substitutes for labor, the higher the elasticity of demand for labor; the fewer substitutes for labor, the lower the elasticity of demand for labor.

7. Screening is the process used by employers to increase the probability of choosing good employees (to promote) from within the firm.

    Screening is the process used by employers to increase the probability of choosing good employees—from within or outside the firm.

8. A firm minimizes costs by buying factors in the combination at which the MPP-to-price ratio for the expensive factors is greater than the MPP-to-price ratio for the less expensive factors.

    A firm minimizes costs by buying factors in the combination at which the MPP-to-price ratio for all factors is the same.

9. The supply curve is upward-sloping for a factor price taker.

    The supply curve is horizontal for a factor price taker.

10. The higher the labor cost-total cost ratio, the lower the elasticity of demand for labor.

    The higher the labor cost-total cost ratio, the higher the elasticity of demand for labor. Alternatively, you could write: The lower the labor cost-total cost ratio, the lower the elasticity of demand for labor.

Multiple Choice
1. a
2. d
3. a
4. a
5. b
6. e
7. c
8. d
9. d
10. c
11. b
12. a
13. a
14. d
15. a

True-False
16. T
17. T
18. T
19. F
20. F

Fill in the Blank
21. Value marginal product (VMP)
22. screening
23. quantity demanded of labor; wage rate
24. MRP = MFC
25. derived

Chapter 28
Answers

Review Questions
1. Employ all members of the union, maximize the total wage bill, and maximize the income of a limited number of union members.
2. Since the demand curve for union labor is downward-sloping, as the wage rate rises, the number of union workers employed falls.
3. It would need to reduce the availability of substitute products or reduce the availability of substitute factors.
4. By increasing the demand for the product it produces, by increasing the price of substitute factors, and by increasing the marginal physical product (productivity) of members.
5. In a closed shop, a person must join the union before he or she can be hired. With a union shop, one can be hired without being a member of the union. However, the worker must join the union within a certain time of becoming employed.
6. Because it is the only (or single) buyer of a factor, just as a monopolist is the only (or single) seller of a good.
7. For a monopsonist, MFC is greater than the wage rate.
8. Suppose labor is homogeneous and mobile. If there is an increase in the wage rate in the union sector (brought about by collective bargaining), there will be fewer people working in the union sector. Some of the people no longer working in the union sector will supply their labor services in the nonunion sector and the wage rate (in that sector) will fall.
9. That labor unions have a negative impact on productivity and efficiency through unnecessary staffing requirements, strikes, and more.
10. The quantity at which MRP = MFC.

Problems

1.

Description	Type of union
A union whose membership is made up of individuals who practice the same craft or trade.	craft (trade) union
A union whose membership is made up of individuals who work for the local, state, or federal government.	public employee union
A union whose membership is made up of individuals who work in the same firm or industry but do not all practice the same craft or trade.	industrial union

2.

Action	Effect on elasticity of demand for union labor (rises, falls, remains unchanged)
reduced availability of substitute products	falls
reduced availability of substitute factors	falls

3.

Action	Effect on demand for union labor (rises, falls, remains unchanged)
MPP of union labor falls	falls
product demand rises	rises
substitute factor prices fall	falls

4.

Action	Does it affect the demand for union labor, or the supply of union labor?
MPP of union labor rises	demand for union labor
substitute factor prices rise	demand for union labor
introduction of union shop	supply of union labor

5. Labor union changes supply curve from SS to S*S.

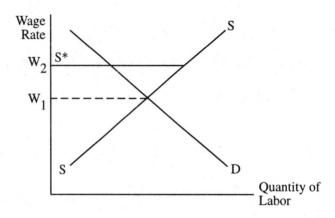

6.

Number of workers	Wage rate	Total labor cost	Marginal factor cost
1	$10.00	$10.00	$10.00
2	$10.10	$20.20	$10.20
3	$10.20	$30.60	$10.40
4	$10.30	$41.20	$10.60
5	$10.40	$52.00	$10.80

What Is the Question?

1. An organization whose members belong to a particular profession.

    What is an employee association?

2. The labor union will want this wage rate to prevail if its objective is to maximize the total wage bill.

    What is the wage rate that corresponds to the unit elastic point on the demand for union labor curve?

3. The wage-employment tradeoff decreases.

    What happens as the demand for labor becomes more inelastic (or less elastic)?

4. The purpose is to convince management that the supply curve is what the union says it is.

    What is the purpose of a strike?

5. MFC is greater than the wage rate.

    What is the relationship between MFC and the wage rate for a monopsonist?

6. An organization in which an employee must belong to the union before he or she can be hired.

    What is a closed shop?

7. Increasing product demand, increasing substitute factor prices, and increasing marginal physical product.

    What will lead to an increase in the demand for union labor?

8. The change in total labor cost divided by the change in the number of workers.

    What is marginal factor cost equal to?

What Is Wrong?

1. Union membership as a percentage of the labor force was about 25 percent in the United States in the late 1990s.

    Union membership as a percentage of the labor force was about 14.1 percent in the United States in the late 1990s.

2. If the objective of the labor union is to maximize the total wage bill, it will want the wage rate that corresponds to the inelastic portion of the labor demand curve.

    If the objective of the labor union is to maximize the total wage bill, it will want the wage rate that corresponds to the unit elastic point on the labor demand curve.

3. The more substitutes for union labor, the lower the elasticity of demand for union labor.

    The more substitutes for union labor, the higher the elasticity of demand for union labor. Alternatively, you could write: The fewer substitutes for union labor, the lower the elasticity of demand for union labor.

4. The National Working Rights Act allowed states to pass right-to-work laws.

    The Taft-Hartley Act allowed states to pass right-to-work laws.

5. The MFC curve lies below the supply of labor curve for a monopsonist.

    The MFC lies above the supply of labor curve for a monopsonist.

6. The percentage of the national income that goes to labor has been rising over the past 30 years.

    The percentage of the national income that goes to labor has been fairly constant over time.

7. If labor is homogeneous and mobile, an increase in the wage rate in the union sector will bring about an increase in the wage rate in the nonunion sector.

    If labor is homogeneous and mobile, an increase in the wage rate in the union sector will bring about a decrease in the wage rate in the nonunion sector.

8. An industrial union is a union whose membership is made up of individuals who practice the same
    craft or trade.

    *A craft or trade is a union whose membership is made up of individuals who practice the same
    craft or trade. Alternatively, you could write: An industrial union is a union whose membership is
    made up of individuals who work in the same firm or industry but do not all practice the same
    craft or trade.*

Multiple Choice
1. b
2. a
3. d
4. b
5. d
6. b
7. a
8. c
9. b
10. e
11. a
12. c
13. d
14. b
15. a

True-False
16. T
17. F
18. T
19. T
20. T

Fill in the Blank
21. right-to-work
22. monopsony
23. unit elastic
24. strike
25. MRP = MFC

Chapter 29
Answers

Review Questions

1. The *ex ante* distribution has not been adjusted for taxes and transfer payments, the *ex post* distribution has been.
2. Labor income, asset income, transfer payments, taxes.
3. The income share of different quintiles is identified. Then cumulative quintile (households) is plotted against cumulative income share. For example, suppose the lowest fifth (of households) has an income share of 10 percent and the second fifth (of households) has an income share of 15 percent. One point on the Lorenz curve identifies 20 percent of households against a 10 percent income share. A second point on the Lorenz curve identifies 40 percent of households against a 25 percent income share. For more details, see Exhibit 4 in the text chapter.
4. By comparing Gini coefficients, we cannot identify the percentage of income earned by a particular income group. For example, even though Country A may have a lower Gini coefficient than Country B, we don't know if the lowest fifth of households in Country A do, or do not, earn more income than the lowest fifth of households in Country B.
5. Innate abilities and attributes, work and leisure, education and other training, risk taking, luck, and wage discrimination.
6. The income distribution that should exist is the income distribution that people would agree to behind the veil of ignorance, where they do not know their position in the income distribution.
7. A person is said to be in absolute poverty if he or she earns an income below a certain dollar amount. A person is said to be in relative poverty if he or she is one of the lowest income earners. For example, if 95 percent of individuals earn more than Smith, Smith might be said to be falling into relative poverty. In short, absolute dollar amounts are relevant to absolute poverty and percentages are relevant to relative poverty.
8. People tend to earn more in middle age than in their youth. A very youthful population, therefore, might skew the income distribution toward greater inequality.
9. It argues that people should be paid their marginal revenue products.
10. It holds that the reduction or elimination of poverty is a public good and therefore everyone will take a free ride on someone else's efforts at trying to eliminate poverty. In this setting, very little poverty will be reduced or eliminated. It follows, then, that government is justified in taxing all persons to pay for the welfare assistance of some.

Problems

1.

Quintile	Percentage of total income, 1998
Lowest fifth	3.6
Second fifth	9.0
Third fifth	15.0
Fourth fifth	23.2
Highest fifth	49.2

2.

Quintile	Income share (percent)	Cumulative percentage of income	Cumulative percentage of households
Lowest fifth	10	10	20
Second fifth	12	22	40
Third fifth	22	44	60
Fourth fifth	25	69	80
Highest fifth	31	100	100

3.

Group	Percent of group in poverty, 1998
Total population	12.7
White	10.5
African-American	26.1
Hispanic	25.6
Under 18 years of age	18.9
18-24 years old	16.6
65 years old and older	10.5

4.

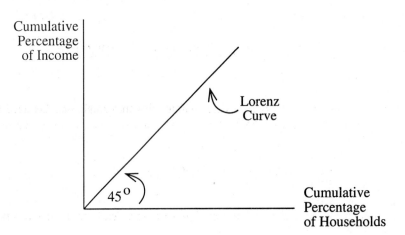

5.

Quintile	Income share
Lowest fifth	10 percent
Second fifth	20 percent
Third fifth	21 percent
Fourth fifth	22 percent
Highest fifth	27 percent

What Is the Question?

1. Payments to persons that are not made in return for goods and services currently supplied.

    What are transfer payments?

2. Labor income plus asset income plus transfer payments minus taxes

    What does an individual's income equal?

3. This exists when individuals of equal ability and productivity are paid different wage rates.

    What is wage discrimination?

4. It is determined in factor markets.

    Where is the income distribution determined?

5. The Gini coefficient is 1.

    What is the Gini coefficient if there is complete income inequality?

6. The income level below which people are considered to be living in poverty.

    What is the poverty income threshold or poverty line?

7. An example is that everyone who earns less than $5,000 is living in poverty.

    What is absolute poverty?

8. An example is that the bottom one-tenth of income earners are living in poverty.

    What is relative poverty?

9. It holds that individuals currently not receiving welfare think they might one day need welfare assistance and thus are willing to take out a form of insurance for themselves by supporting welfare programs.

    What is the social insurance justification of welfare assistance?

What Is Wrong?
1. The income distribution in the United States in 1998 was more nearly equal than it was in 1967.

    The income distribution in the United States in 1998 was more nearly unequal (or less equal) than it was in 1967.

2. The government can change the distribution of income through taxes, but not through transfer payments.

    The government can change the distribution of income through taxes and transfer payments.

3. The Lorenz curve is a measurement of the degree of inequality in the distribution of income.

    The Gini coefficient is a measurement of the degree of inequality in the distribution of income. Alternatively, you could write: The Lorenz curve is the graphical representation of the income distribution.

he Rawlsian normative standard of the income distribution holds that there should be complete income equality.

> *The absolute income equality standard holds that there should be complete income equality. Alternatively, you could write, The Rawlsian normative standard holds that the income distribution should be what is decided behind the veil of ignorance.*

5. Asset income is equal to the wage rate an individual receives multiplied by the number of hours he or she works.

> *Labor income is equal to the wage rate an individual receives multiplied by the number of hours he or she works. Alternatively, you could write: Asset income consists of such things as the return to saving, the return to capital investment, and the return to land.*

6. In general, human capital refers to the increases in productivity brought about by humans when they use physical capital goods.

> *In general, human capital refers to the labor productivity brought about through education, developing one's skills, and so on.*

7. The Gini coefficient is zero (0) if there is an unequal income distribution.

> *The Gini coefficient is zero if there is an absolutely equal income distribution. Alternatively, you could write: The Gini coefficient is between 0 and 1 if there is an unequal income distribution.*

Multiple Choice
1. a
2. b
3. b
4. e
5. a
6. e
7. b
8. d
9. d
10. c

True-False
11. T
12. T
13. T
14. T
15. T

Fill in the Blank
16. Transfer payments
17. Gini coefficient
18. Wage discrimination
19. One (1)
20. *ex ante*

Chapter 30
Answers

Review Questions
1. A person borrows $100 and repays $120. Twenty dollars ($20) is interest; 20 percent is the interest rate, or the interest/principal ratio.
2. It means the person slightly prefers earlier to later availability of goods.
3. Instead of digging holes by hand, a person takes out time to produce a shovel to use to dig the holes.
4. People would not pay positive interest rates if they didn't have a positive rate of time preference or roundabout methods of production weren't productive.
5. Interest rates differ because loans are not the same with respect to all factors, such as risk, term of the loan, and cost of making the loan.
6. The present value of the income stream is $4,920, which is less than the cost of the capital good. The firm should not buy the capital good for $5,000.
7. He meant that it was because prices were high that land rent was high, not the other way around.
8. Suppose opportunity cost is $10 and the wage rate is $12. Economic rent is $2. Now suppose opportunity cost is $0 and the wage rate is $12. Pure economic rent is $12. Pure economic rent exists when opportunity costs are zero. Whenever opportunity costs are positive, we are dealing with economic rent instead of pure economic rent.
9. A rent is real if it has not been artificially brought about some way. Artificial rent is economic rent that is artificially contrived (usually by government).
10. One theory of profit states that profit would not exist if uncertainty did not exist. One theory of profit states that profit is the return to innovation.
11. Profit and loss are signals to resources. Resources flow toward profits and away from losses.

Problems
1.

Dollar amount received	Number of years before dollar amount is received	Interest rate (percent)	Present value
$1,000	2	5	$907.03
$10,000	3	6	$8,396.31
$100	2	7	$87.34

2.

Cost of capital good	Life of capital good	Income from capital good each year	Interest rate (percent)	Should the firm buy the capital good? (yes, no)
$4,000	3 years	$1,500	2	yes
$19,000	5 years	$4,000	5	yes
$20,000	6 years	$5,000	4	yes

3.

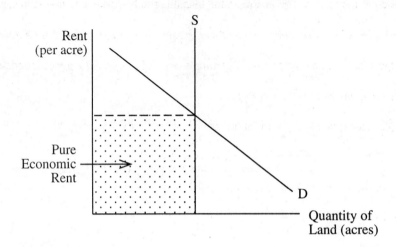

4.

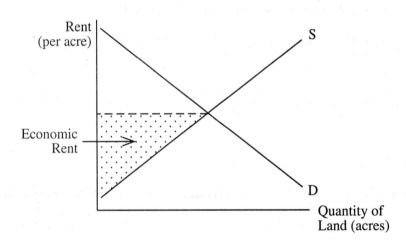

5.

Wage rate	Next best wage rate	Economic rent
$12	$11	$1
$10	$10	$0
$100	$66	$34

What Is the Question?

1. The production of capital goods that enhance productive capabilities and ultimately bring about increased consumption.

    What is the roundabout method of production?

2. It is composed of the demand for consumption loans and the demand for investment loans.

    What are the components of the demand for loans?

6. A decreased threat of war would probably raise peoples' rate of time preference.

    A decreased threat of war would probably lower peoples' rate of time preference. Alternatively, you could write: An increased threat of war would probably raise peoples' rate of time preference.

7. As the interest rate falls, present value falls.

    As the interest rate falls, present value rises. Alternatively, you could write: As the interest rate rises, present value falls.

8. Uncertainty exists when a potential occurrence is so unpredictable that the probability of it occurring is less than 1.

    Uncertainty exists when a potential occurrence is so unpredictable that a probability cannot be estimated.

9. Economists emphasize accounting profit over economic profit because economic profit determines entry into and exit from an industry.

    Economists emphasize economic profit over accounting profit because economic profit determines entry into and exit from an industry.

Multiple Choice
1. c
2. d
3. a
4. c
5. d
6. a
7. d
8. d
9. c
10. c
11. e
12. e
13. d
14. c
15. c

True-False
16. F
17. F
18. F
19. F
20. T

Fill in the Blank

21. roundabout methods
22. equality
23. nominal, real
24. one
25. increase

Chapter 31
Answers

Review Questions

1. No, when there are no externalities (positive or negative), the market output and the socially optimal output are the same.
2. Market failure is the situation that exists when the market does not produce the optimal amount of a good.
3. They matter if there are positive transaction costs but not if transaction costs are trivial or zero.
4. The objective is to move from the market output to the socially optimal output. A corrective tax does not always work because sometimes the tax is more or less than the external cost.
5. No, since there are costs and benefits to eliminating pollution.
6. Government issues pollution permits and allows them to be bought and sold. In the end, the entities that can eliminate pollution at the lowest cost will end up eliminating pollution.
7. Both a nonexcludable and excludable public good are nonrivalrous in consumption, but a nonexclucable public good cannot be denied to a person while an excludable public good can be.
8. Because of the existence of free riders, who will be able to consume the good without paying for it. In short, because of free riders, no seller of a nonexcludable public good would be able to extract payment from people who benefit from the good.
9. With symmetric information the demand for a good may be lower than it would be with asymmetric information. It follows then that the market output is larger with asymmetric information than with symmetric information.
10. With symmetric information the supply of a factor may be less than it would be with asymmetric information. It follows then that more factor units will be employed with asymmetric information than with symmetric information.
11. Consider it in the used car market. The owners of lemons offer their cars for sale because they know, and only they know, that the average price they are being offered for their below-average car is a good deal. Through adverse selection, the supply of lemons rises on the market and the supply of good used cars falls. There is now a new average price that is less than it was earlier. Only people with below average cars think the average price is a good price. The people with above-average used cars drop out of the market. In time, the process continues and more and more owners of above-average cars drop out of the market. In the end there is no longer a market for good used cars but only for lemons.
12. Jones buys a health insurance policy. Afterward, she doesn't watch her health as much as she would have otherwise, but the seller of the health insurance policy does not know this.

Problems

1. a) $3,800; b) $1,800
2. The tax moves the output from Q_1 to Q_3 instead of from Q_1 to Q_2.

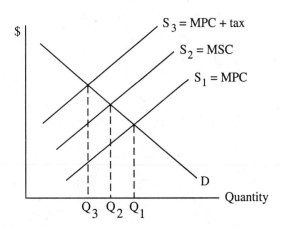

3. Because there are net costs of moving from the socially optimal output (Q_2) to the market output (Q_1). In other words, the costs of moving from Q_2 to Q_1 are greater than the benefits by the amount of the triangle.
4. When the tax equals external cost.
5. With asymmetric information the demand curve is D_1, and with symmetric information it is D_2. If the outcome really would be Q_1 with asymmetric information and Q_2 with symmetric information, then the difference between Q_1 and Q_2 represents a market failure.

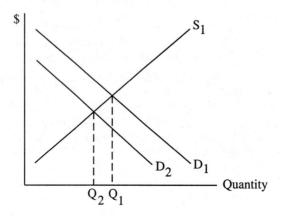

What Is the Question?

1. This exists when a person's or group's actions cause a cost to be felt by others.

    What is a negative externality?

2. MSC > MPC.

    What is the relationship between MSC and MPC when a negative externality exists?

3. MSB > MPB.

    What is the relationship between MSB and MPB when a positive externality exists?

4. In this case property rights assignments do not matter to the resource allocative outcome.

    Do property rights assignments matter to the resource allocative outcome when transaction costs are zero?

5. He stressed the reciprocal nature of externalities.

    Who is Ronald Coase?

6. Consumption by one person reduces consumption by another person.

    What does it mean if there is rivalry in consumption?

7. The person who makes it difficult, if not impossible, for the market to produce nonexcludable public goods.

    Who is the free rider?

8. This exists when either the buyer or the seller in a market exchange has some information that the other does not have.

    What is asymmetric information?

9. This exists when the parties on one side of the market, who have information not known to others, self-select in a way that adversely affects the parties on the other side of the market.

    What is adverse selection?

What Is Wrong?

1. The economist holds that less pollution is always better than the current amount of pollution because pollution is a bad.

    The economist does not always hold that less pollution is always better than the current amount of pollution. The economist knows that the costs of eliminating some units of pollution may be greater than the benefits derived.

2. A negative externality is a type of subsidy.

    A negative externality is an adverse side-effect of an individual's or group's actions.

3. Given a positive externality, the marginal private benefit curve lies to the left of the demand curve, with the market output above the socially optimal output.

    Given a positive externality, the marginal private benefit curve lies to the right of the demand curve, with the market output below the socially optimal output.

4. The side effect of an action that increases the well-being of others is called a neutral benefit.

    The side effect of an action that increases the well-being of others is called a positive externality.

5. If private property were established in the air, there would probably be more air pollution.

    If private property were established in the air, there would probably be less air pollution.

6. If a person who generates a negative externality incorporates into his private cost-benefit calculations the effects that this externality will have on third parties, the externality has been complementarized.

    If a person who generates a negative externality incorporates into his private cost-benefit calculations the effects that this externality will have on third parties, the externality has been internalized.

7. Generally, negative externalities result in too little of a good being produced.

    Generally, negative externalities result in too much of a good being produced.

8. If there are no externalities, then the socially optimum output occurs where MPB > MPC.

    If there are no externalities, then the socially optimum output occurs where MPB = MPC.

9.   Exchange is a zero sum game.

     Exchange is a positive sum game.

10. Marginal social costs equal marginal private costs plus internal costs.

     Marginal social costs equal marginal private costs plus external costs.

Multiple Choice
1.   c
2.   d
3.   a
4.   e
5.   d
6.   d
7.   d
8.   b
9.   d
10. c

True-False
11. T
12. F
13. T
14. T
15. T

Fill in the Blank
16. Market failure
17. internalized
18. nonrivalrous in consumption
19. Moral hazard
20. socially optimal

Chapter 32
Answers

Review Questions

1. Yes. To speak in specific terms is more likely to get a person labeled as being "to the right" or "to the left." Candidates do not want to be seen as "to the right" or "to the left," but instead "in the middle."
2. Yes. See answer to number 1.
3. They are more likely to take polls to determine their position. It is harder to move from an off-center position to a center position than it is to locate at the center position from the beginning.
4. The general answer is: because the costs of voting outweigh the benefits. Specifically, the reason the benefits may be so low (relative to the costs) is because the person only perceives benefits to voting if he believes his vote can affect the outcome. Since this isn't likely in a larger-numbers election (where there are many eligible voters), there are no benefits to voting and therefore the person chooses not to vote.
5. There are some benefits she gets from voting that are unrelated to her vote's impact on the outcome of the election.
6. No matter who you voted for in the last presidential election, the outcome would have been the same.
7. It may have everything to do with rational ignorance. Jim may not know the names of his U.S. senators because he perceives the benefits of acquiring this information as less than the costs.
8. Probably so. It is unlikely that anyone finds the benefits of learning all those things there are to learn greater than the costs of learning all those things there are to learn. People usually prioritize and therefore find some things worth learning and other things not worth learning.
9. Subsets of the population who hold intense preferences with respect to some issue, action, or policy.
10. Because agricultural policy will have a bigger monetary effect on the farmer than on the member of the general public.
11. Because the costs of doing anything might be greater than the benefits. Suppose a piece of legislation will take $2 away from Joe. To lobby against the legislation, Joe might have to pay $40. Is it worth Joe paying $40 to save $2? No. Joe may decide to do nothing.
12. Rent is a payment in excess of opportunity cost. Rent seeking is the expenditure of scarce resources to bring about a pure transfer.
13. Because resources that are used to bring about a pure transfer could, instead, be used to produce goods.

Problems

1. The group will buy good X because this is the preference of a simple majority of the group. The purchase of good X is inefficient because the total benefits ($388) are less than the total cost ($500).

What Is the Question?

1. The branch of economics that deals with the application of economic principles and tolls to public-sector decision making.

   What is public choice?

2. Candidates will speak in general terms; candidates will label their opponent in extreme terms; candidates will label themselves in moderate terms; candidates will take polls and if they are not doing well in their polls they will adjust their positions.

   What are the predictions of the median voter model?

3. The state of not acquiring information because the costs of acquiring the information are greater than the benefits.

   What is rational ignorance?

4. The exchange of votes to gain support for legislation.

   What is logrolling?

5. In this case rent is usually called profit.

   When rent is the result of entrepreneurial activity designed to either satisfy a new demand or rearrange resources in an increasingly valuable way, what is it called?

6. The expenditure of scarce resources to capture a pure transfer.

   What is rent seeking?

What Is Wrong?

1. Legislation that concentrates the benefits on many and disperses the costs over a few is likely to pass, because the beneficiaries will have an incentive to lobby for it, whereas those who pay the bill will not lobby against it because each of them pays such a small part of the bill.

   Legislation that concentrates the benefits on few and disperses the costs over many is likely to pass, because the beneficiaries will have an incentive to lobby for it, whereas those who pay the bill will not lobby against it because each of them pays such a small part of the bill.

2. A public choice economist would likely state that people will not behave differently in different settings.

   A public choice economist believes that people do behave differently in different settings if costs and benefits are different in different settings.

3. In a two-person race, the candidate on the right of the median voter is more likely to win the race than the candidate on the left of the median voter.

   In a two-person race, the candidate closer to the median voter is more likely to win.

4. One of the predictions of the median voter model is that candidates will speak in specific terms instead of general terms because this is what the median voter wants.

   One of the predictions of the median voter model is that candidates will speak in general instead of specific terms.

5. Younger people are more likely to be rationally ignorant of various subjects than older people.

   There is no evidence that younger people are more likely to be rationally ignorant than older people. Rational ignorance appears to be independent of age.

6. A government bureau maximizes profit and minimizes costs.

   A government bureau does not attempt to maximize profit.

7. Farmers, lobbying for a legislative bill, are more likely to openly state, "We need this legislation because it will be good for us," instead of "We need this legislation for America's future."

   It's just the opposite. Farmers are more likely to say "We need this legislation for America's future." That is, they are more likely to utter the public-interest words than the special-interest words.

Multiple Choice
1. d
2. a
3. a
4. d
5. b
6. c
7. d
8. c
9. b
10. a

True-False
11. T
12. F
13. T
14. T
15. F

Fill in the Blank
16. Government failure
17. costs, benefits
18. general; specific
19. closer
20. James Buchanan

Chapter 33
Answers

Review Questions

1. People in different countries trade with each other for the same reason that people within a country trade with each other—to make themselves better off.
2. Through specialization, countries (as a group) can end up producing more than if they don't specialize. Since they can produce more through specialization, the possibility certainly exists that they can consume more, too. This is accomplished by their trading with each other.
3. A tariff will lower consumers' surplus.
4. A tariff will raise producers' surplus.
5. The benefits of the tariff may be concentrated over relatively few producers and the costs of the tariff may be dispersed over relatively many consumers. As a result, the average producer may receive more in gains than the average consumer loses, although consumers (as a group) lose more than producers (as a group) gain. This means the average producer has a sharper incentive to lobby for the tariff than the average consumer has to lobby against it.
6. Industries that are new (infants) in one country may have a hard time competing against their counterparts in other countries that have been around for awhile (and therefore are adults). The infant industries may need some assistance (protection) until they grow up and mature and are ready to compete on an equal basis.
7. A country is said to be dumping goods if it sells a good for less than its cost and below the price charged in the domestic market. Some people argue that this is unfair to domestic industries and therefore they should be protected from this action.
8. No, not necessarily. An economist might ask: What was the price to save the domestic job? If consumers have to pay $60,000 (in higher prices) to save every $40,000 job, it isn't worth saving those jobs.
9. The WTO's objective is to help trade flow "smoothly, freely, fairly, and predictably." It does this by administering trade agreements, assisting developing countries in trade-policy issues, and cooperating with other international organizations.
10. It means that the gains to the winners (or beneficiaries) of tariffs are less than the costs (or losses) to the losers.

Problems

1.

Opportunity cost of one unit of X for Country A	Opportunity cost of one unit of Y for Country A	Opportunity cost of one unit of X for Country B	Opportunity cost of one unit of Y for Country B
1.5Y	0.67X	1Y	1X

2. Area 1
3. Area 2
4. Change in consumers' surplus is the loss of areas 3, 4, 5, 6. Change in producers' surplus is the gain of area 3.
5. Gain from the tariff is area 3 (for producers) and area 5 (for government). Loss is the areas 3, 4, 5, and 6 (for consumers).
6. Net loss is the areas 4 and 6.
7. Area 5

8.

Price after quota	Loss in consumers' surplus due to the quota	Gain in producers' surplus due to the quota	Increase in revenue received by importers due to the quota	Net loss due to the quota
P_Q	Areas 3, 4, 5, 6	Area 3	Area 5	Areas 4 and 6

What Is the Question?

1. This will allow the country to consume beyond its production possibilities frontier (PPF).

   What will specialization and trade do for a country (in terms of its consumption)?

2. As a result, imports decrease.

   What will happen to imports as a tariff or quota is imposed.

3. The sale of goods abroad at a price below their cost and below the price charged in the domestic market.

   What is dumping?

4. The situation in which a country can produce a good at lower opportunity cost than another country.

   What does comparative advantage refer to?

5. The gains are less than the losses plus the tariff revenues.

   What is the net effect of a tariff?

What Is Wrong?

1. A PPF for the world can be drawn when 1) countries do not specialize and trade and 2) when they do specialize and trade. The world PPF will be the same in both cases.

   The world PPF will be further to the right when countries specialize and trade than when they do not.

2. The national-defense argument states that certain goods are necessary to the national defense and therefore should be produced only by allies.

   The national-defense argument states that certain goods are necessary to the national defense and therefore should be produced only by the domestic country.

3. A quota raises more government revenue than a tariff.

   A quota doesn't raise tariff revenue.

4. Consumers' surplus and producers' surplus fall as a result of a tariff being imposed on imported goods.

   Only consumers' surplus falls as a result of a tariff. Producers' surplus rises.

5. What producers gain from a quota is greater than what consumers lose from a quota.

    What producers gain from a quota is less than what consumers lose from a quota.

6. If the United States sells a good for less in France than it does in Brazil, then the United States is said to be dumping goods in France.

    The United States may not be dumping goods in this situation. Dumping requires the United States to sell goods for less than cost and less than the price charged in the domestic economy.

7. A voluntary export restraint is an agreement between two countries in which importing countries voluntarily agree to limit their imports of a good from another country.

    A voluntary export restraint is an agreement between two countries in which the exporting country voluntarily agrees to limit its exports of a good to another country.

8. A quota is a tax on the amount of a good that may be imported into a country.

    A tariff is a tax on the amount of a good that may be imported into a country.

Multiple Choice
1. c
2. a
3. d
4. a
5. a
6. c
7. d
8. d
9. a
10. e
11. d
12. e
13. b
14. d
15. c

True-False
16. F
17. T
18. T
19. T
20. T

Fill in the Blank
21. antidumping
22. fall
23. falls
24. less
25. more (greater)

Chapter 34
Answers

Review Questions

1. A person in the United States wants to buy a British good. The American has to supply dollars in the foreign exchange market in order to buy pounds.
2. A German wants to buy a U.S. good. The German has to supply marks (in the foreign exchange market) in order to demand dollars.
3. The current account balance takes into account more items than the merchandise trade balance. The merchandise trade balance looks at the difference between merchandise exports and merchandise imports. The merchandise account balance takes into account exports of goods and services (one component of which is merchandise exports), imports of goods and services (one component of which is merchandise imports) and net unilateral transfers abroad.
4. Outflow of U.S. capital and inflow of foreign capital.
5. With a flexible exchange rate system, the demand for and supply of currencies determine equilibrium exchange rates. It is no different than supply and demand determining the price of corn, television sets, or houses. In this case supply and demand simply determine the price of one currency in terms of another currency. With a fixed exchange rate system, governments determine the exchange rate. Under a fixed exchange rate system, exchange rates are determined by government edict, not market forces.
6. If a person in the United States wants to buy a British good, he must pay for the British good with pounds. Thus he will have a demand for pounds. How will he get these pounds? He will have to supply dollars in order to demand pounds in order to buy the British good.
7. If a person in the UK wants to buy a U.S. good, he must pay for good with dollars. Thus he will have a demand for dollars. How will he get these dollars? He will have to supply pounds in order to demand dollars in order to buy the U.S. good.
8. The dollar has appreciated. When it takes less of currency X to buy currency Y, currency X is said to have appreciated. It took $0.0094 to buy one yen on Tuesday, and $0.0090 to buy one yen on Wednesday.
9. A difference in income growth rates (among countries), a difference in relative inflation rates (among countries), and changes in real interest rates (among countries).
10. Suppose the equilibrium exchange rate is $1 = 106$ yen and the official exchange rate is $1 = 150$ yen. The dollar is overvalued.
11. Devaluation is an act of government; depreciation is an act of markets.

Problems
1. $-\$10$
2. $+\$4$
3. $+\$17$
4. $-\$1$
5. $\$0$
6.

If the	Then the
demand for dollars rises in the foreign exchange market	supply of pesos rises on the foreign exchange market
demand for pesos falls on the foreign exchange market	supply of dollars falls on the foreign exchange market
demand for dollars rises in the foreign exchange market	supply of pesos rises on the foreign exchange market

7.

If	Then
$1 = 106 yen	1 yen = $0.0094
$1 = 74 Kenyan shillings	1 shilling = $0.135
$1 = 1,500 Lebanese pounds	1 pound = $0.000667

8.

The exchange rate is	And the item costs	What does the item cost in dollars?
$1 = 106 yen	18,000 yen	$169.81
$1 = £0.50	£ 34	$68
$1 = 9.44 pesos	89 pesos	$9.43

9.

The exchange rate changes from	Has the dollar appreciated or depreciated?
$2 = £1 to $2.50 = £1	depreciated
109 yen = $1 to 189 yen = $1	appreciated
10 pesos = $1 to 8 pesos = $1	depreciated

10.

If ...	The dollar will (appreciate, depreciate)
the real interest rate in the U.S. rises relative to real interest rates in other countries	appreciate
income in foreign countries (that trade with the U.S.) rises relative to income in the United States	appreciate
the inflation rate in the U.S. rises and the inflation rate in all other countries falls	depreciate

11.

If the equilibrium exchange rate is $1 = £ 0.50 and the official exchange rate is	Then the dollar is (overvalued, undervalued)
$1 = £ 0.60	overvalued
$1 = £ 0.30	undervalued

What is the Question?

1.   Any transaction that supplies the country's currency in the foreign exchange market.

   What is a debit?

2.   Any transaction that creates a demand for the country's currency in the foreign exchange market.

   What is a credit?

3. The summary statistic for the exports of goods and services, imports of goods and services, and net unilateral transfers abroad.

    What is the current account balance?

4. The difference between the value of merchandise exports and the value of merchandise imports.

    What is the merchandise trade balance?

5. One-way money payments.

    What are unilateral transfers?

6. The price of one currency in terms of another currency.

    What is the exchange rate?

7. It predicts that the exchange rates between any two currencies will adjust to reflect changes in the relative price levels of the two countries.

    What does the purchasing power parity theory predict?

8. Raising the official price of a currency.

    What is revaluation?

What Is Wrong?

1. The balance of payments is the summary statistic for the current account balance, capital account balance, net unilateral transfers abroad, and statistical discrepancy.

    The balance of payments is the summary statistic for the current account balance, capital account balance, official reserve balance, and statistical discrepancy.

2. The demand for dollars on the foreign exchange market is linked to the supply of dollars on the foreign exchange market. In short, if the demand for dollars rises, the supply of dollars rises, too.

    The demand for dollars on the foreign exchange market is linked to the supply of other currencies on the foreign exchange market. In short, if the demand for dollars rises, the supply of other currencies rise, too.

3. There are two countries, A and B. The income of Country B rises and the income of Country A remains constant. As a result, the currency of Country B appreciates.

    There are two countries, A and B. The income of Country B rises and the income of Country A remains constant. As a result, the currency of Country B depreciates.

4. There are two countries, C and D. The price level in Country C rises 10 percent and the inflation rate in Country D is zero percent. As a result, the demand for Country C's goods rises and the supply of its currency falls.

    There are two countries, C and D. The price level in Country C rises 10 percent and the inflation rate in Country D is zero percent. As a result, the demand for Country C's goods falls and the supply of other countries' currencies fall. Alternatively, you could write: As a result, the demand for Country C's goods falls and the demand for its currency falls.

5. A change in real interest rates across countries cannot change the exchange rate.

    A change in real interest rates across countries can change the exchange rate.

6. If the equilibrium exchange rate is £1 = $1.50, and the official exchange rate is £1 = $1.60, then the dollar is overvalued and the pound is undervalued.

    If the equilibrium exchange rate is £1 = $1.50, and the official exchange rate is £1 = $1.60, then the dollar is undervalued and the pound is overvalued.

7. A international monetary fund right is a special international money crated by the IMF.

    A special drawing right is an international money crated by the IMF.

Multiple Choice
1. c
2. a
3. c
4. b
5. c
6. a
7. e
8. c
9. a
10. a
11. b
12. d
13. d
14. b
15. a

True-False
16. T
17. T
18. T
19. F
20. T

Fill in the Blank
21. merchandise trade balance
22. purchasing power parity theory
23. fix
24. devaluation
25. fixed; flexible

Chapter 35
Answers

Review Questions

1. A developed country is a country with a relatively high per capita GDP; a less developed country is a country with a relatively low per capita GDP.
2. The Rule of 72 is a simple arithmetical rule for compound calculations. It says that the time required for any variable to double is calculated by dividing its percentage growth rate into 72. For example, suppose a person's income grows 4 percent a year. It will take 18 years (72 ÷ 4) for the person's income to double.
3. Capital, of which there is physical and human, assists economic development. Strictly speaking, it assists people in producing goods and services.
4. Increases in labor productivity are critical to economic development. In short, without increases in labor productivity, most poor countries do not develop.
5. The property rights structure influences the incentive to produce. Some property rights structures reward risk and hard work more than others.
6. Some economists say a rapid population growth rate increases the dependency ratio and therefore puts a burden on the working-age population. Supposedly, without this burden, people are more productive, more likely to start new businesses, and so on.
7. It is equal to the number of children under a certain age plus the number of the elderly divided by the population.
8. It is the idea that because people in less developed countries have low incomes, they save little. Low savings translates into low investment, which keeps productivity low, and this, in turn, keeps income low.
9. It may be cheaper to accomplish a given task without the technology.

What Is the Question?

1. It is a country with a relatively low GDP per capita.

   What is a less developed country?

2. The number of children who die before their first birthday out of every 1,000 live births.

   What is the infant mortality rate?

3. Natural resources, capital formation, labor productivity, technological advances, property rights structure, and economic freedom.

   What are the factors that promote economic development?

4. Any unit is substitutable for another.

   What does it mean if something is fungible?

5. The combination of higher birthrates and declining death rates.

   What is the reason for the higher population growth rates in less developed countries (as compared with developed countries)?

6. The number of children under a certain age plus the number of the elderly divided by the total population.

    What is the dependency ratio?

7. Low income leads to low savings, which leads to low investment, which leads to low productivity, which leads to low income, and so on.

    What is the idea implicit in the vicious circle of poverty?

What Is Wrong?

1. If a country has an annual growth rate in GDP per capita of 4 percent, it will take 15 years for its GDP per capita to double.

    If a country has an annual growth rate in GDP per capita of 4 percent, it will take 18 years for its GDP per capita to double.

2. Natural resources are a necessary but not sufficient factor for economic development.

    Natural resources are neither a necessary nor sufficient factor for economic development.

3. One way to calculate labor productivity is to divide the number of labor hours worked by GDP.

    One way to calculate labor productivity is to divide GDP by the the number of labor hours worked.

4. The infant mortality rate tends to be lower in less developed countries than in developed countries.

    The infant mortality rate tends to be higher in less developed countries than in developed countries.

5. Countries poor in natural resources do not experience economic development.

    Countries poor in natural resources may experience economic development. Some countries poor in natural resources have experienced economic development.

6. A high dependency ratio is something that most economists think promotes economic development.

    A high dependency ratio is something that most economists think hinders economic development.

7. The vicious circle of poverty holds that low productivity leads to low savings, which leads to low income.

    The vicious circle of poverty holds that low productivity leads to low income, which leads to low savings.

Multiple Choice

1. c
2. b
3. a
4. a
5. b
6. d
7. c
8. c
9. c
10. b

True-False

11. T
12. T
13. T
14. F
15. T

Fill in the Blank

16. property rights
17. Fungible
18. infant mortality rate
19. Technological advances
20. sufficient; necessary